IMAGES
of America

ARCATA

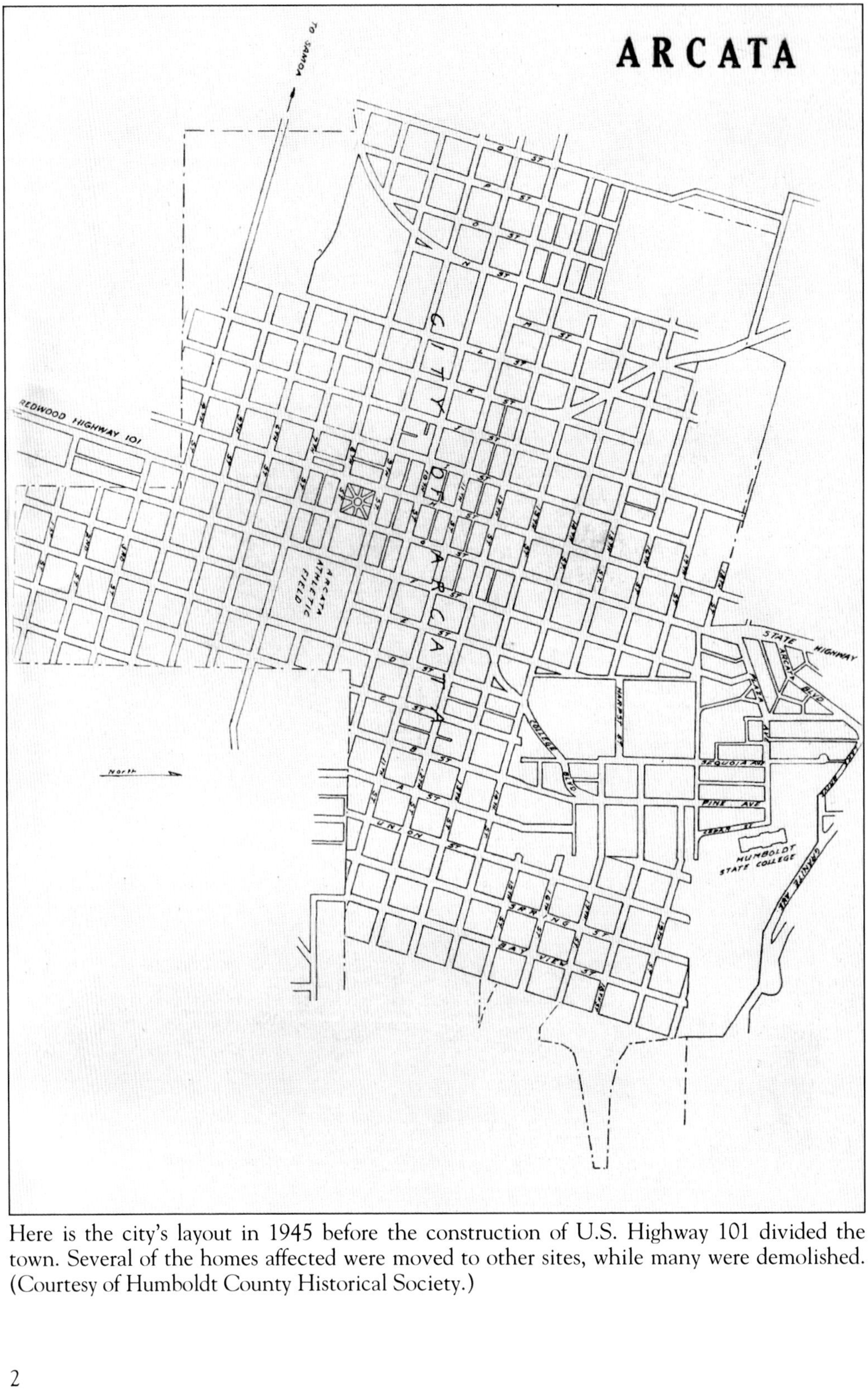

Here is the city's layout in 1945 before the construction of U.S. Highway 101 divided the town. Several of the homes affected were moved to other sites, while many were demolished. (Courtesy of Humboldt County Historical Society.)

IMAGES
of America

ARCATA

Jessie Faulkner
Humboldt County Historical Society

ARCADIA
PUBLISHING

ISBN 978-0-7385-2906-6

Published by Arcadia Publishing
Charleston, South Carolina

Printed in the United States of America

Library of Congress Catalog Card Number: 2004106340

For all general information contact Arcadia Publishing at:
Telephone 843-853-2070
Fax 843-853-0044
E-mail sales@arcadiapublishing.com
For customer service and orders:
Toll-Free 1-888-313-2665

Visit us on the Internet at www.arcadiapublishing.com

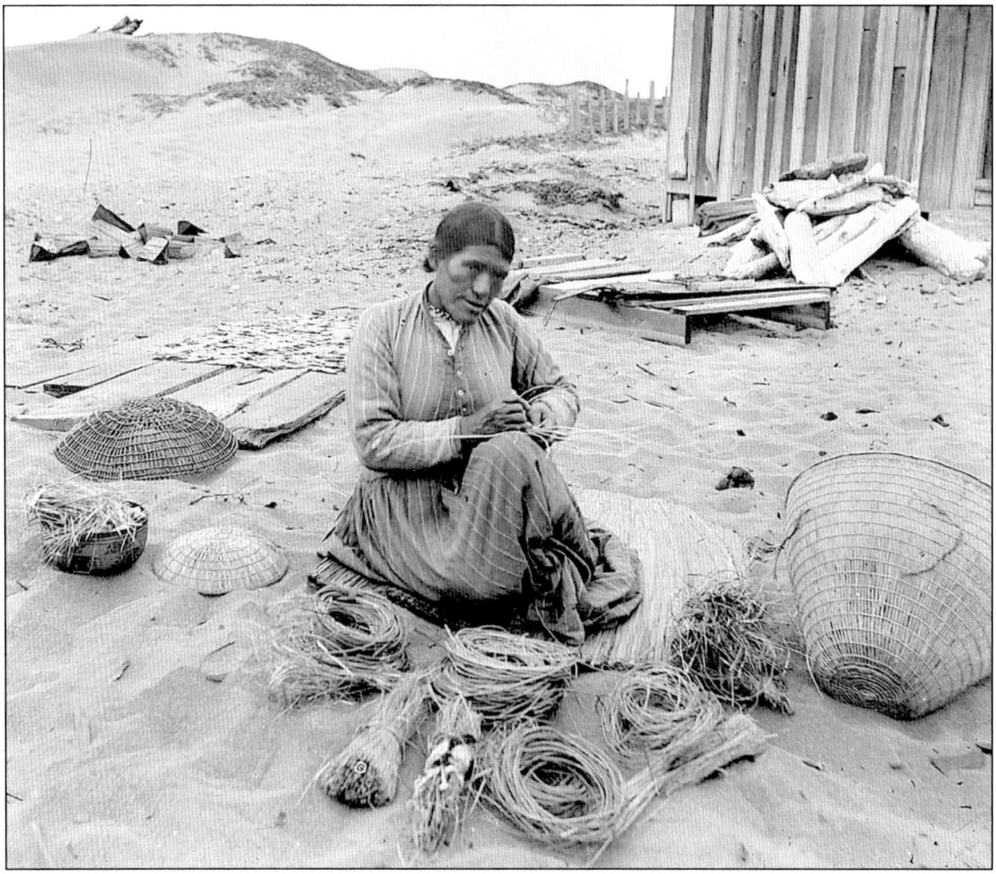

A basket weaver known as Mad River Annie demonstrates her skills in 1905. (Courtesy of Ericson Collection, Humboldt State University Library.)

CONTENTS

Acknowledgments

We are indebted to many for their help with this book. First, the Humboldt County Historical Society thanks the many members and non-members, near and far, who have donated their families' images and records of time spent in Humboldt County, some of which are shared here. The photos featured come from the collections of Helen DeZordo Cates, Kay Gott Chaffey, Harriet Tracy DeLong, Jon Humboldt Gates, Franny and Bess Givins, Robert Goss, Roy Gustafson, Don and Lila Lea Haffner, H. Brett Melendy, Leonard Nielson, Martha Roscoe, Robert Titlow, and Tom Woods. We're honored by your trust and your contribution to the ever-changing puzzle of the North Coast's past.

To Edie Butler of Humboldt State University's Humboldt Room, thank you for making many of long-time Arcata resident and professional photographer A.W. Ericson's images part of this collection. Edie deserves credit also for access to the Ruth Horel Collection, property of the Historic Sites Society of Arcata, and, of course, the balance of the HSU photos that complete the depiction of Humboldt Normal School, Humboldt State College, and, finally, Humboldt State University.

Anyone with the slightest interest in Arcata's history may have long admired Pete Hess's photographic collection hanging on the walls of his business, Hensel Hardware, at the corner of Tenth and I Streets in Arcata. We're thrilled and grateful to include a sample of those precious images—especially of the cows on the plaza. The willingness of lifelong Arcata resident Vivian Ziegler to loan her family's images to this effort is much appreciated. Ziegler's mother and father were among the many Swedish immigrants who made Arcata their home around the turn of the 20th century.

The actual work of putting this volume together would not have been possible without the many hours of effort put in by Humboldt County Historical Society research assistant Catherine Mace, a sixth-generation resident of Humboldt County. Despite busy days and few available hours, Catherine brought together the materials used to provide a deeper context for the images. Her efforts were aided immensely by Arcata historian Susie Van Kirk's 1979 volume, *Reflections on Arcata's History: Eighty Years of Architecture*.

Research and collections manager Matina Kilkenny's assistance in creating a path to the historical society's many images of Arcata and offering encouragement was invaluable, as was her help in fine-tuning both photo credits and captions. Humboldt County Historical Society executive director Denise Giltzow's well-refined eye for detail and penchant for order were crucial to making all the parts fall into place, tasks she took on between the many administrative duties that more than fill her hours at the Gross-Wells-Barnum House, the society's beloved office and research center. She remained confident in the project's outcome. Thank you, Denise. Thank you, reader, for peeking between these covers.

INTRODUCTION

Since its beginning in 1850 as Union, the namesake of the founding Union Company (a short-lived association to secure land for settlement), the community of Arcata, California, has exhibited all that makes up the diverse essence of Humboldt County: a deep sense of community, hard work, strong opinions, tolerance and intolerance, and a distinct consciousness of its place in the larger world. Much of that history has played out on the plaza—the center of the community and a gathering spot carefully watched over for the last century by a statue of President William McKinley.

The earliest history of this town was sometimes dark and violent. Bret Harte, who would go on to literary fame, penned a riveting, widely read editorial in 1860 condemning white men from the southern part of the county who massacred Wiyot men, women, and children on a nearby Humboldt Bay island. The whites attacked the Wiyot with hatchets in the dead of night just after the Indians had observed an annual religious celebration. Harte's denouncement of these murders led to his departure from Arcata about a month later.

But there were rays of light in the darkness. Methodist Rev. Asa White, credited with establishing the first Humboldt County church in the summer of 1850, defended the equality of all, regardless of ethnicity. As described in Gayle Karsher's book, *A Bell Rang in Uniontown*, White agreed to lead 120 wagons west along the Oregon Trail in 1847 on the condition that none of the travelers shoot an Indian except in self-defense. White's sensibilities helped to smooth what were often difficult relations between the settlers and the Indians in Humboldt County. Karsher wrote, "According to a family account, Rev. White went among the Indians, talking to them as a friend . . . Many came to trust him and to bring him their troubles and problems, which often involved the white settlers who had cheated or robbed them."

Other episodes of violence or discrimination against ethnic groups came when the city's Chinese residents were ordered to leave town following the fatal shooting of a Eureka city councilman on February 6, 1885. Arcata's Chinese residents were given until February 11 to leave—one day longer than the residents of Eureka's Chinatown were given. World War II gave rise to other fears that made no distinction between Italians, deemed the enemy, and Italian Americans. Those of Italian descent were forbidden to live west of G Street and were instructed to visit that portion of town only with a police escort.

Despite these episodes, the history of the city, officially incorporated in 1856, has a remarkable record of determined and often successful community efforts and progressive thinking and education. Opinions vary regarding the meaning of the name Arcata, as the city was christened in 1860. It is often noted as coming from the language of the nearby Indians; the Wiyot name for the land is "Goad-la-nah." Arcata is credited as the location of the first county school, established in 1852. Arcata High School, which until the early 1960s served all the teens from Arcata north to Orick, is the oldest high school in the county, having gotten its start in 1895. The clever members of the Arcata Women's Club, fueled by determination, used their refinement and social skills to convince the state board of education to establish Humboldt Normal School in their city in 1914, a victory that seemed to catch the Eureka promoters off-guard.

Arcata, while it was still known as Union or Uniontown, managed to secure the county seat but held it for only three years before it was snatched away by Eureka in 1856. Yet the city can lay permanent claim to the first church in Humboldt County and the first railroad in the state.

Flanked by the agricultural plains of the Arcata Bottom to the northwest, the gently sloping coastal hills to the east, and Humboldt Bay to the south, Arcata is the ancestral homeland of the Wiyot people. The recent establishment of the United Indian Health Services complex on the north edge of the city, site of an early Wiyot village that stood along a former path of the Mad River, renews that ancient connection to the land.

And despite early episodes of intolerance, Arcata has historically been home to diverse ethnic enclaves. The Portuguese, most of whom emigrated from the Azores, often made their living on the thriving dairy farms of the green and windswept Arcata Bottom. The Portuguese influence remains strong in Arcata with an annual celebration of Holy Ghost Day on Trinity Sunday. In the first three decades of the 20th century, nearly 1,000 Yugoslavians came to Humboldt County, many settling in the eastern section of Arcata. The Swedish have also had a cultural impact on Arcata, with one of its early merchants, Isaac Cullberg, arriving in 1853. He soon established a thriving business that served customers at his plaza store and, via pack trains, the miners seeking fortunes in the eastern hills.

In more recent years progressive thinking has gained Arcata national attention for such developments as the first city council in the nation with a Green Party majority and the widely acclaimed Arcata Marsh. The marsh uses thoughtful innovation to convert a wastewater treatment system into a favorite resting spot for hundreds of bird species and a like number of birdwatchers.

As in any collection, there are gaps here. Where, some may ask, are the photos of the Big 4 Inn, an extremely popular dinner house in Arcata, or why weren't photographs of the Arcata Theater included? Neither have yet made their way into the Humboldt County Historical Society's collection. The Humboldt County Historical Society thanks Peter Hess, the Humboldt State University Library, and the Historic Sites Society of Arcata for enriching this depiction of Arcata's past. If you have photographs that should be preserved for posterity, please consider sharing them with the Humboldt County Historical Society.

Nineteenth-century author Bret Harte spent part of his early career at *The Northern Californian*, Arcata's newspaper. In February 1860, Harte wrote an editorial damning those who massacred Wiyot men, women, and children during a nighttime attack on Indian Island. "He became the target of all those who upheld the white men," the *Humboldt Standard* reported in 1928. Hart soon left for San Francisco. (Courtesy of Humboldt County Historical Society.)

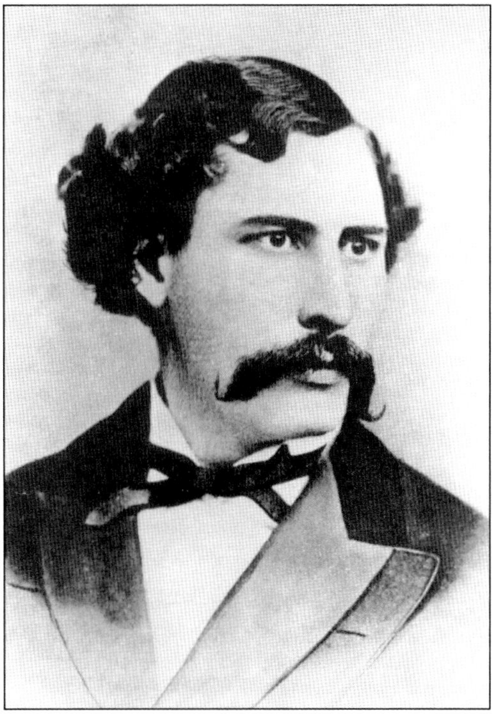

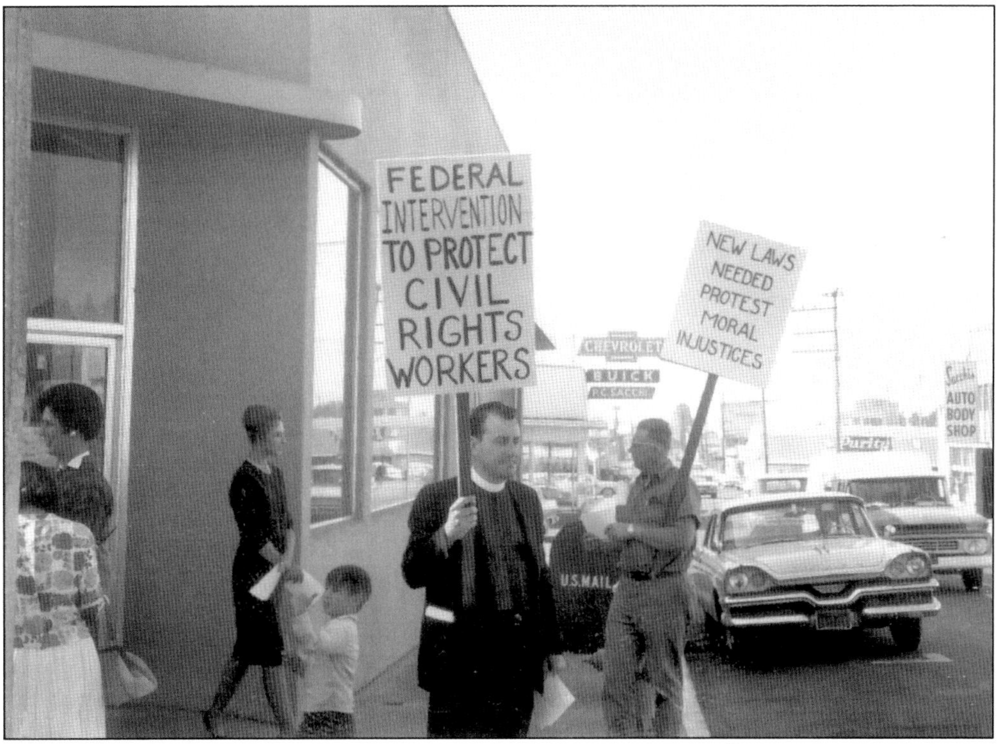

Episcopal Rev. John Downing pickets in front of the U.S. Post Office on October 1, 1965, calling upon the federal government to protect civil rights workers. (Courtesy of Humboldt County Historical Society, KIEM Collection.)

One

Plaza

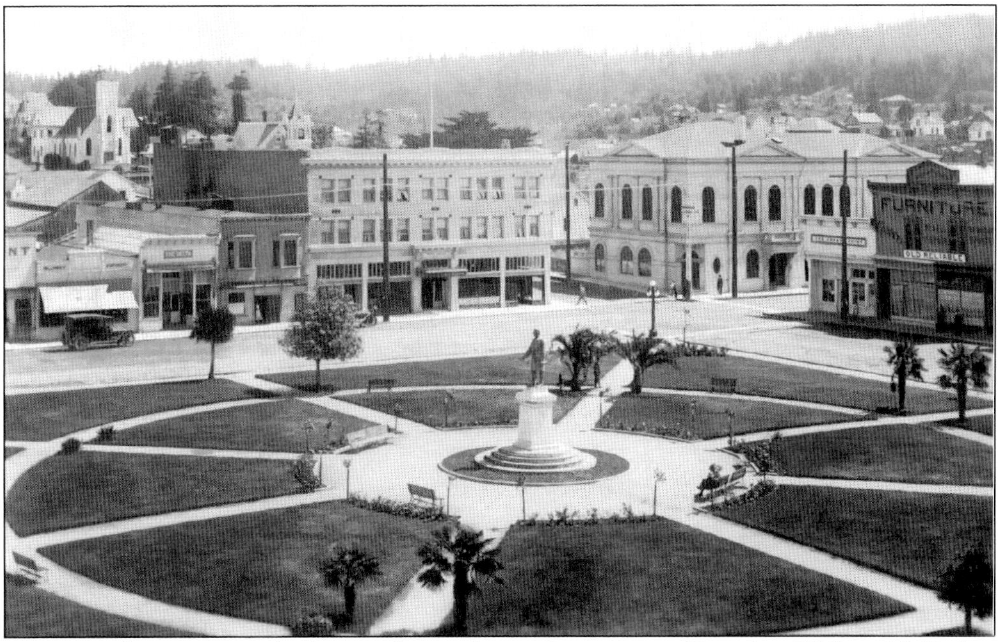

Arcata resident George Zehndner, wishing to honor the memory of President William McKinley, commissioned a statue of the late president in 1906—a work that nearly became a casualty of the 1906 earthquake and fire. Sculptor Haig Patigian's statue, which was thrown to the floor of the San Francisco foundry, escaped damage when its backward fall was broken by a plaster cast. Although charred, McKinley's bronze likeness survived the fire that followed when workers removed it to the middle of the street. Arcatans celebrated the sculpture's unveiling on July 4, 1906. (Courtesy of Humboldt County Historical Society.)

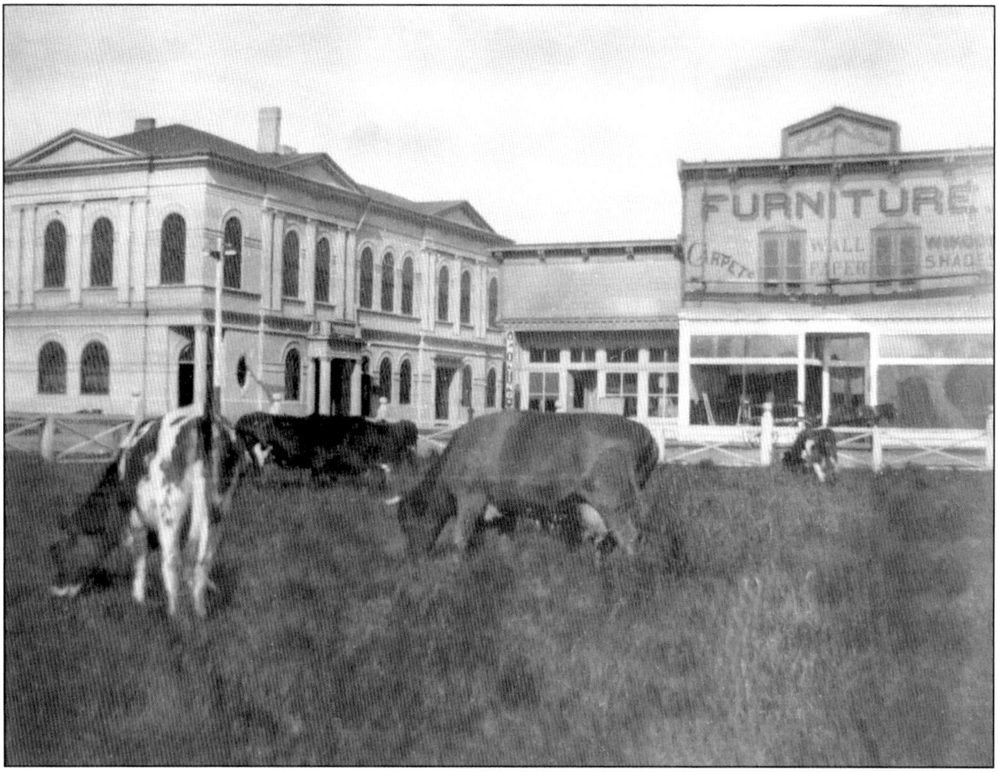

The Plaza Improvement Committee banned cows from the plaza after the bandstand was completed in 1901. Livestock had likely grazed on the plaza since the Union Company deemed Block 167 a park or plaza. Mule corrals were common on the plaza during the days of pack trains. By the time of the 1901 ban, plaza livestock included cows and at least one goat. (Courtesy of Peter Hess.)

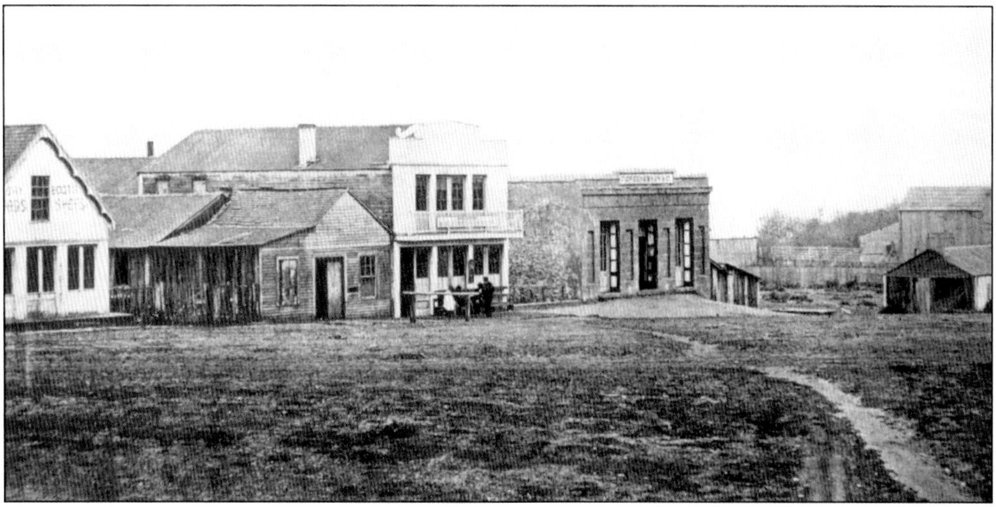

One of the earliest images of the plaza, this 1870 view looking southwest shows Augustus Jacoby's fireproof store, built in 1857, on the far right. The white building to the left is the hotel and saloon run by Jacoby and Alexander Paskesher. (Courtesy of Humboldt County Historical Society, Roscoe Collection.)

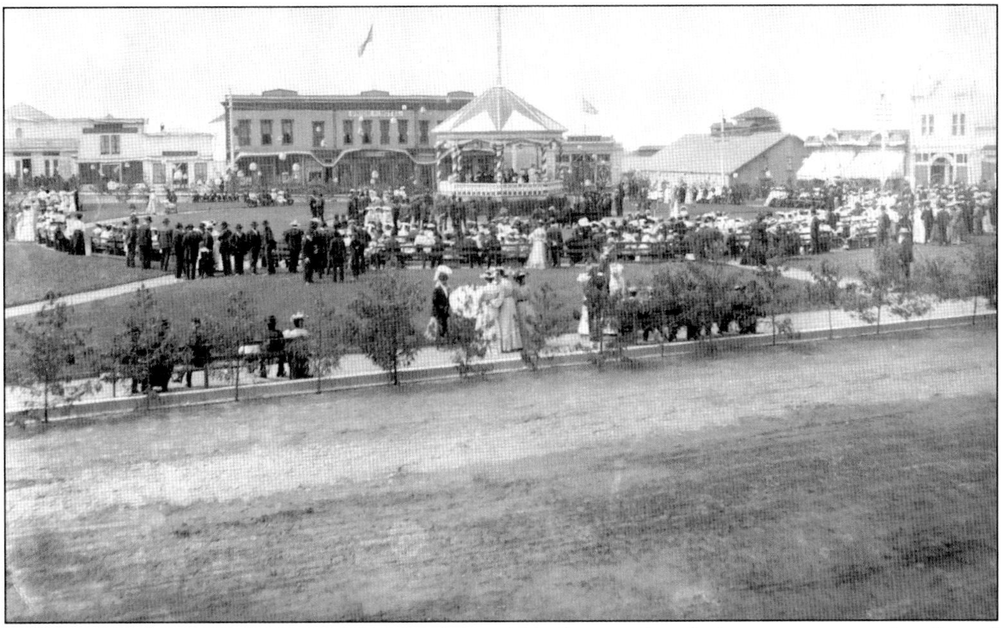

The Plaza Improvement Committee planned and completed this impressive bandstand in 1901, but it was removed just five years later to make way for the statue of President William McKinley. The fence that surrounded the green was torn down shortly after the bandstand appeared and the first palm trees were planted in 1903. (Courtesy of Humboldt County Historical Society.)

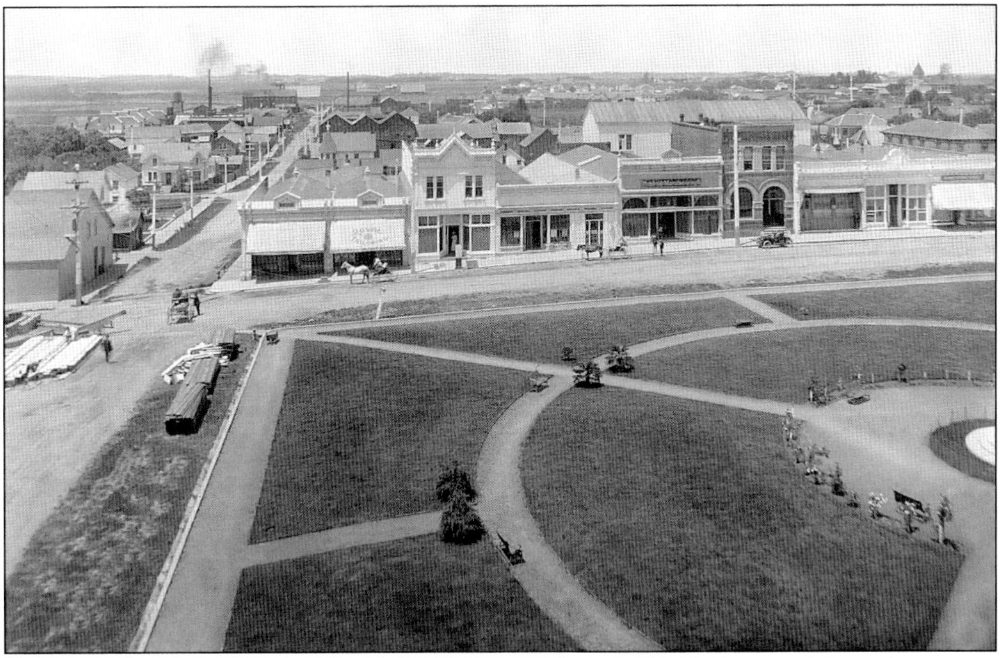

The west plaza businesses in this undated photo show a tailor shop second from the corner, on the left, and the Humboldt Manufacturing Company office fourth from left. The peaked bell tower of Arcata Grammar School can be seen in the upper right background. (Courtesy of Ericson Collection, Humboldt State University Library.)

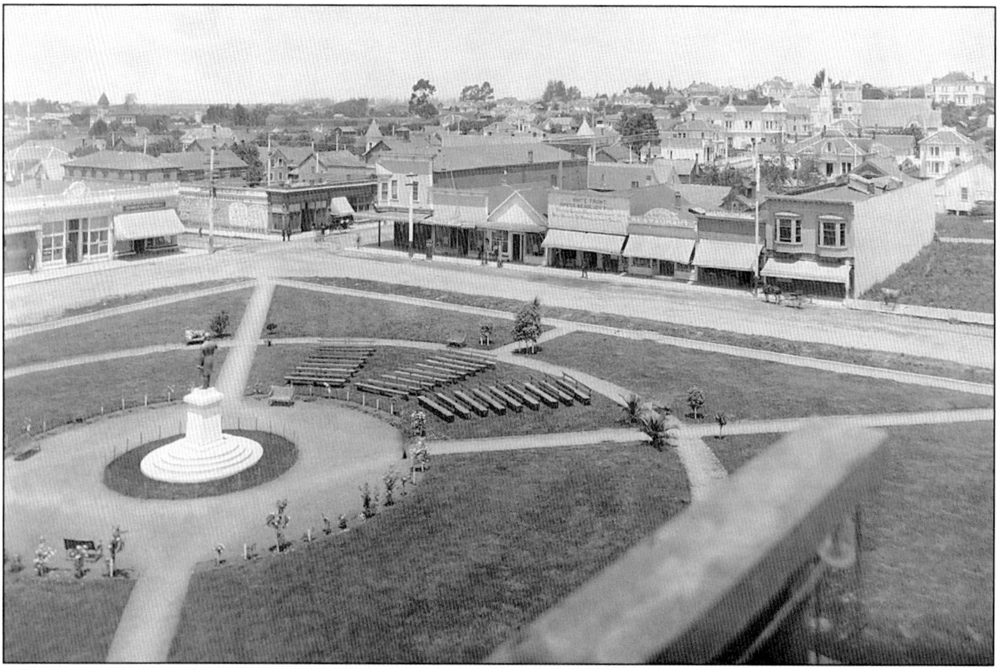

This view shows the north and west sides of the plaza between 1906 and 1914. Benches are set out for an unknown event. (Courtesy of Humboldt State University Library.)

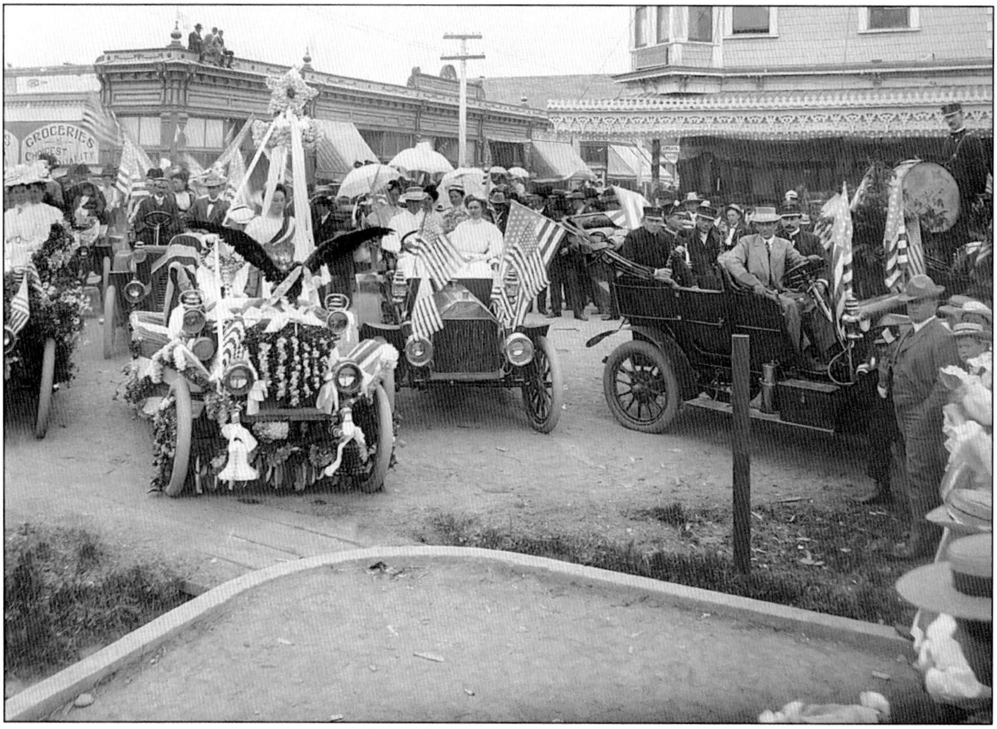

These well-decorated Fourth of July celebrants round the corner of Ninth and G Streets to join the community-wide celebration on the plaza. (Courtesy of Ericson Collection, Humboldt State University Library.)

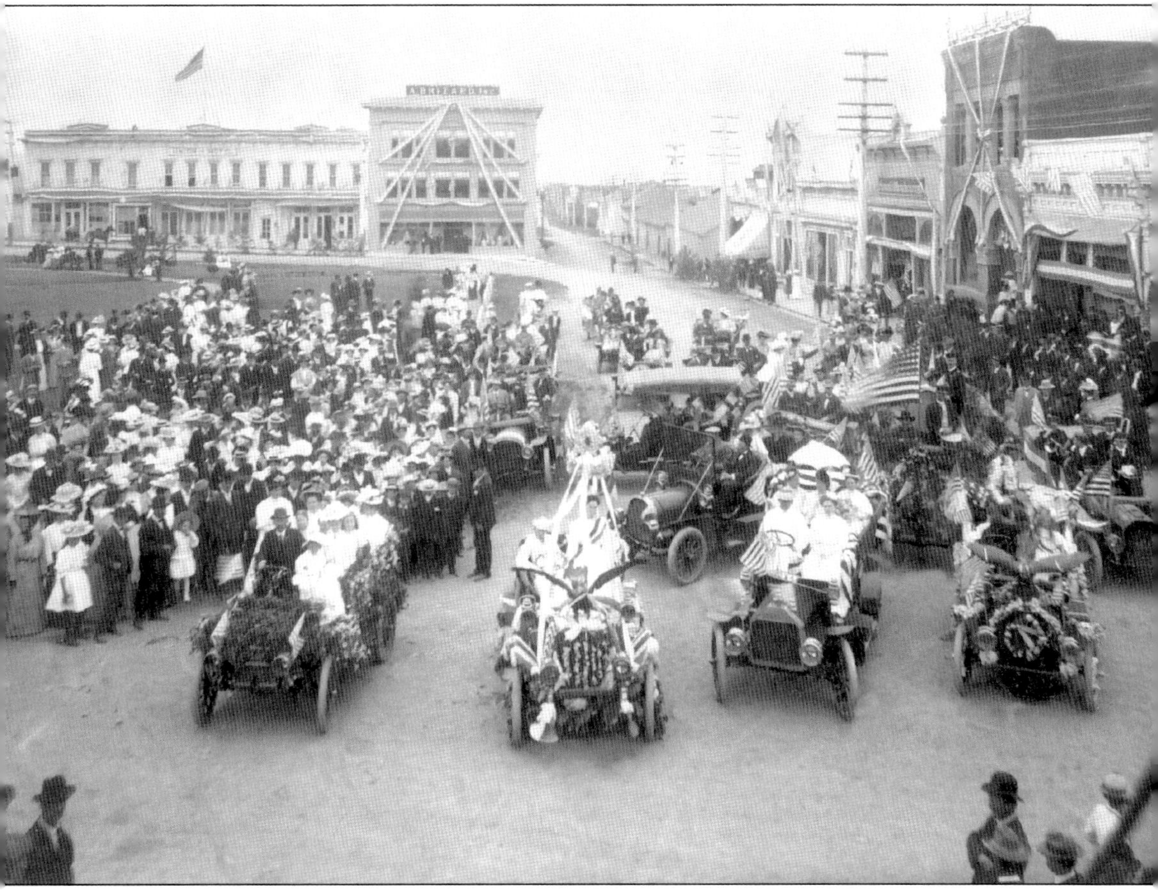

Arcata residents gather on the plaza on Independence Day 1908. The Union Hotel, just left of the bunting-decorated Brizard's in the background, included the Union Restaurant and Saloon in the 1860s and was owned by several parties. Jacob Richert eventually took over management from 1871 to 1881, the same year the 1860s structure was removed and rebuilt. A variety of retail businesses were opened in the hotel's first floor over the years. The top story burned in 1936. (Courtesy of Humboldt County Historical Society.)

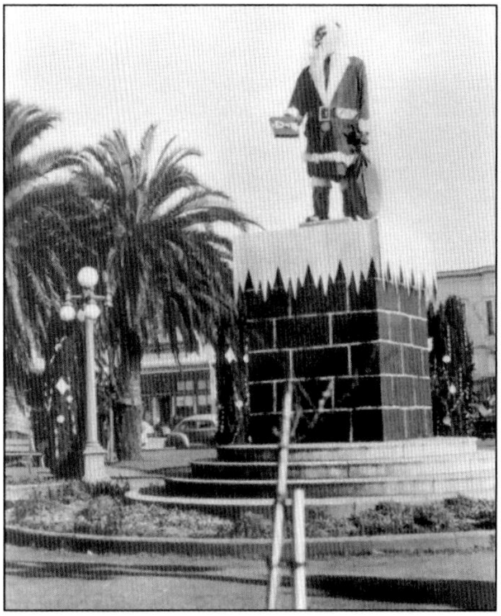

President McKinley's likeness gets into the plaza's holiday spirit in this *c.* 1930s image. Townspeople continue to decorate the statue whenever the spirit moves them. (Courtesy of Humboldt County Historical Society.)

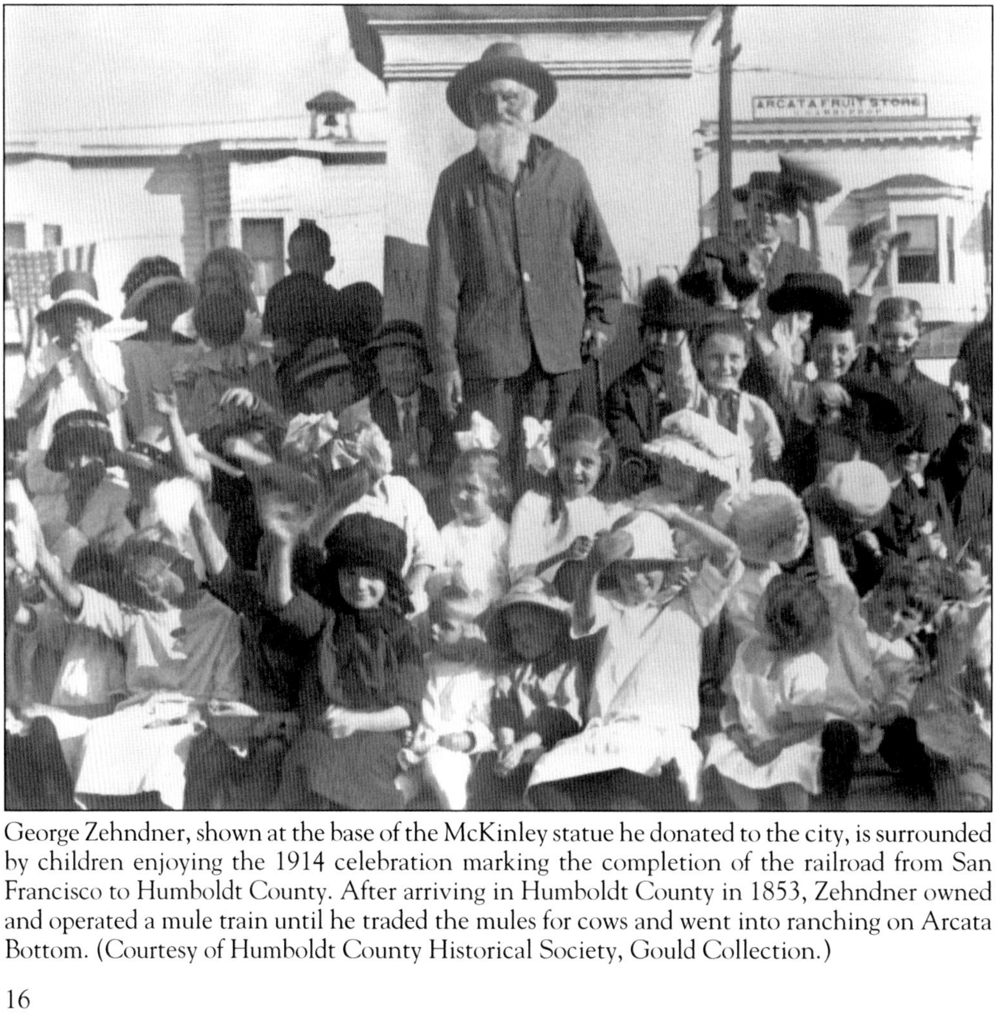

George Zehndner, shown at the base of the McKinley statue he donated to the city, is surrounded by children enjoying the 1914 celebration marking the completion of the railroad from San Francisco to Humboldt County. After arriving in Humboldt County in 1853, Zehndner owned and operated a mule train until he traded the mules for cows and went into ranching on Arcata Bottom. (Courtesy of Humboldt County Historical Society, Gould Collection.)

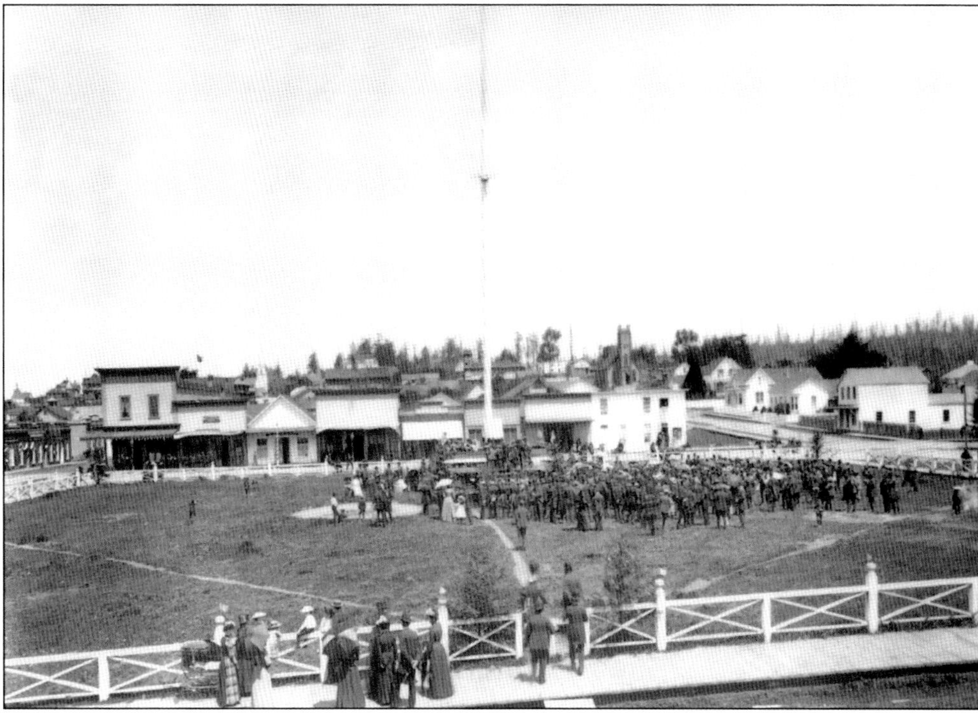

Taken prior to 1900—as a fence still surrounds the plaza—this image shows a gathering for an unknown reason. Among the buildings visible on the north side are Buck's Saloon, the first building left of the corner, with a dance floor on the second story, and Bull's Meat Market, second from the right corner. The two-story white building on the right corner would come down to make way for the Hotel Arcata in 1914. (Courtesy of Humboldt County Historical Society, Roscoe Collection.)

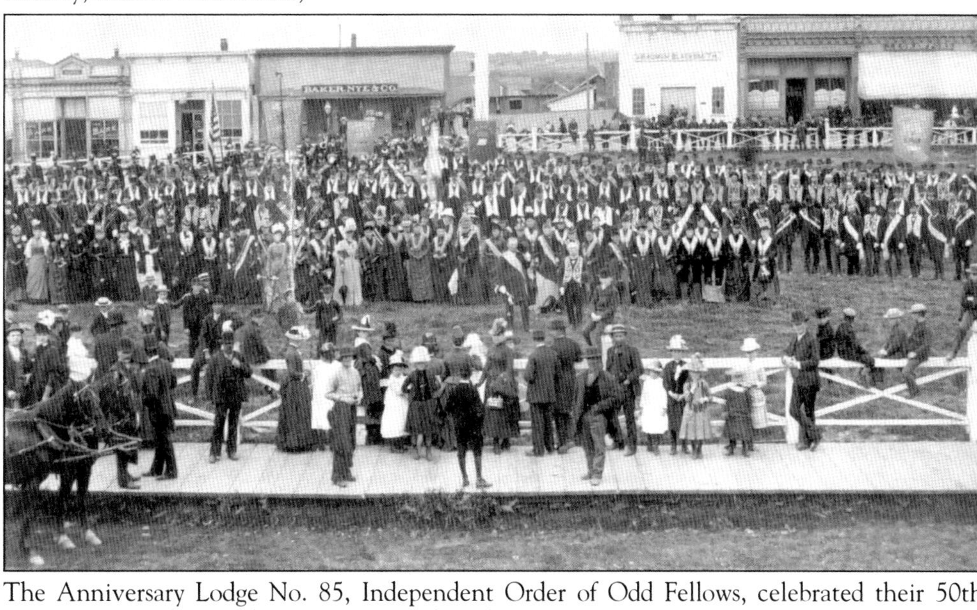

The Anniversary Lodge No. 85, Independent Order of Odd Fellows, celebrated their 50th anniversary with grand festivities on the plaza April 26, 1909. (Courtesy of Humboldt State University Library.)

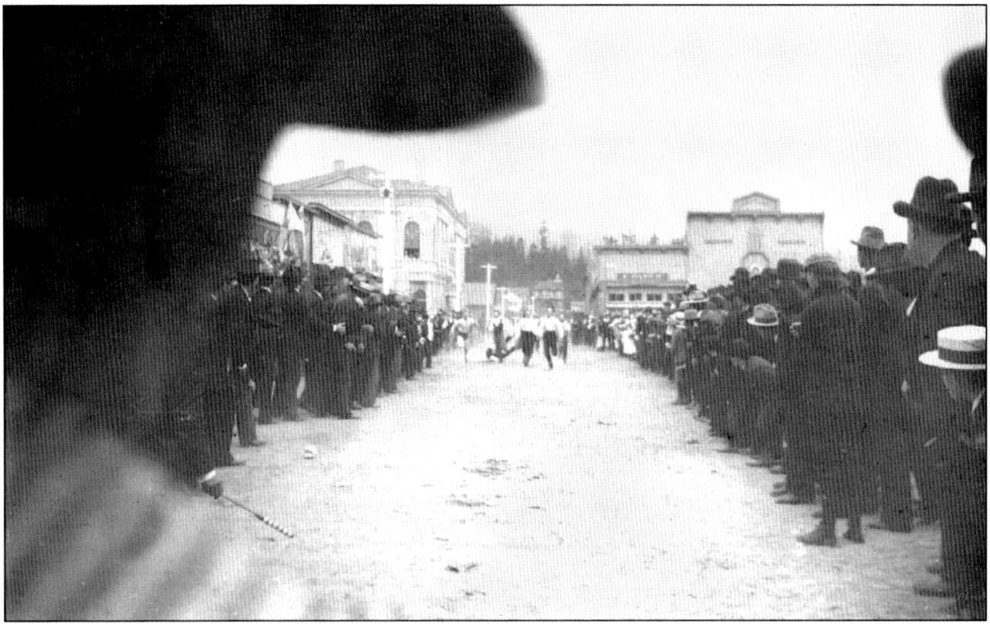

Quick-moving men race west on Ninth Street sometime between 1896, when the city hall was built, and 1914, when Hotel Arcata went up. (Courtesy of Historic Sites Society of Arcata, Ruth Horel Collection.)

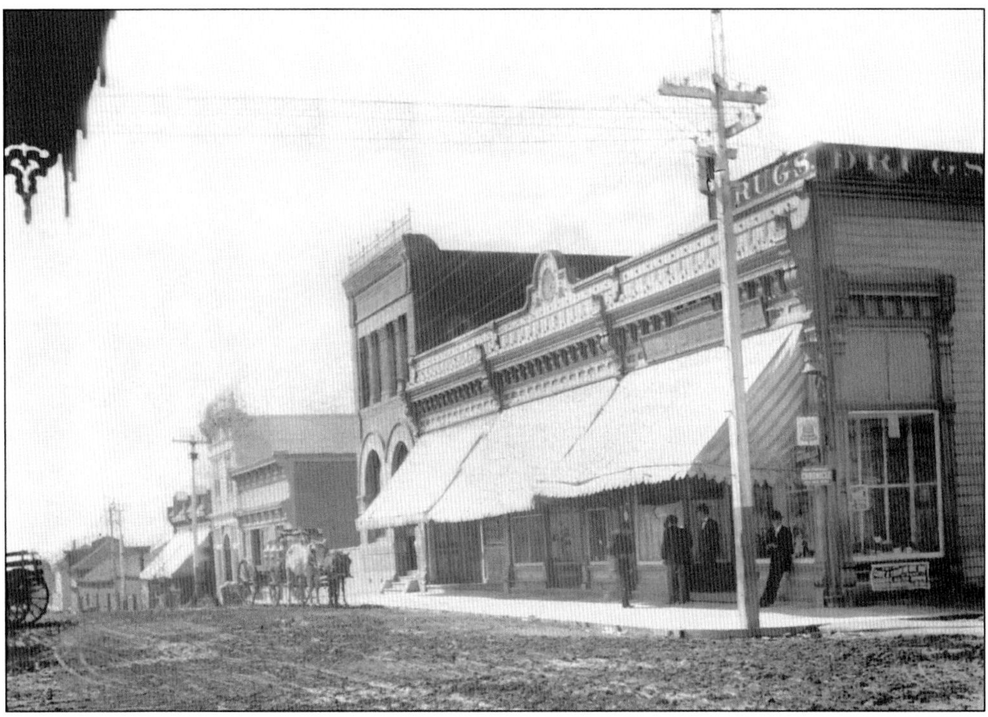

Dirt streets were the standard throughout Arcata until well into the 20th century. The Davies & Ericson Drugstore, shown here in 1887, stood on the northwest corner of the plaza and lasted just three years, from 1886 to 1889. (Courtesy of Historic Sites Society of Arcata, Ruth Horel Collection.)

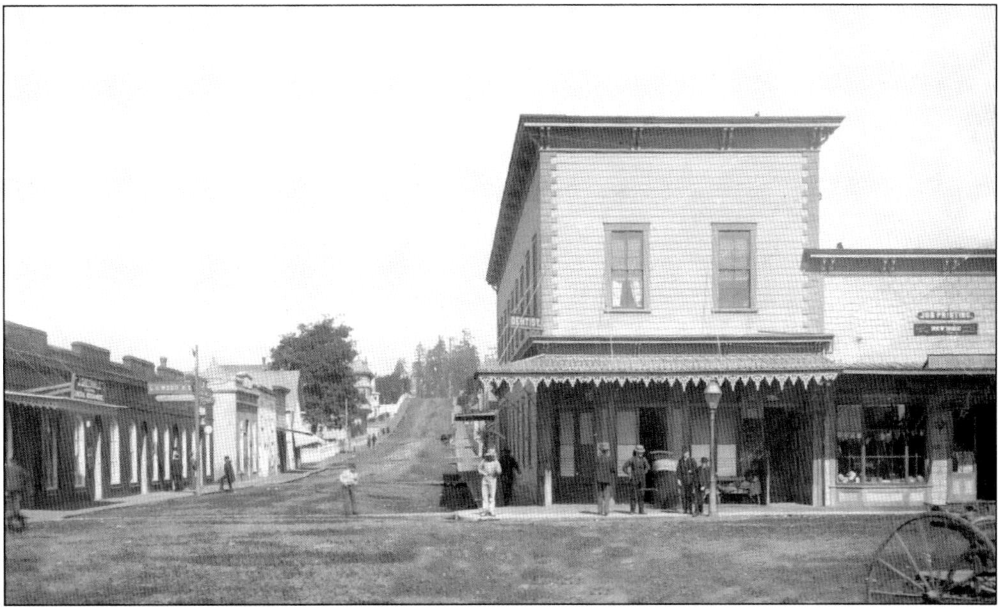

This prominent structure at the corner of Ninth and G Streets was built in 1876. The unique porch, the last of its kind on the plaza, was removed in 1922. The downstairs was most often a liquor store or saloon, but it was also the home of the Arcata Safeway from 1931 to 1942. The upstairs housed the Knights of Pythias until they built their own hall farther up G Street in 1885. Woodmen of the World also gathered upstairs. (Courtesy of Humboldt State University Library.)

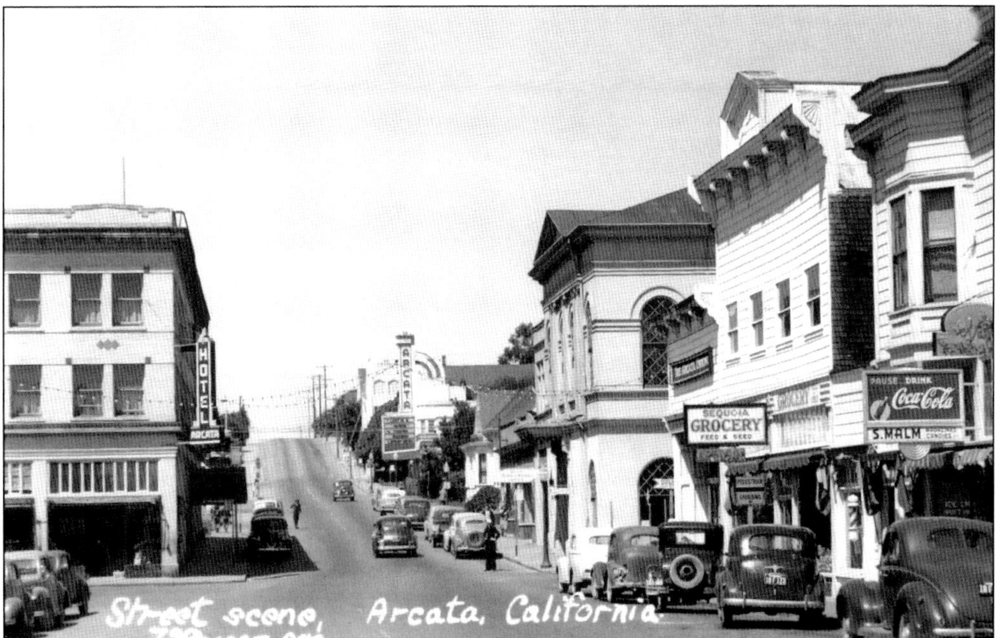

The Sequoia Grocery Store at right was one of the many enterprises that occupied the Bull Building on Arcata's G Street. The store ran for 12 years, from 1943 to 1955. (Courtesy of Humboldt County Historical Society, Woods Collection.)

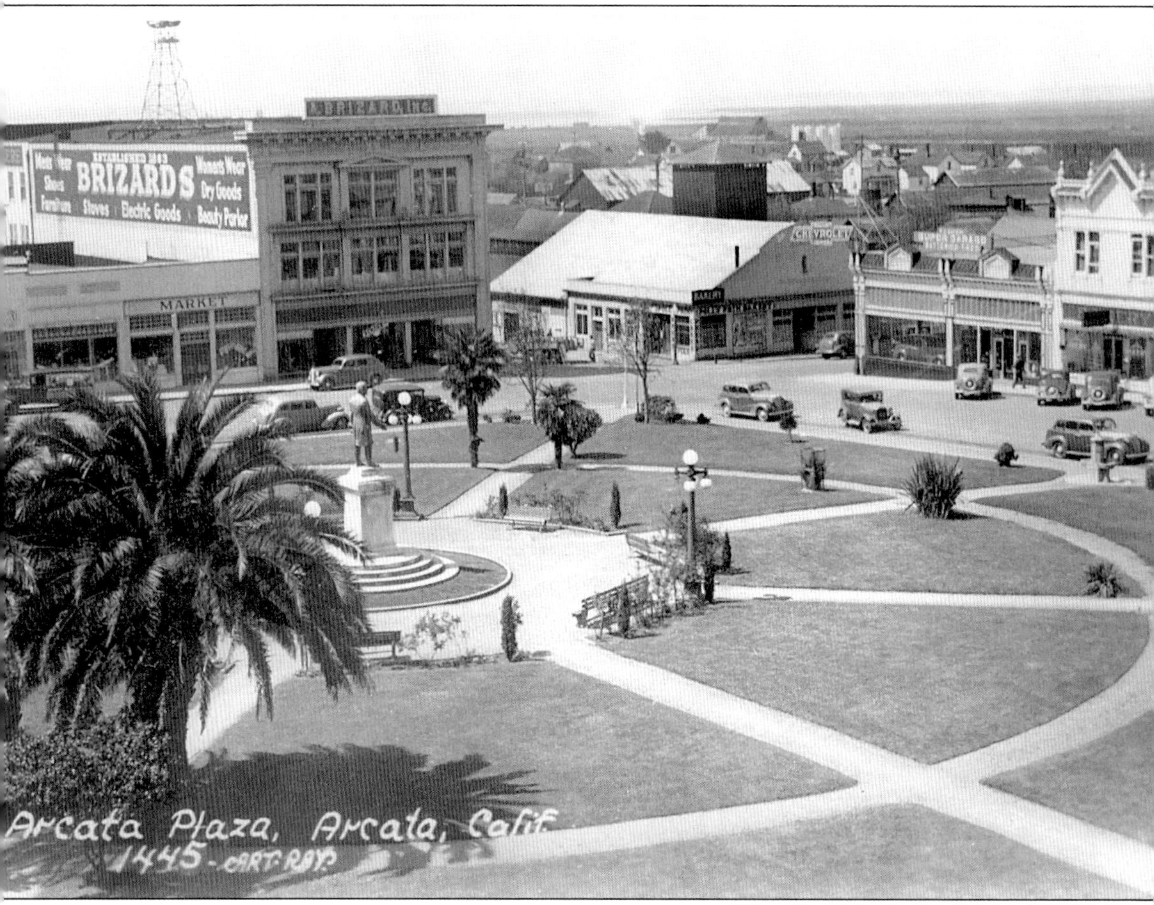

This view of Eighth and H Streets shows the starting point for the railroad track built to the Union Wharf in 1855. A new passenger depot and warehouse were built at the site in 1887. The corner, home to the post office since 1950, served as a repair and storage space for Brizard's as well as a depot for McConnaha's Humboldt Motor Stages, Pickwick Stage Company, and the Greyhound Bus Company. (Courtesy of Humboldt County Historical Society.)

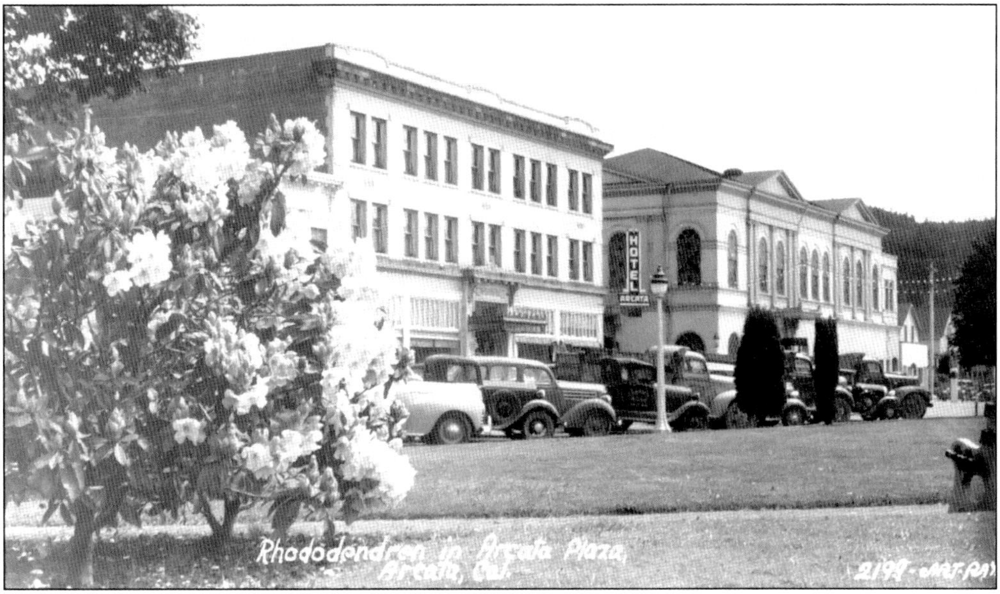

Hotel Arcata opened for visitors on April 26, 1915, to much acclaim. The *Arcata Union* filled an entire page describing the city's newest hostelry on April 29, 1915, from the $80,000 price tag to the more than 1,000 people who visited on the opening day, to detailed descriptions of "massive oak Mission furniture." George Marken, Noah Falk, Ralph Bull, S. Myers, and Henry Brizard were the first directors of the Arcata Hotel Company. (Courtesy of Humboldt County Historical Society, Titlow Collection.)

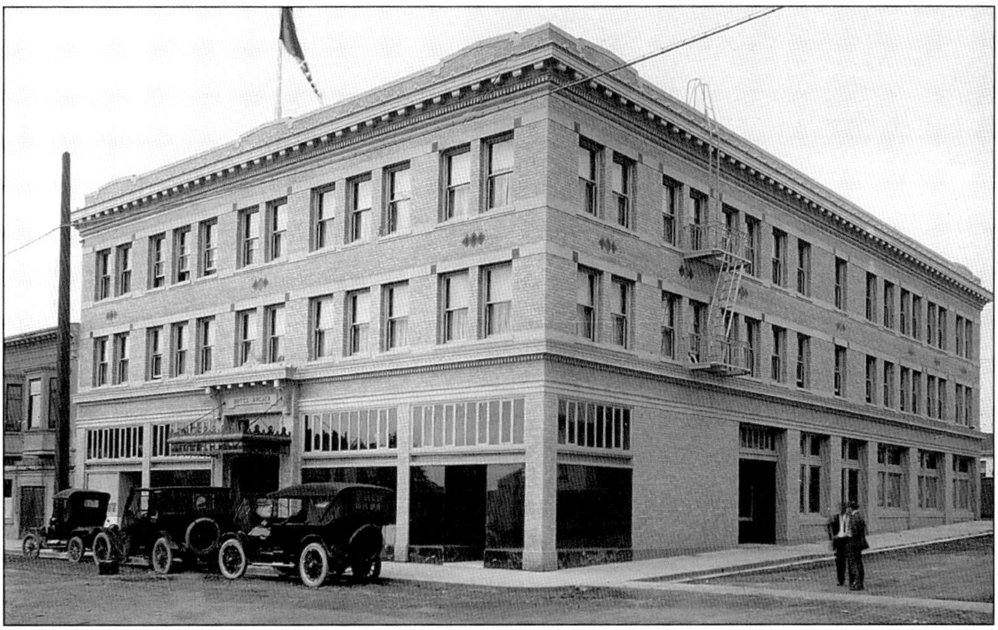

The three-story brick Hotel Arcata drew both temporary and permanent residents in its early days. The well-known establishment, which still anchors the plaza's northeast corner, initially included separate lobbies for men and women. The hotel helped relieve a Humboldt State College student housing shortage in 1967 by renting rooms for $10 a week. (Courtesy of Humboldt State University Library.)

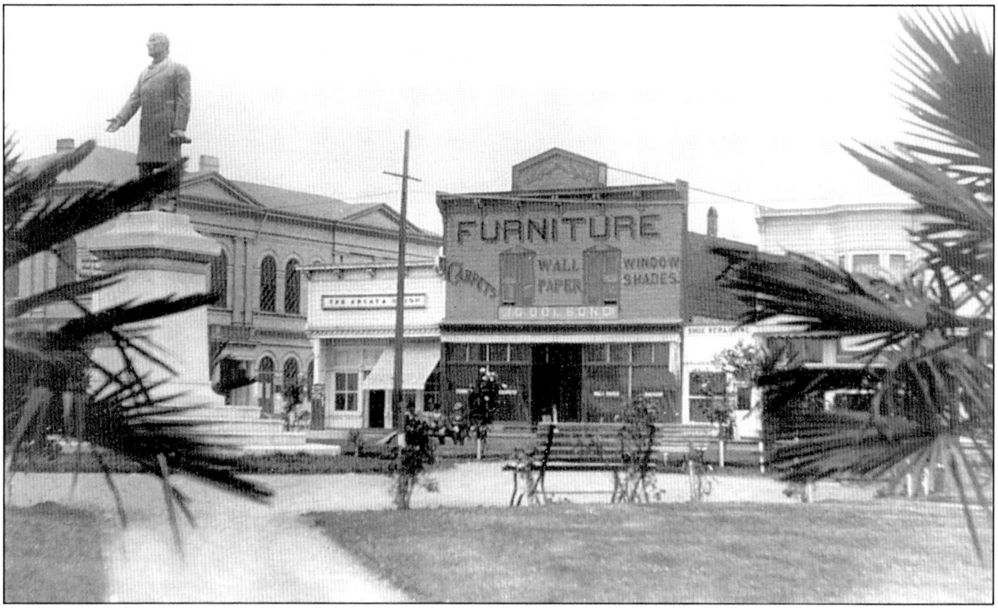

John C. Bull Jr. built this false-front structure in 1890 and included corrugated galvanized iron on the roof as a fire precaution; a year earlier the structure at the site had fallen to just such a blaze. Originally a livery stable, the G Street building has been home to furniture stores, an undertaker, a meat market, a shoe shop, a Buick dealership, a variety store, a grocery, a thrift store, and an outdoor equipment retailer. (Courtesy of Humboldt County Historical Society.)

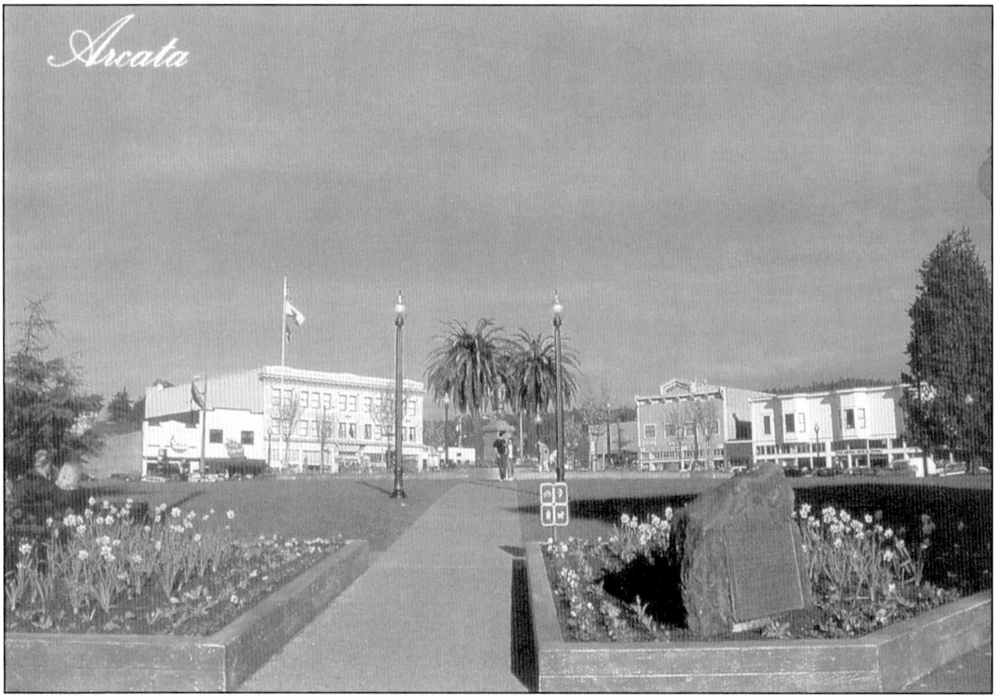

This postcard image provides a late 20th century northeastern perspective on the Arcata Plaza. A plaque on the boulder in the right flowerbed describes the history of the Jacoby Storehouse. (Courtesy of Humboldt County Historical Society, Woods Collection.)

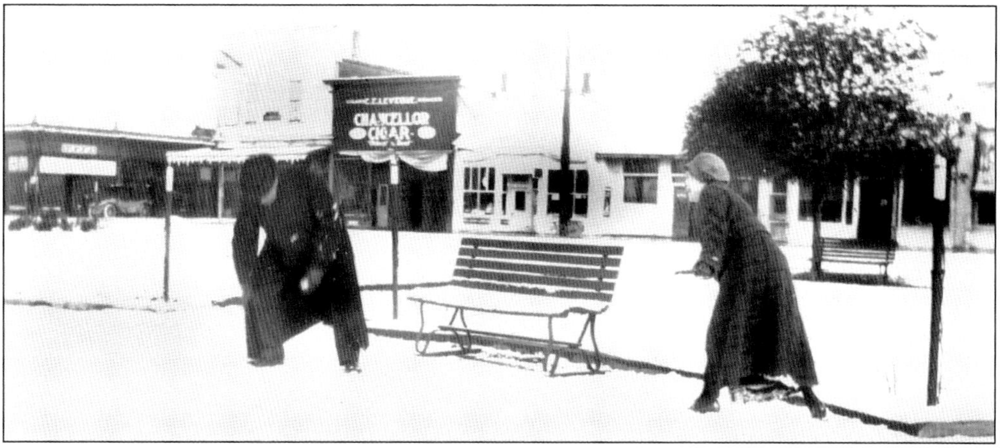

Snowfall is rare and a bit of a novelty for those living on Northern California's coast. Here the plaza lies under a blanket of white, probably around 1915, providing a chance for a few well-placed snowballs by these frolickers. (Courtesy Historic Sites Society of Arcata, Ruth Horel Collection.)

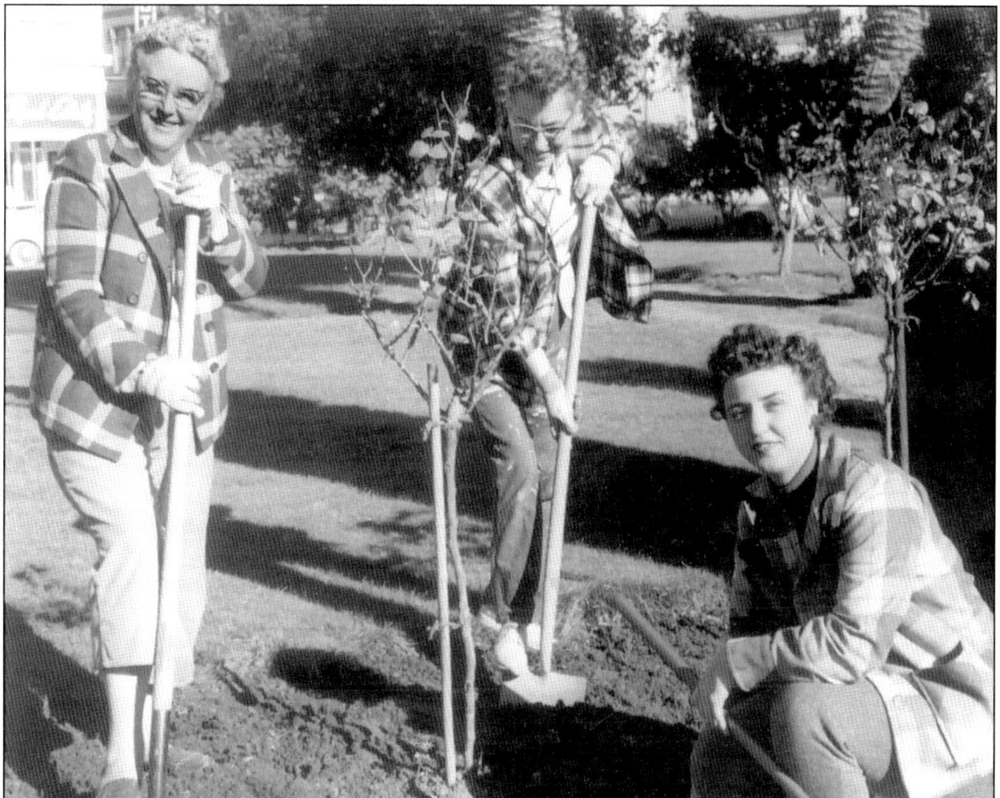

The Arcata Business and Professional Women's Club put some muscle behind their effort to beautify the plaza in late 1957 and early 1958 by planting more than 600 tulip, daffodil, narcissus, and crocus bulbs around the McKinley statue. Shown, from left to right, are club members Alice Beer, Cynthia Schwenson, and Irene Krellwitz taking a brief break from their work. (Courtesy of Humboldt County Historical Society, Roscoe Collection.)

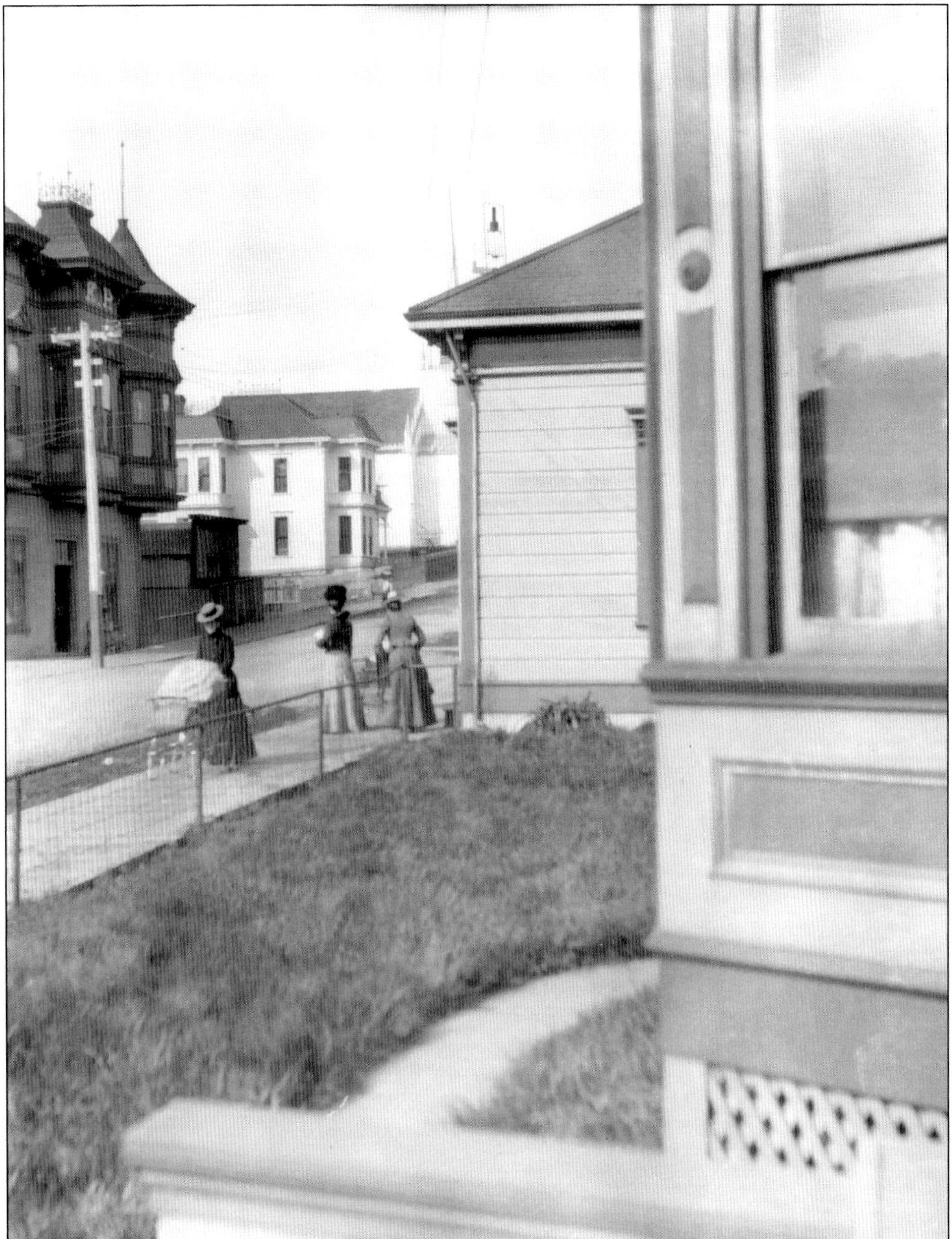

H Street's wooden sidewalks provided a means for these women to visit and roll their baby buggies with a minimum of dust and inconvenience. On the left, across Eleventh Street, the Pythian Castle looms with a glimpse of Atlanta Methodist Church and parsonage visible farther up the street. (Courtesy of Humboldt County Historical Society, Woods Collection.)

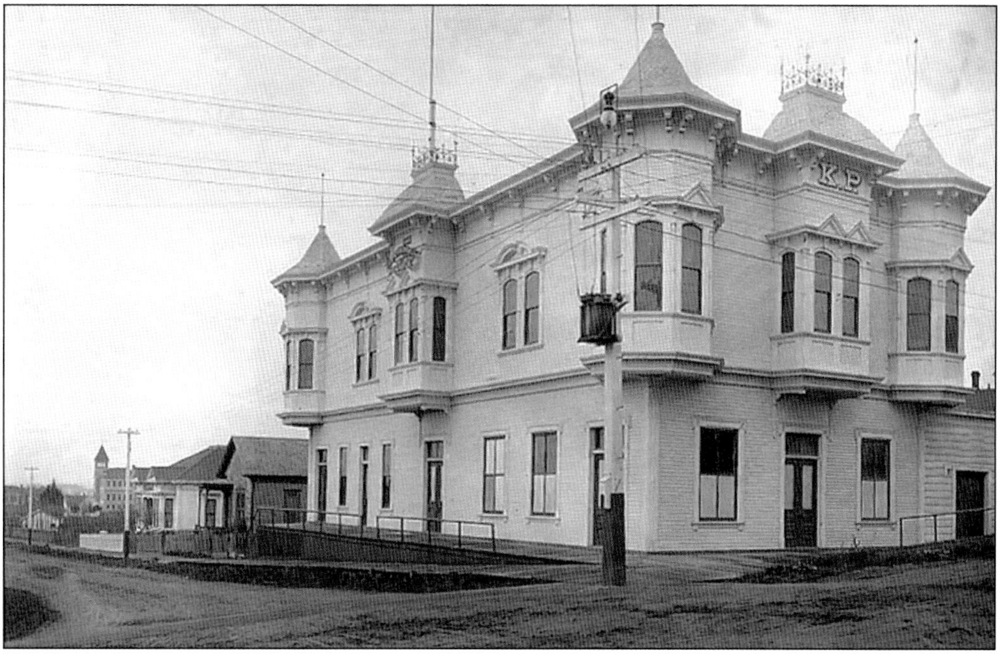

The Pythian Castle still anchors the corner of H and Eleventh Streets and has been home to numerous businesses since its construction in 1885 for North Star Lodge No. 39, Knights of Pythias. The lodge was organized in 1876 as a fraternal organization. (Courtesy of Peter Hess.)

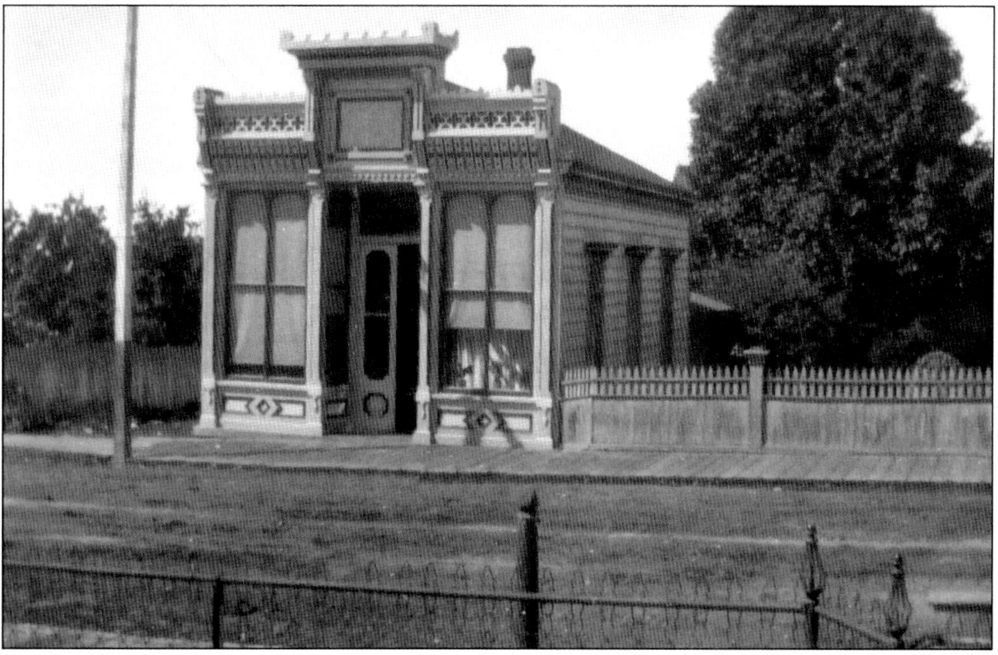
The small false-front establishment on H Street was originally built in 1884 as a milliner's shop for Mrs. David Minor at the direction of businessman Isaac Minor. The enterprise was expanded to dressmaking and taken over by Mrs. Joseph Otto in the following years. Between 1902 and the present, the single-story shop has been a dentist's office, shoe shop, paint store, and several restaurants. (Courtesy of Peter Hess.)

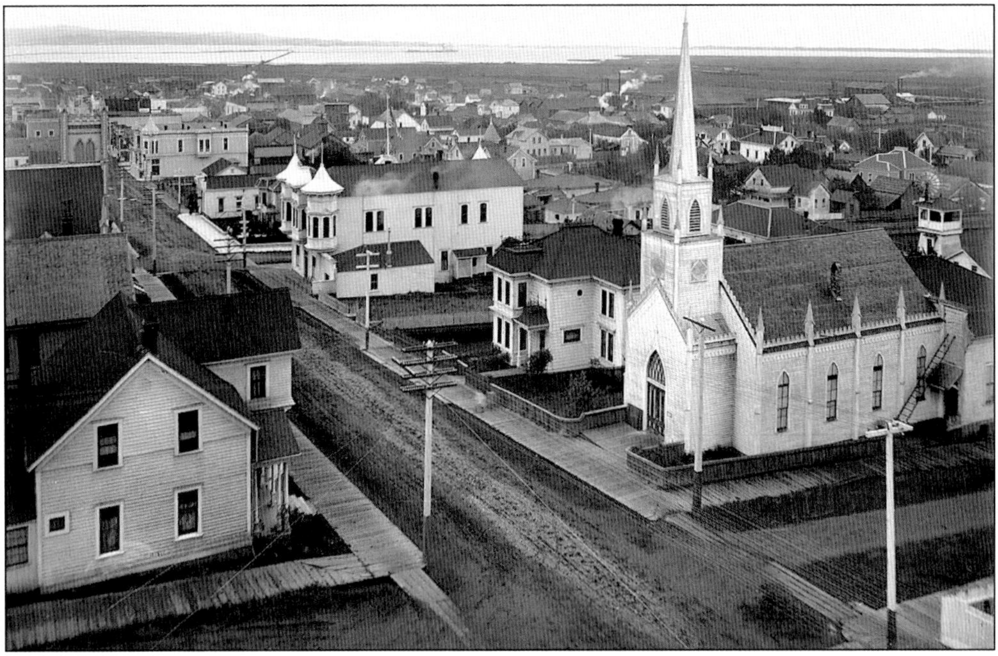

The Methodists got an early start in Arcata in the summer of 1850 under the direction of the dynamic Rev. Asa White. The *c.* 1866 Atlanta Methodist Church building seen on the right underwent a major renovation in 1911 and served the congregation until 1960 when its successor was built closer to the bay on Eleventh Street. (Courtesy of Humboldt County Historical Society.)

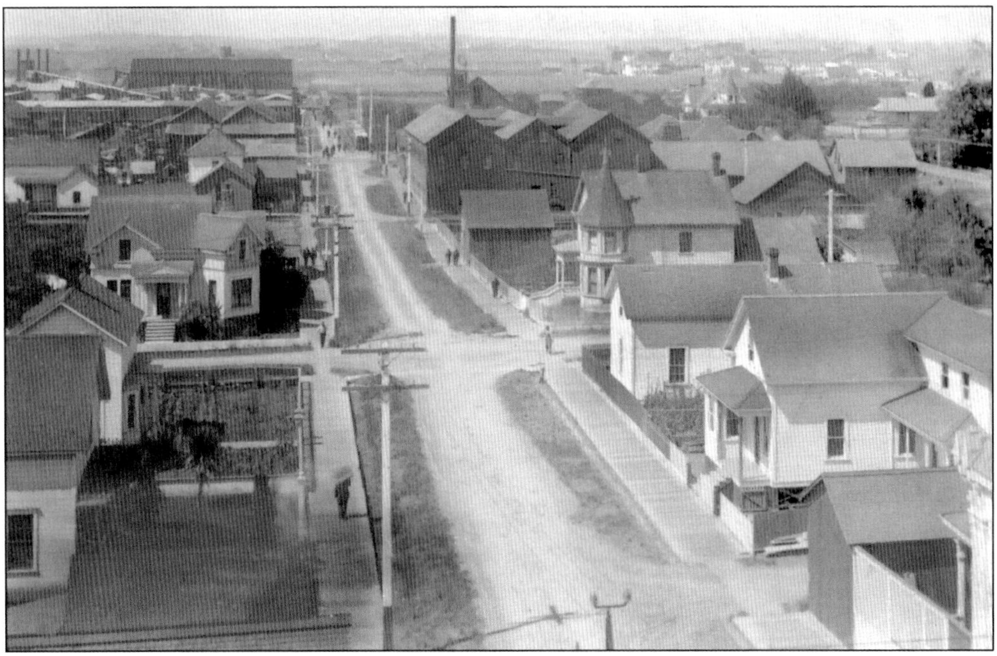

This 1915 image looks away from the plaza west on Eighth Street. At J Street, the three peaked roofs of the Thomas Devlin Tanning Company tower over surrounding homes. (Courtesy of Humboldt County Historical Society, Roscoe Collection.)

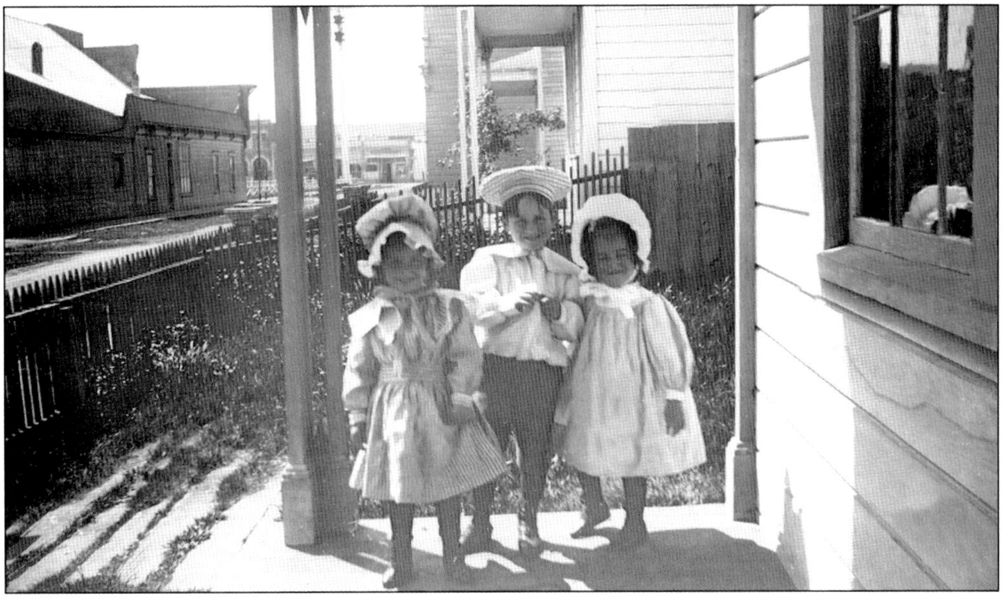

Almost a century ago, three youngsters graced the porch of a house that still stands today on the corner of Ninth and F Streets. (Courtesy of Historic Sites Society of Arcata, Ruth Horel Collection.)

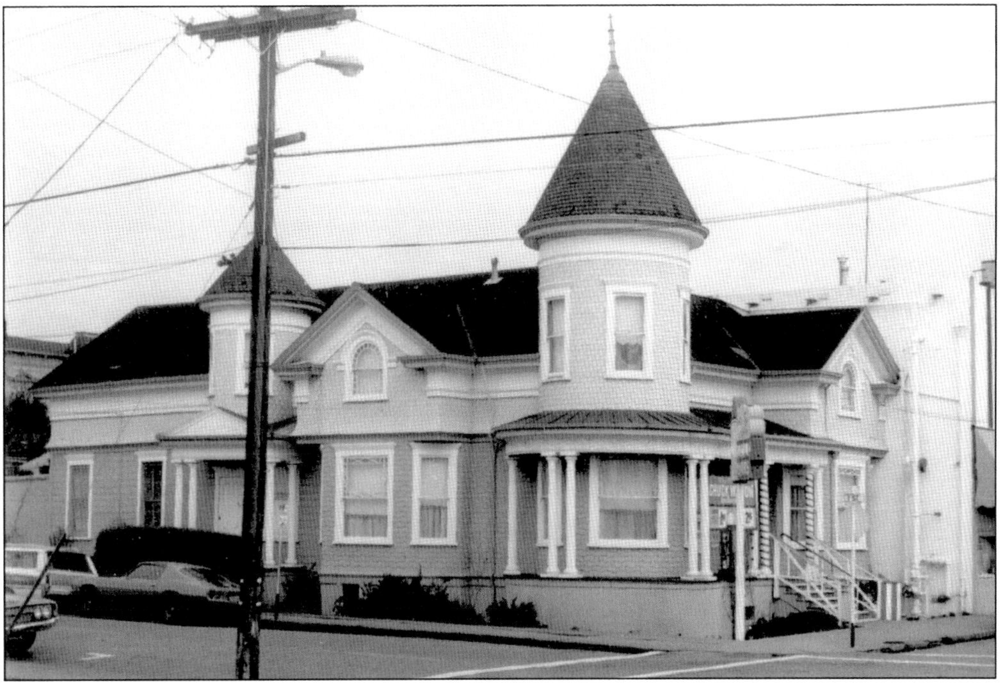

A well-known landmark at Tenth and I Streets and home to several restaurants over the years, this home was originally built for John Chapman in 1876 and was extensively remodeled and expanded in 1902. The house was home to James Kirk in 1883 and was leased to Humboldt Normal School's first president, N.B. Van Matre, in 1914. Walter and Tessa Wood purchased the house in 1925 and Mr. Wood, Arcata High School music teacher, provided private lessons to students there. (Courtesy of Vivian Ziegler.)

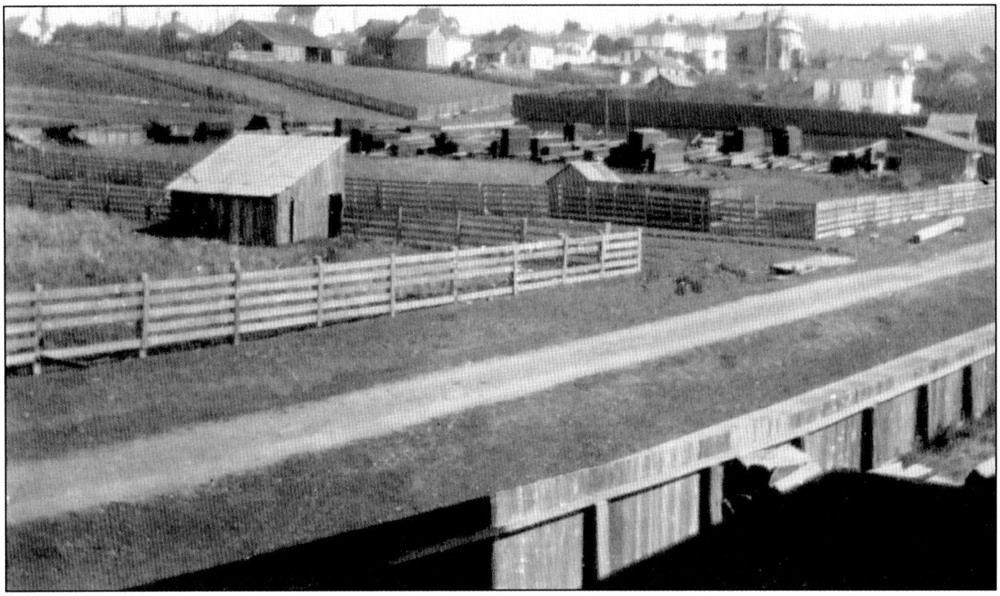

This early vista looks north from the western portion of the city. (Courtesy of Peter Hess.)

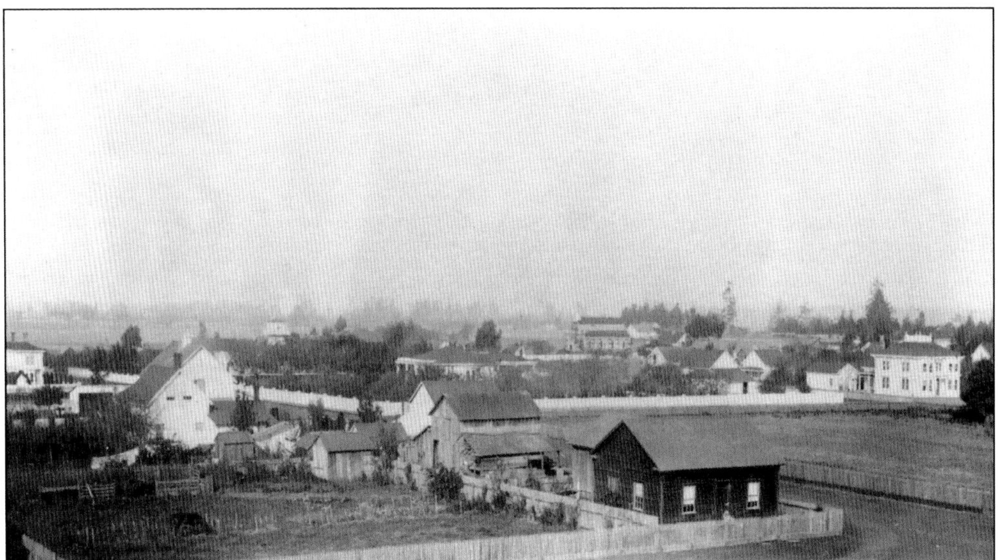

West Arcata, a portion of which is shown here, provided plenty of open space for gardening and livestock. (Courtesy California State Library, Humboldt County Historical Society.)

Two

Business

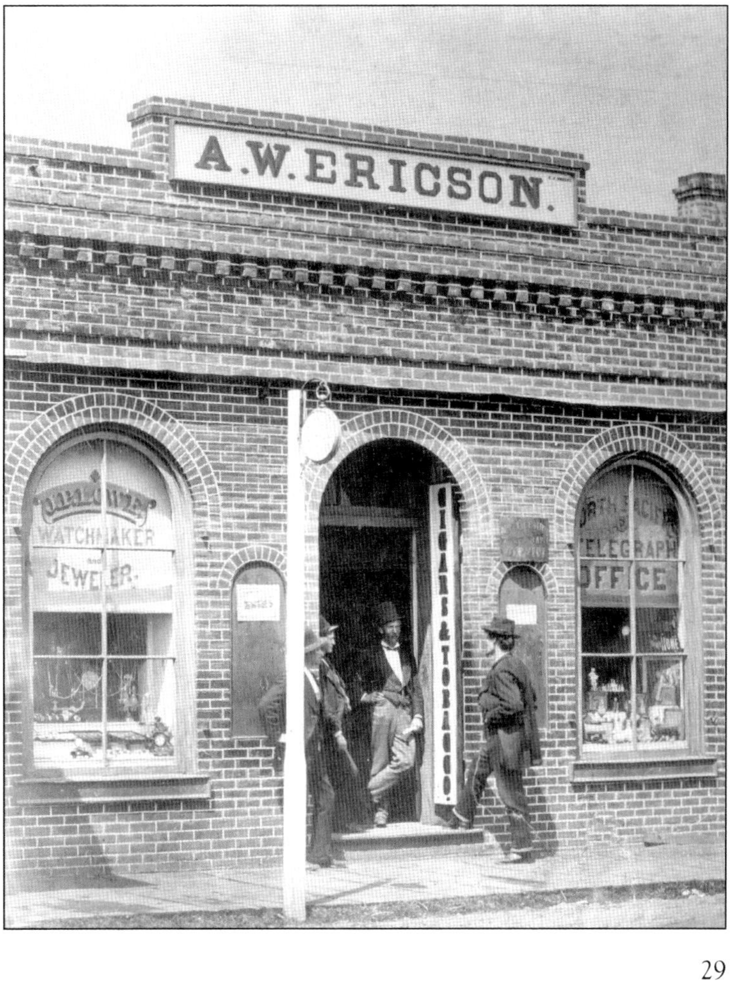

Customers at Arcata photographer A.W. Ericson's Ninth and H Streets store stop to visit on July 4, 1877. Ericson offered music and books in his establishment, which was part of the brick structure built that year. Also located here in the 1880s were the Arcata Reading Room, a telegraph office, and post office. (Courtesy of Humboldt County Historical Society, Stine Collection.)

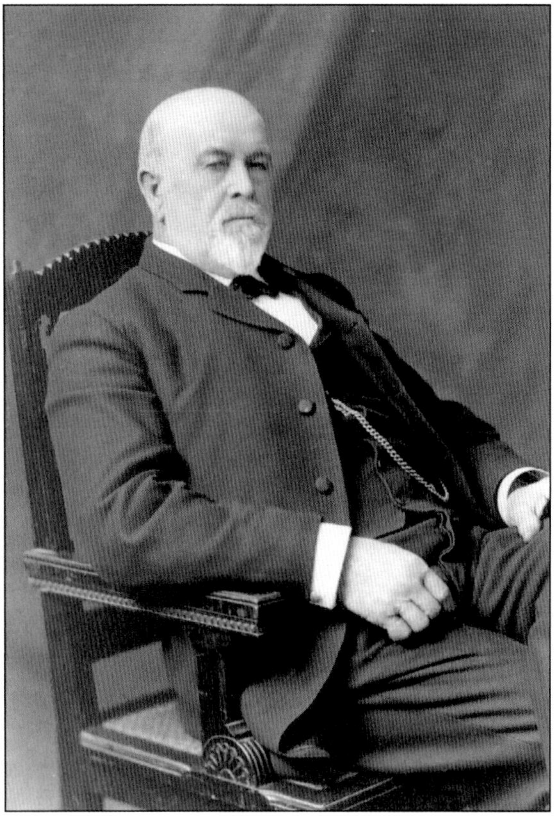

Isaac Minor, a native of Pennsylvania, was just 23 when he arrived in Union. (Courtesy of Humboldt County Historical Society.)

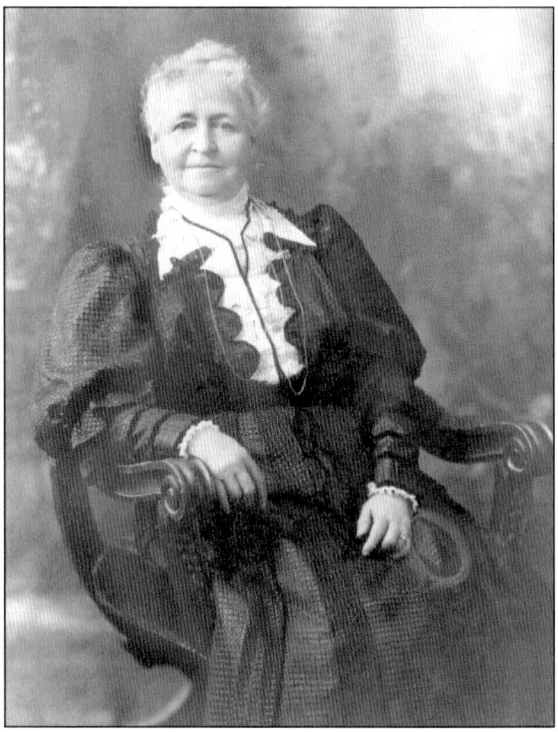

Hannah Nixon Minor, who arrived in Union with her parents in 1853, married Issac in 1855. She had 12 children, six of whom died as children. She was a 45-year member of the Presbyterian Church of Arcata. (Courtesy of Humboldt County Historical Society.)

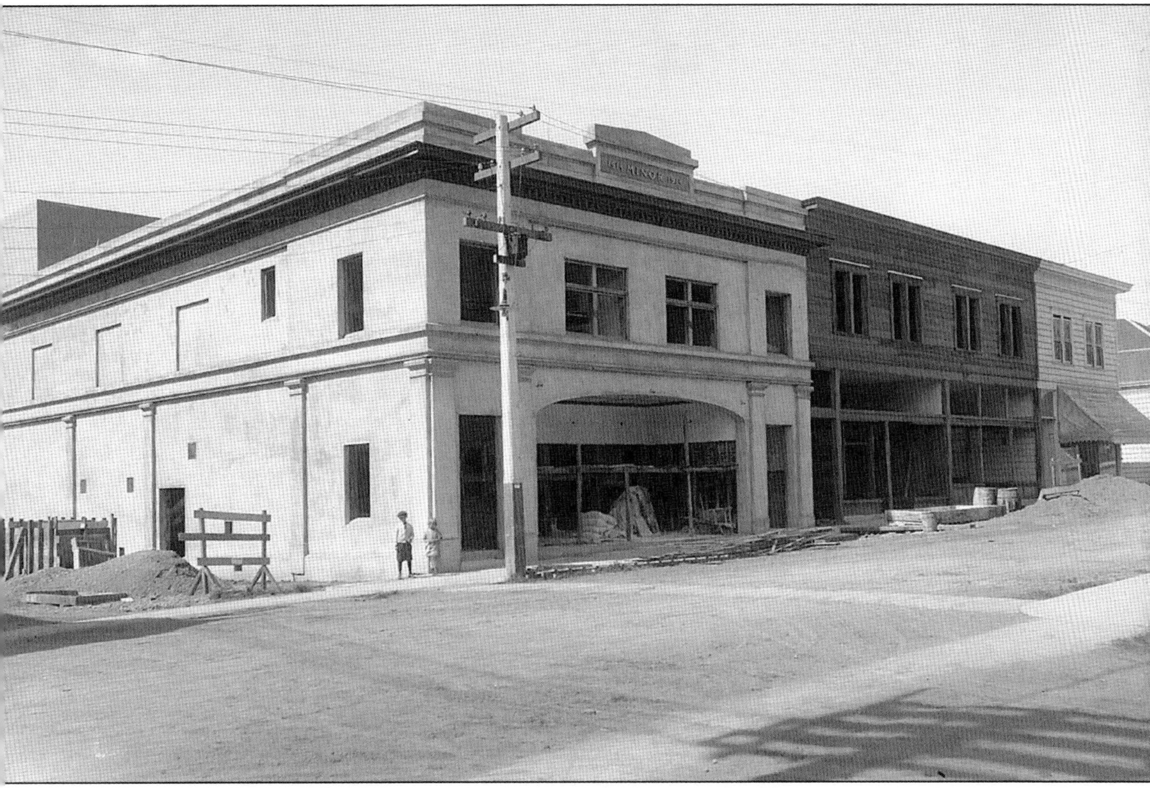

The 1914 construction of the Minor Theater and adjoining buildings on H Street was just one of businessman Isaac Minor's many enterprises. Arriving in Union in 1853, he ran pack trains; owned a cattle ranch; cut and hauled timber; built several mills, including Dolly Varden, Mad River, and Glendale; acquired and ran a granite quarry; and gave nearby McKinleyville its start with the construction of a store and creamery. He died in 1915. (Courtesy of Ericson Collection, Humboldt State University Library.)

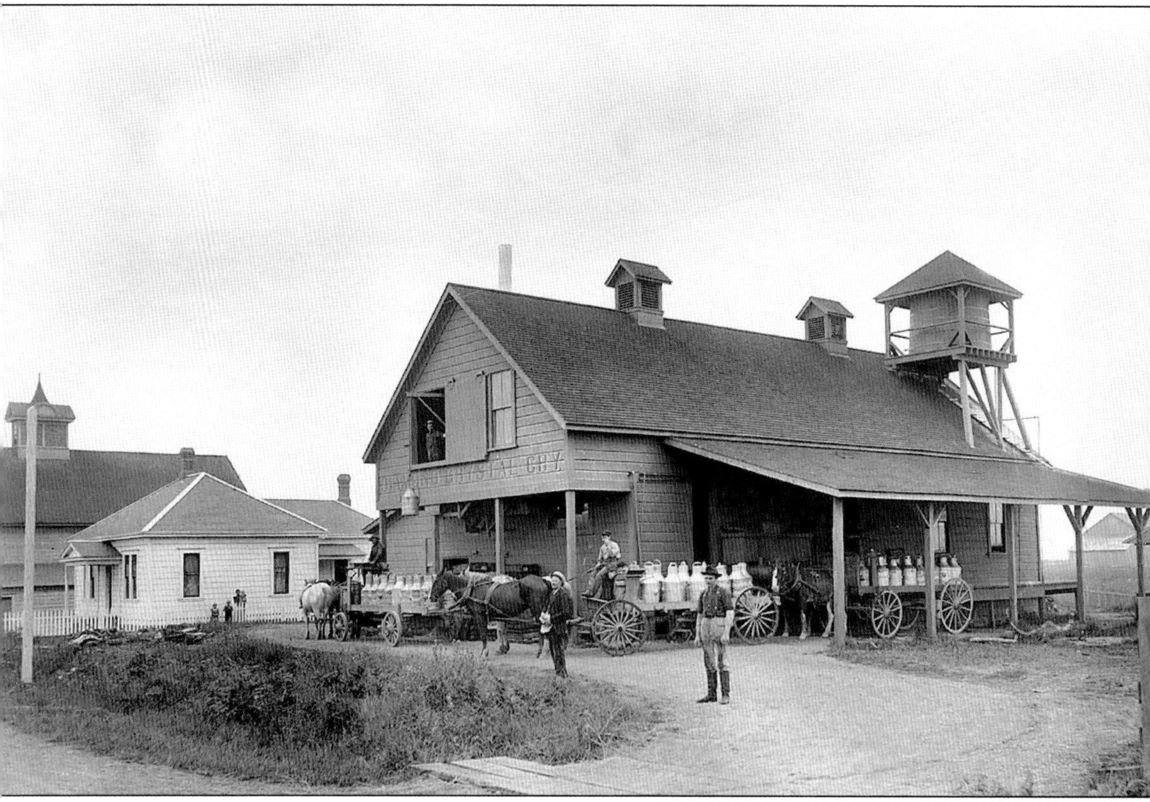

This is a photo of the Diamond Crystal Creamery. (Courtesy of Ericson Collection, Humboldt State University Library.)

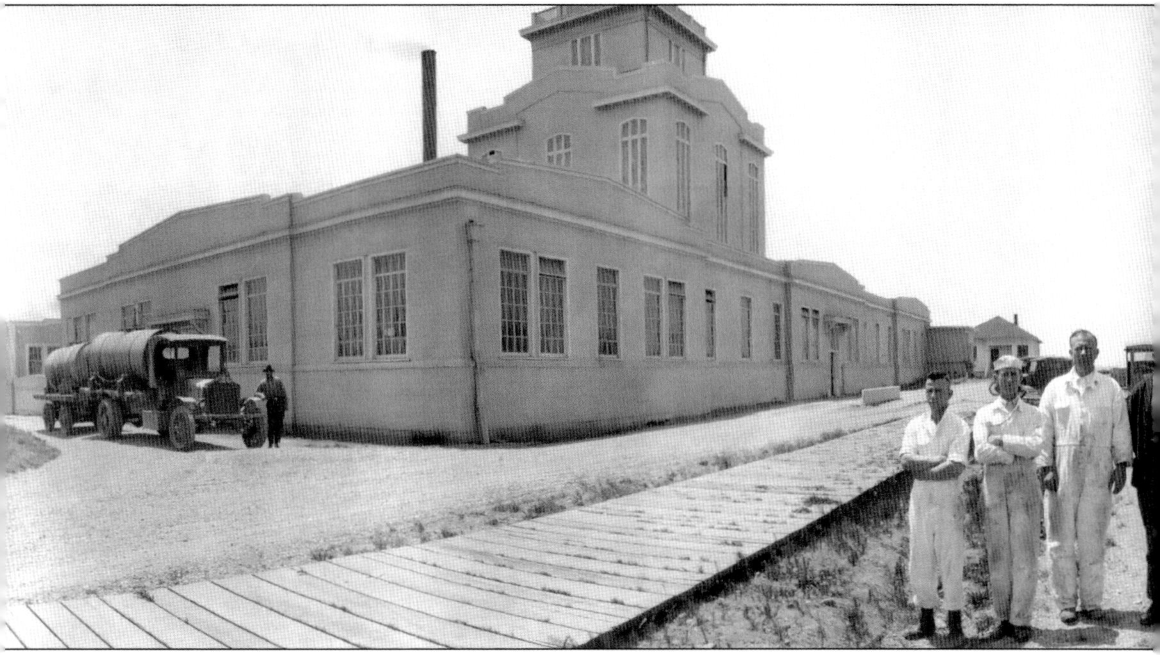

In announcing plans for the California Central Creameries Arcata Plant on Ninth Street, the *Humboldt Times* enticed its readers to apply for jobs with headlines such as the one from August 30, 1917, declaring, "Pay Roll Will be Large—Many Skilled Hands Will be Employed." The operation covered two city blocks and was estimated to cost $100,000 to construct. The business became part of Golden State Creameries in 1923. The creamery has, over the years, been reinvented as a theater, art gallery, roller skating rink, ballet school, martial arts studio, and more. (Courtesy of Humboldt County Historical Society.)

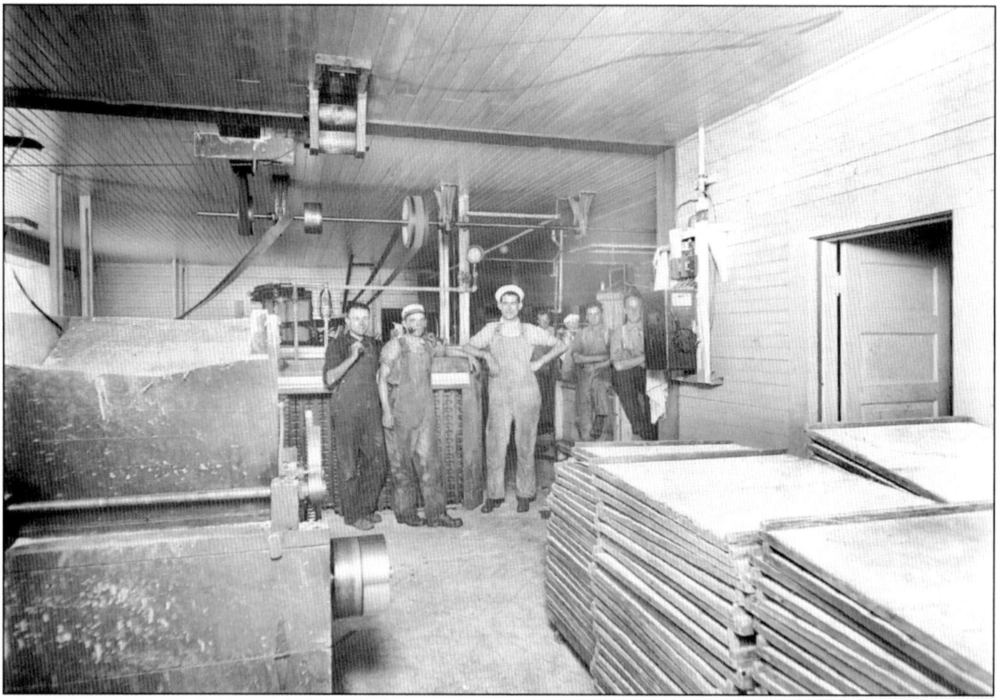

These unidentified United Creamery workers take a break from their work. (Courtesy of Humboldt County Historical Society, Chaffey Collection.)

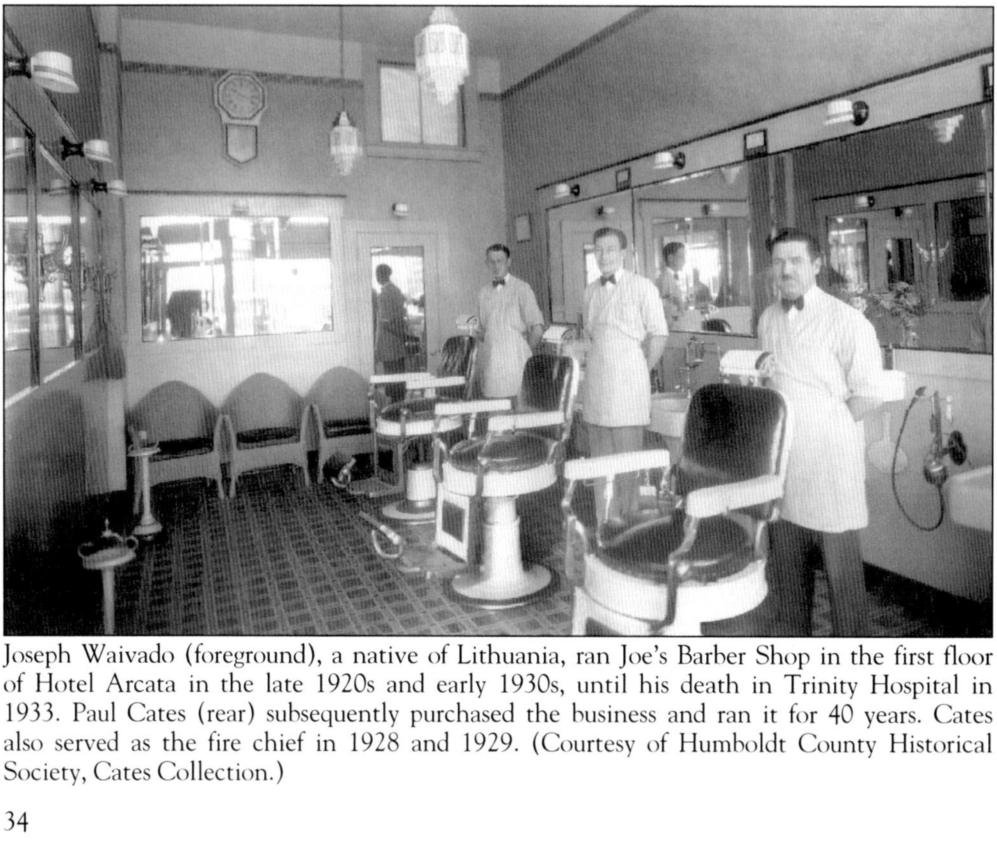

Joseph Waivado (foreground), a native of Lithuania, ran Joe's Barber Shop in the first floor of Hotel Arcata in the late 1920s and early 1930s, until his death in Trinity Hospital in 1933. Paul Cates (rear) subsequently purchased the business and ran it for 40 years. Cates also served as the fire chief in 1928 and 1929. (Courtesy of Humboldt County Historical Society, Cates Collection.)

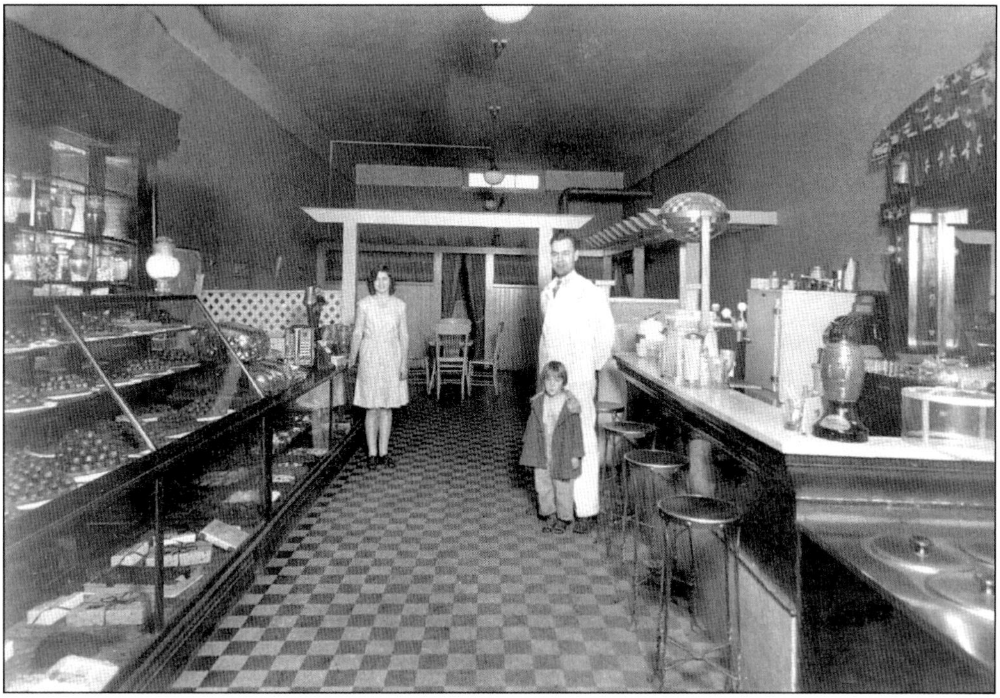

The Varsity Cafe on the plaza's east side enjoyed a long life and went through many transformations. It first emerged as the Varsity Sweet Shoppe, shown here, which was owned by George Rossi in the mid-1920s. (Courtesy of Humboldt State University Library.)

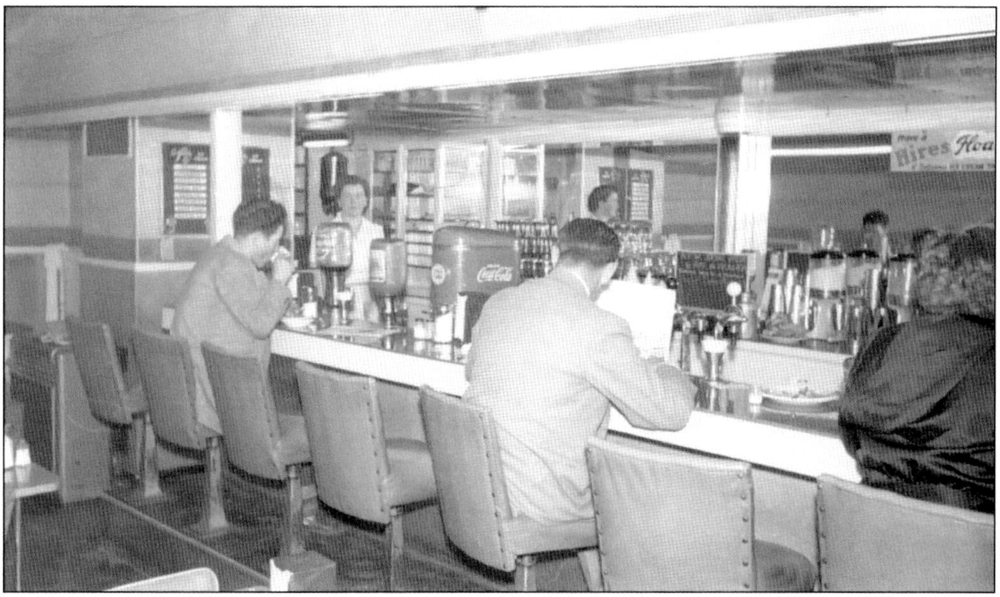

The popular restaurant's interior was photographed shortly after a renovation, most likely in the early 1960s. (Courtesy of Humboldt State University Library.)

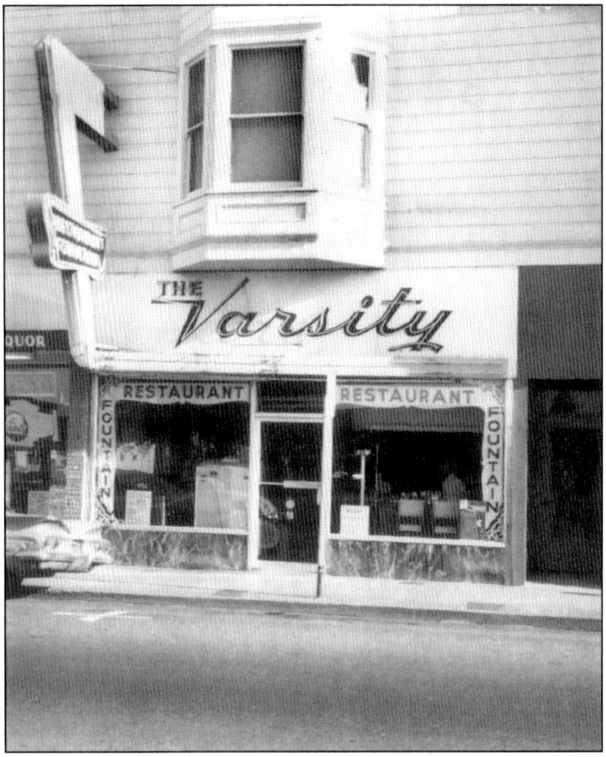

This 1960s view shows the Varsity from the outside. (Courtesy of Humboldt County Historical Society.)

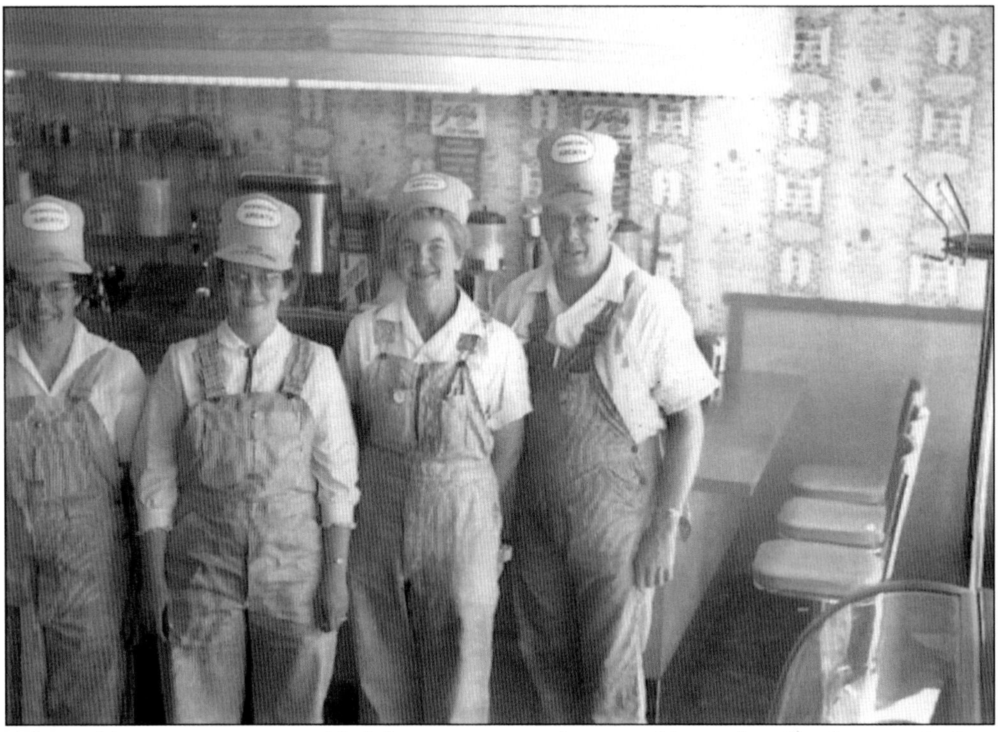

A happy Varsity crew are most likely honoring some element of Arcata's railroad past with their hats and overalls. (Courtesy of Humboldt County Historical Society.)

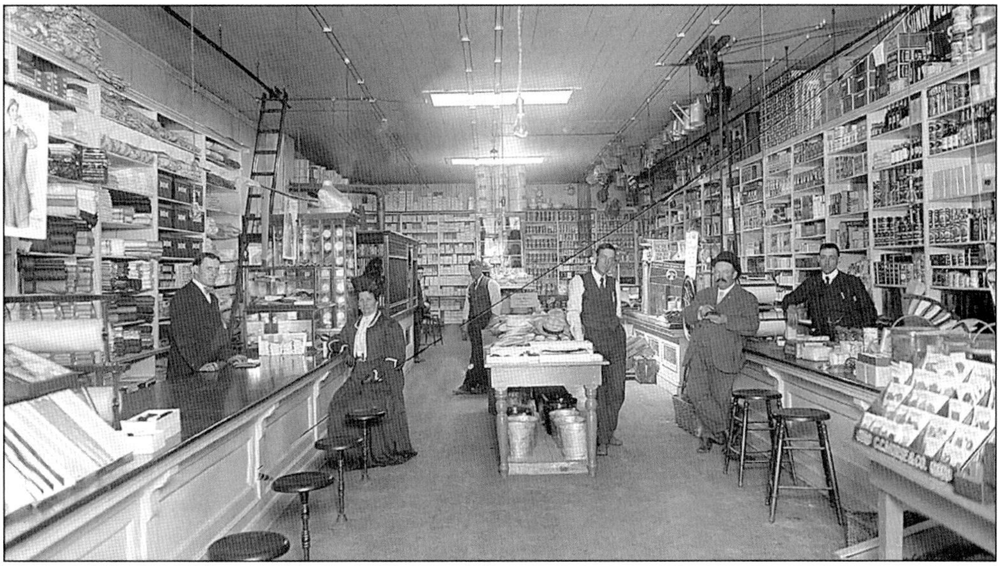

Seely & Titlow's at Tenth and I Streets included a dry goods store as well as hardware and animal feed. The selection ranged from fabric to canned goods to laundry soap to hats and more. (Courtesy of Ericson Collection, Humboldt State University Library.)

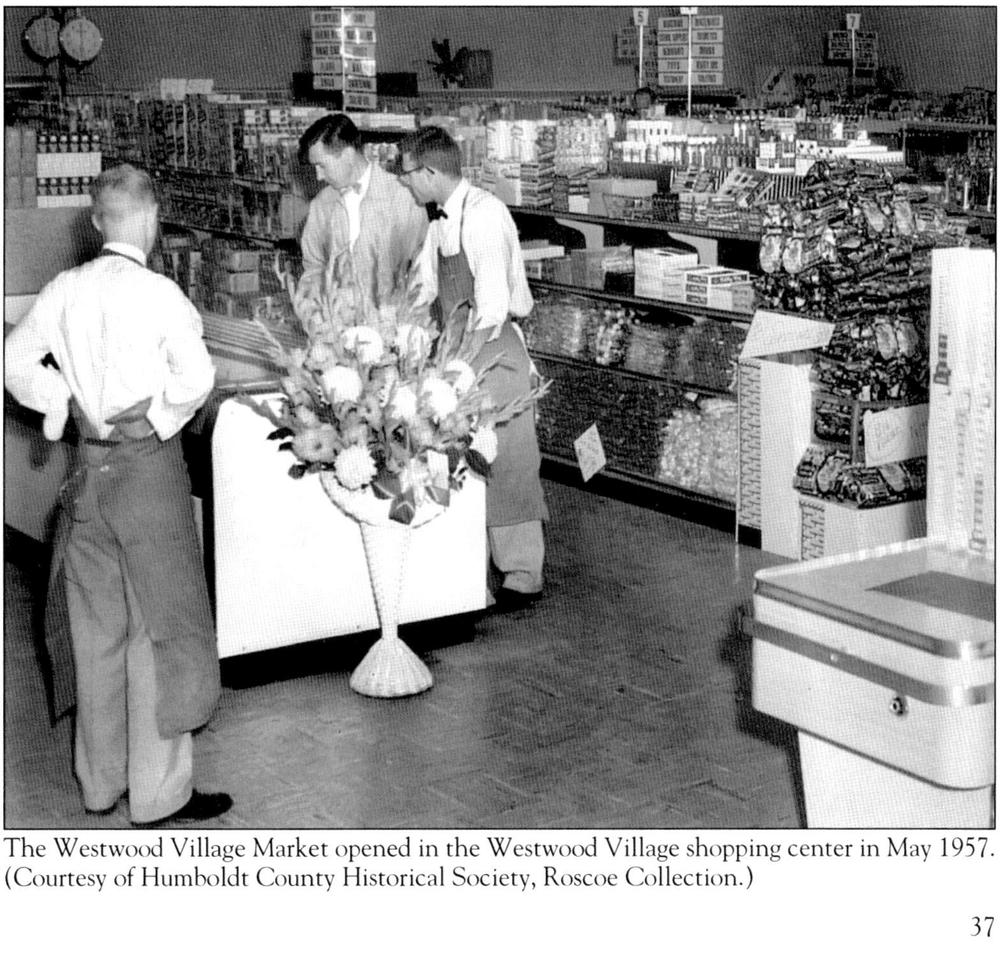

The Westwood Village Market opened in the Westwood Village shopping center in May 1957. (Courtesy of Humboldt County Historical Society, Roscoe Collection.)

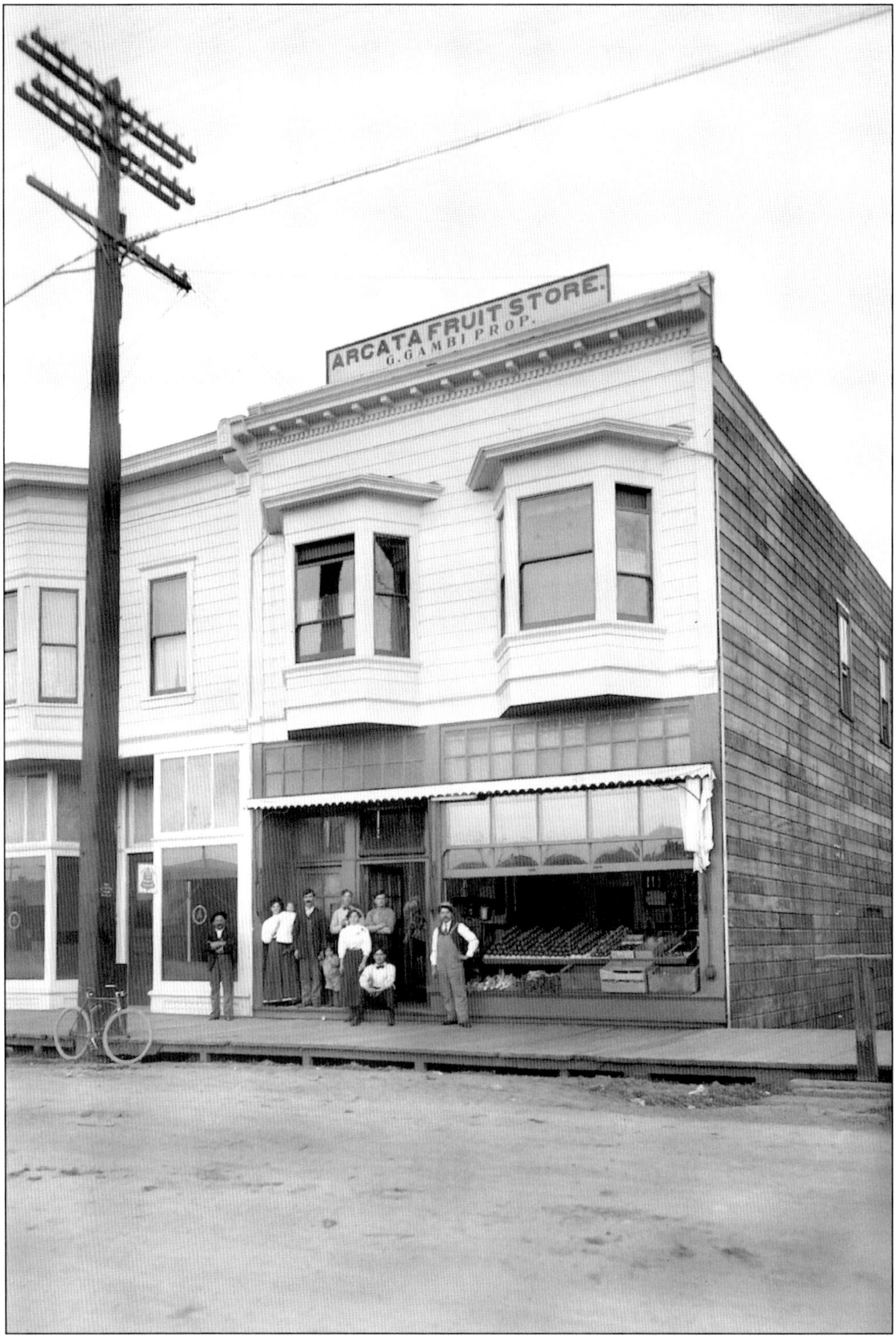

Gambi's Arcata Fruit Store was located on the plaza. (Courtesy of Ericson Collection, Humboldt State University Library.)

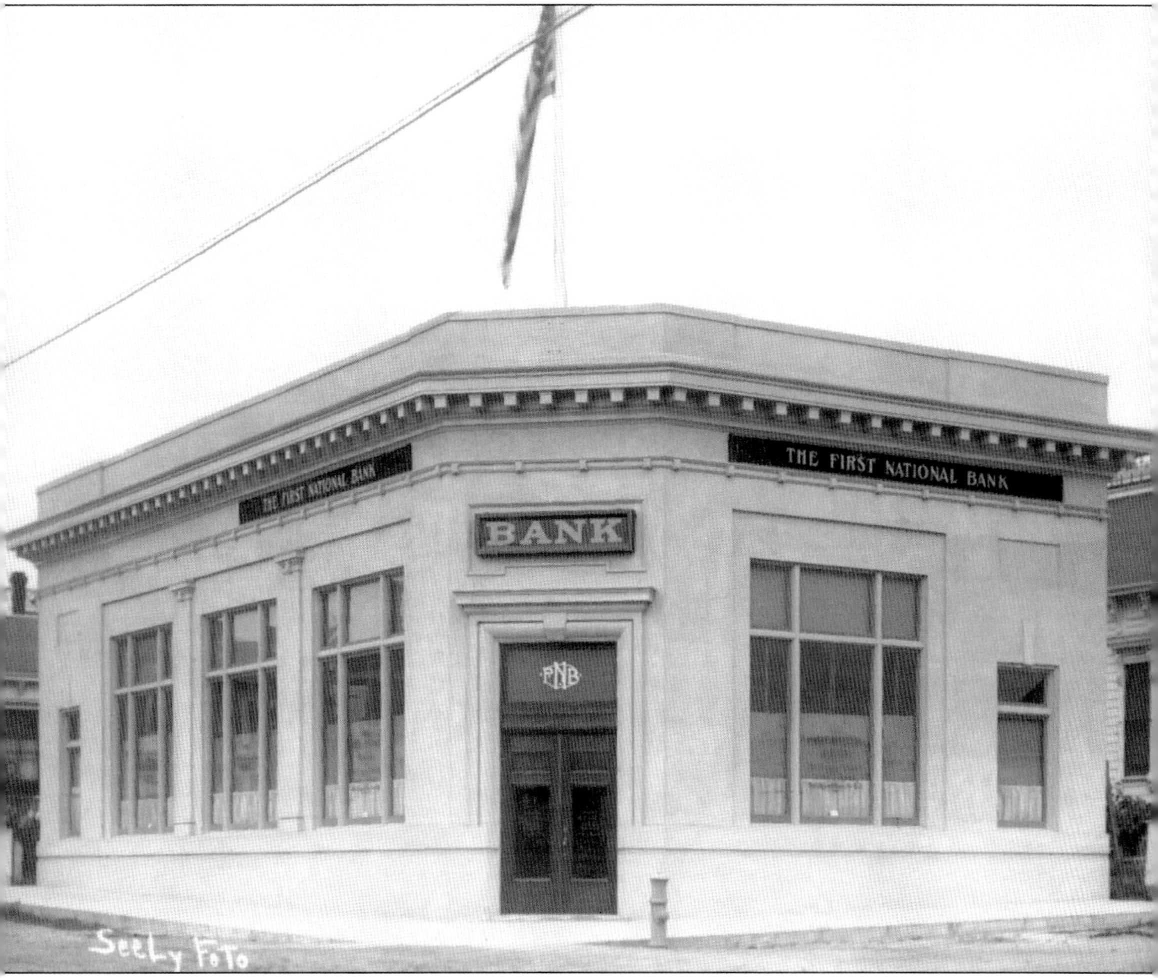

The First National Bank of Arcata, built by Isaac Minor in 1913 at the corner of Tenth and H Streets, became a branch of the Security Bank and Trust Company in 1927. The building was purchased by Bank of America in 1928 and over the years has been the site of Deluxe Cleaners, the first home of the Humboldt Open Door Clinic, and the used bookstore Tin Can Mailman. (Courtesy of Humboldt State University Library.)

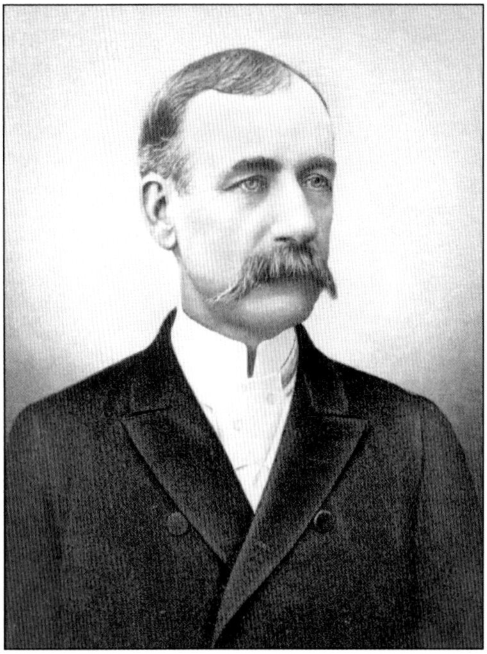

Alexander Brizard, a native of France, began his career as a clerk before establishing his namesake business that would remain active until the 1970s. (Courtesy of Humboldt County Historical Society.)

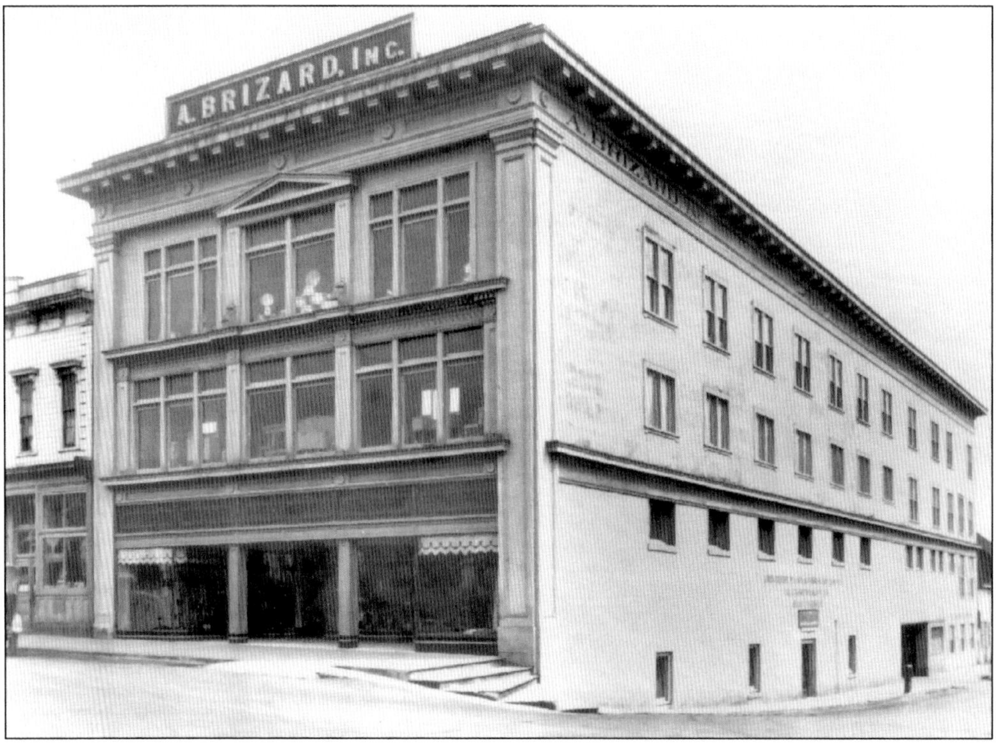

Alexander Brizard purchased August Jacoby's 1857 store warehouse in 1880. Twenty-seven years later, with retail success under his belt, he expanded the department store to its present size, a project that took roughly a year. In 1977 the tallest plaza building underwent a complete renovation restoring the original Classic Revival architecture. (Courtesy of Humboldt County Historical Society.)

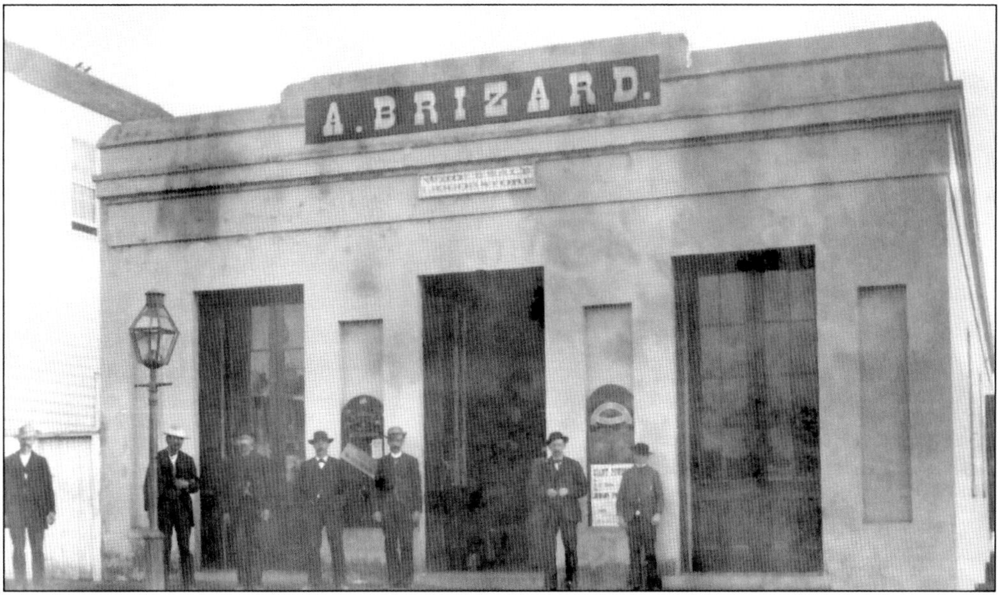

Augustus Jacoby built this one-story Ninth Street store in 1857 and was soon providing supplies to the mining camps to the east. Jacoby left the area in the mid-1860s, but the business continued under the auspices of others until 1880 when Alexander Brizard purchased the property. The storehouse, advertised as fireproof, provided shelter to settlers during the height of the Indian Wars in the early 1860s. (Courtesy of California State Library, Humboldt County Historical Society.)

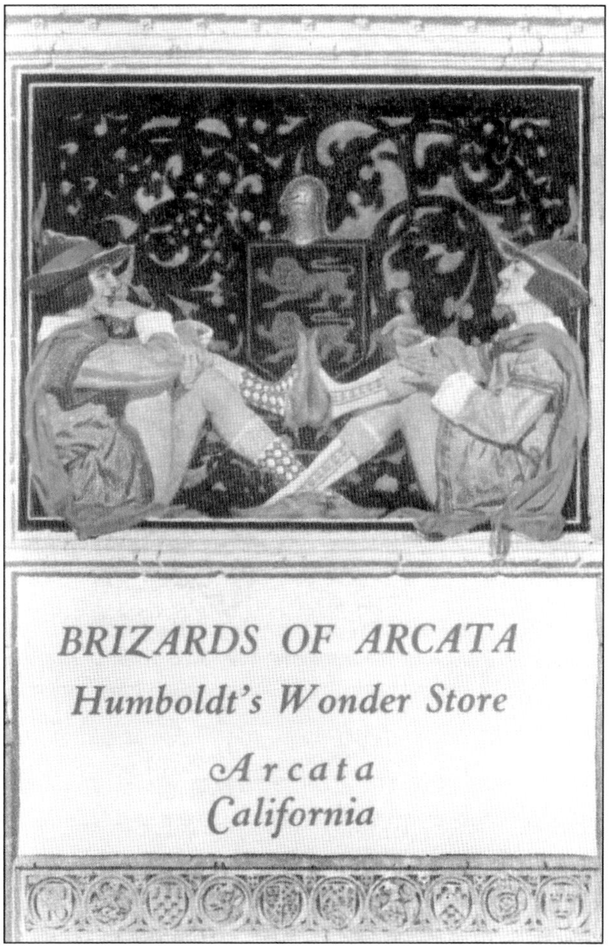

Shown here is an undated promotion of Arcata's largest retail store. (Courtesy of Humboldt County Historical Society, Ephemera Collection.)

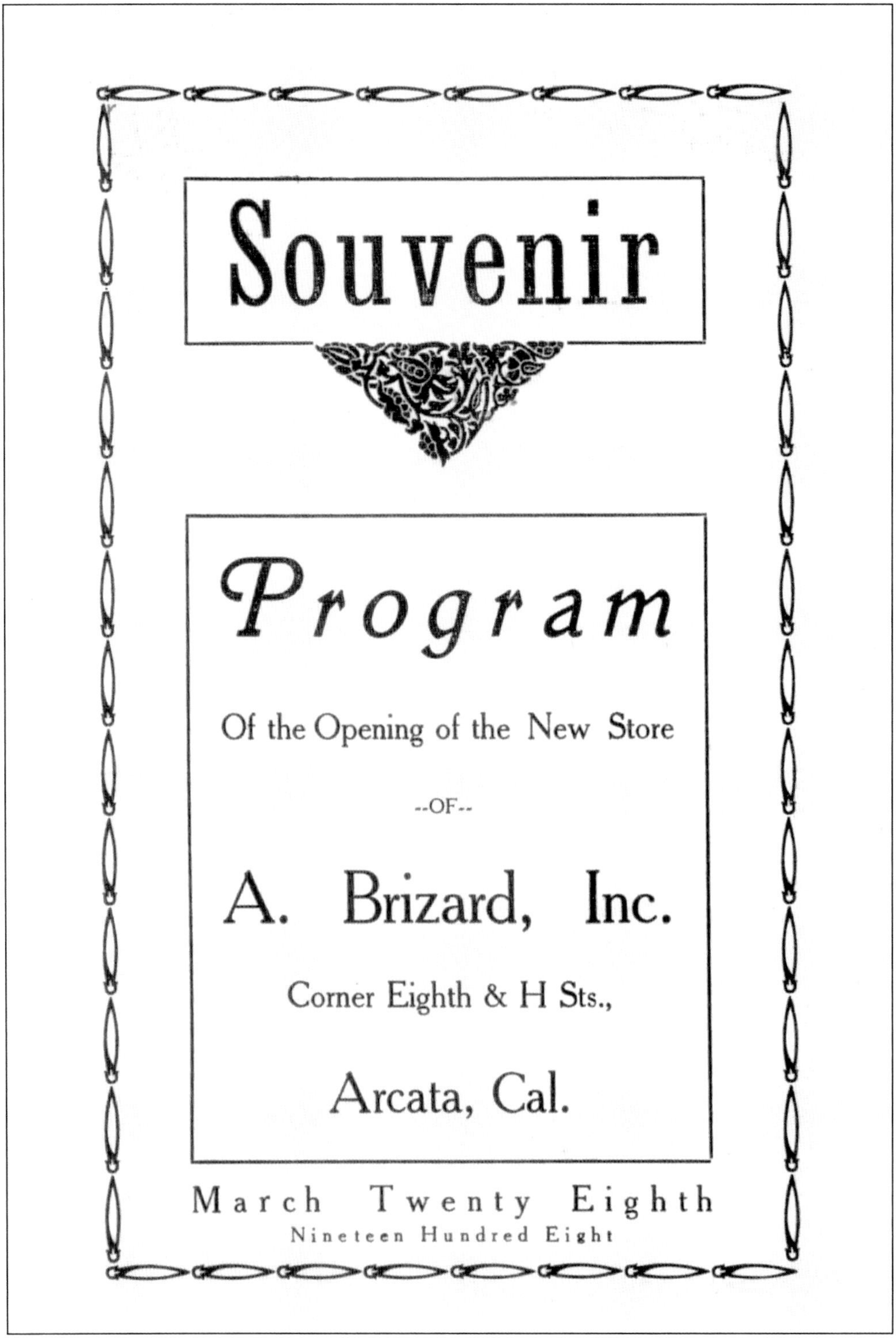

Souvenir

Program

Of the Opening of the New Store

--OF--

A. Brizard, Inc.

Corner Eighth & H Sts.,

Arcata, Cal.

March Twenty Eighth

Nineteen Hundred Eight

A program was issued for the grand celebration noting the opening of the new, four-story Brizard's store on the plaza in 1908. (Courtesy of Humboldt County Historical Society.)

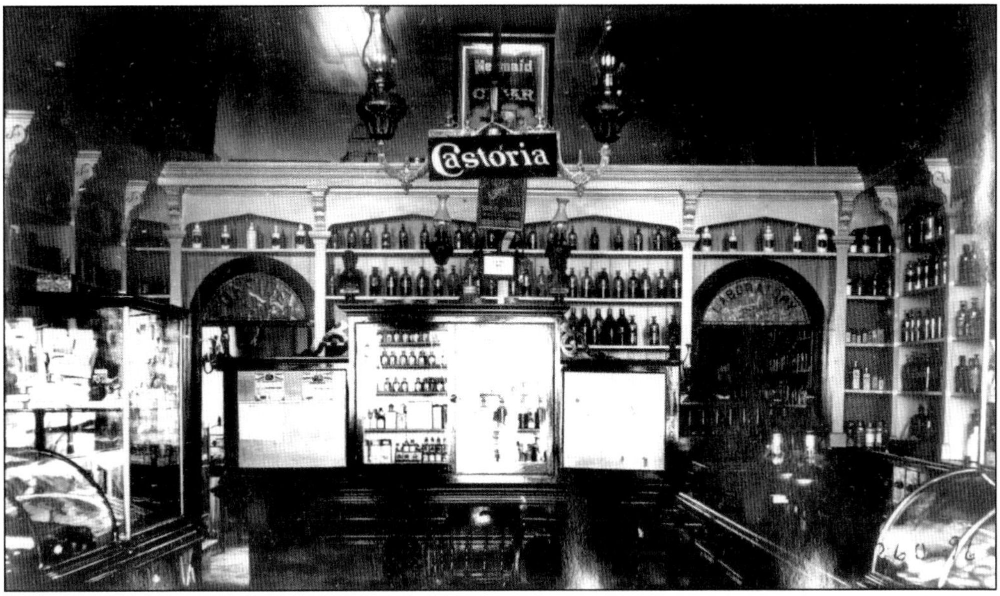

The Arcata Drug Store on H Street was the site of a primitive electric plant that provided the city residents with their first electric lights. The power plant was built in the rear of the business in 1895, which was known as Tilley's and Simmon's Drug Store by then. "It consisted of a five-horsepower Pelton water wheel operated by water delivered through a three-inch pipe under 80 pounds of pressure from the city's water mains and a belt connected to a Westinghouse 60-light generator." (Courtesy of California State Library, Humboldt County Historical Society.)

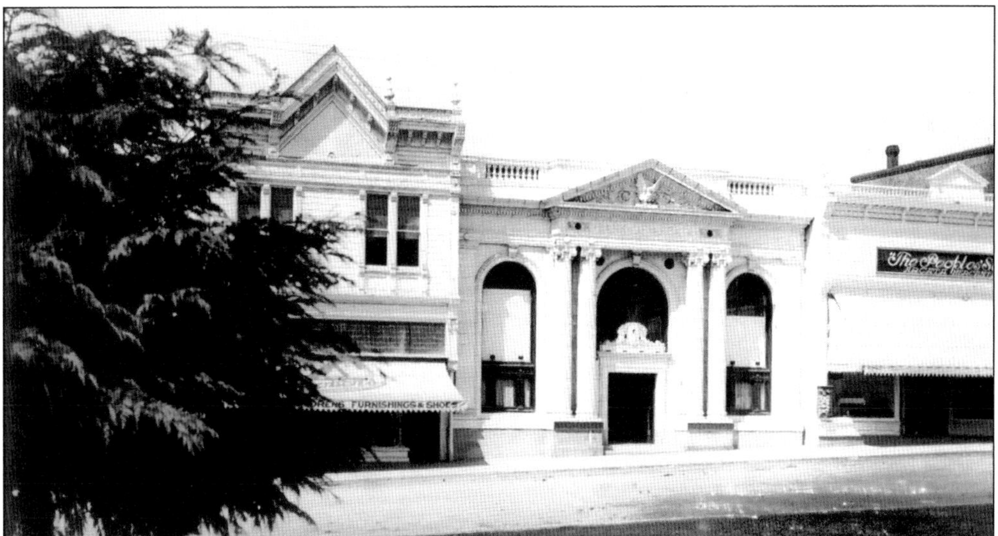

The Bank of Arcata's style and solidity impressed residents when the building was opened on the west side of the plaza in 1914. From its Corinthian columns to its detailed exterior, the substantial building served the banking needs of the community, first as Bank of Arcata, then Liberty Bank of San Francisco, Bank of Italy, and Bank of America. The interior included floors of California and Italian marble and mahogany ceilings and woodwork. As beautiful as it was, the building facade was sacrificed to progress only 40 years later. (Courtesy of Humboldt County Historical Society, Roscoe Collection.)

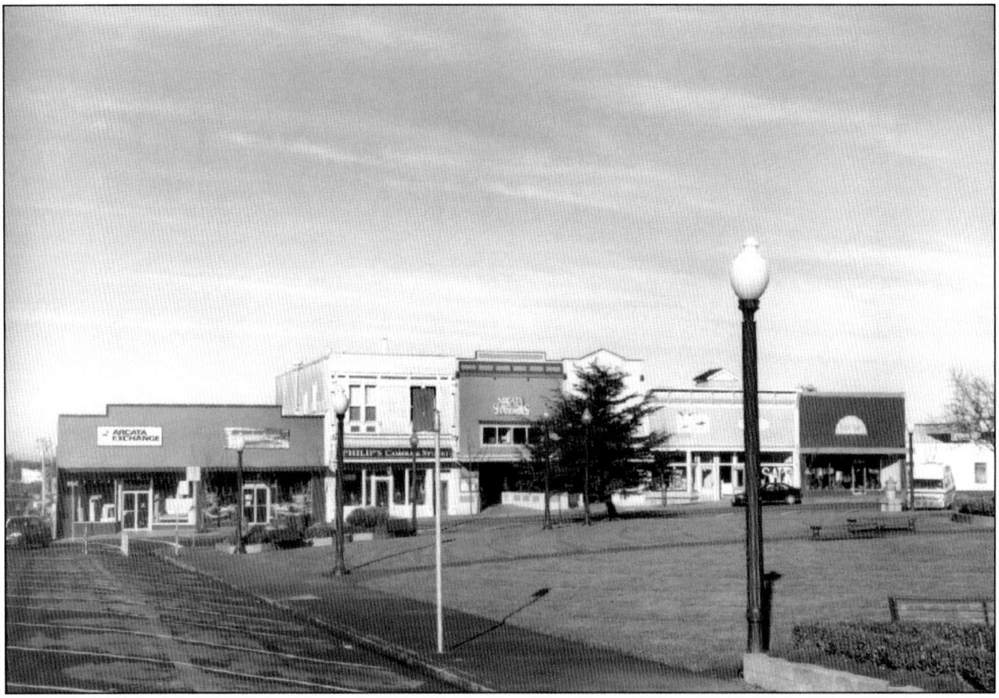

Shown here is a modern view of the west side of the plaza. (Courtesy of Humboldt County Historical Society.)

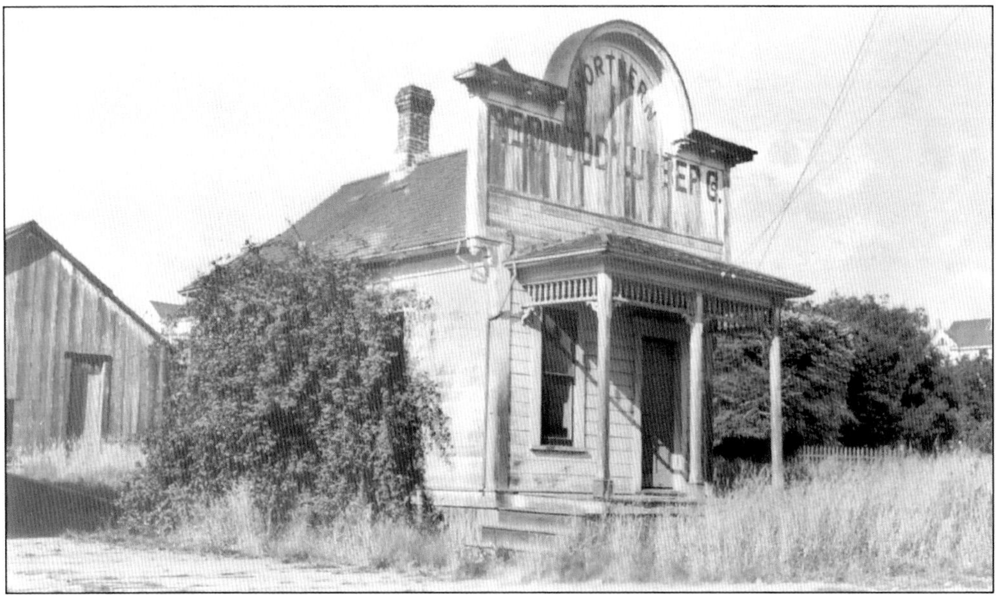

Lloyd Stine captured this image of the Northern Redwood Lumber Company's abandoned lumberyard office at Twelfth and K Streets. The Northern Redwood Lumber Company resulted from the merger of the Riverside Lumber Company and the Korbel brothers' interests in 1903. The Korbel-based mill closed in 1933, reopened in 1942, and was purchased by Simpson Logging Company of Washington in 1955. (Courtesy of Humboldt County Historical Society, Stine Collection.)

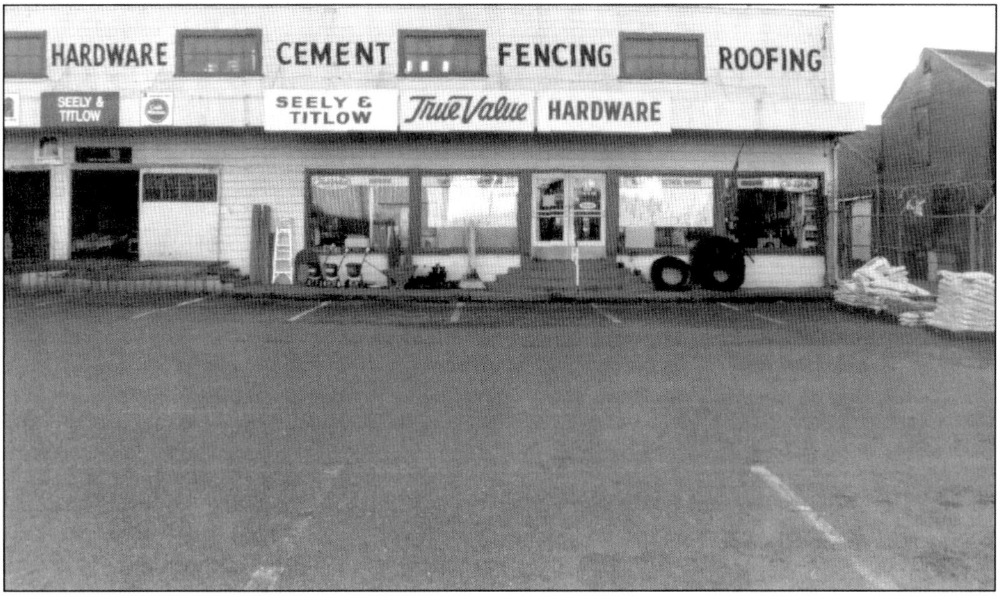

Shown here is the Seely & Titlow feed and hardware store on I Street. (Courtesy of Peter Hess.)

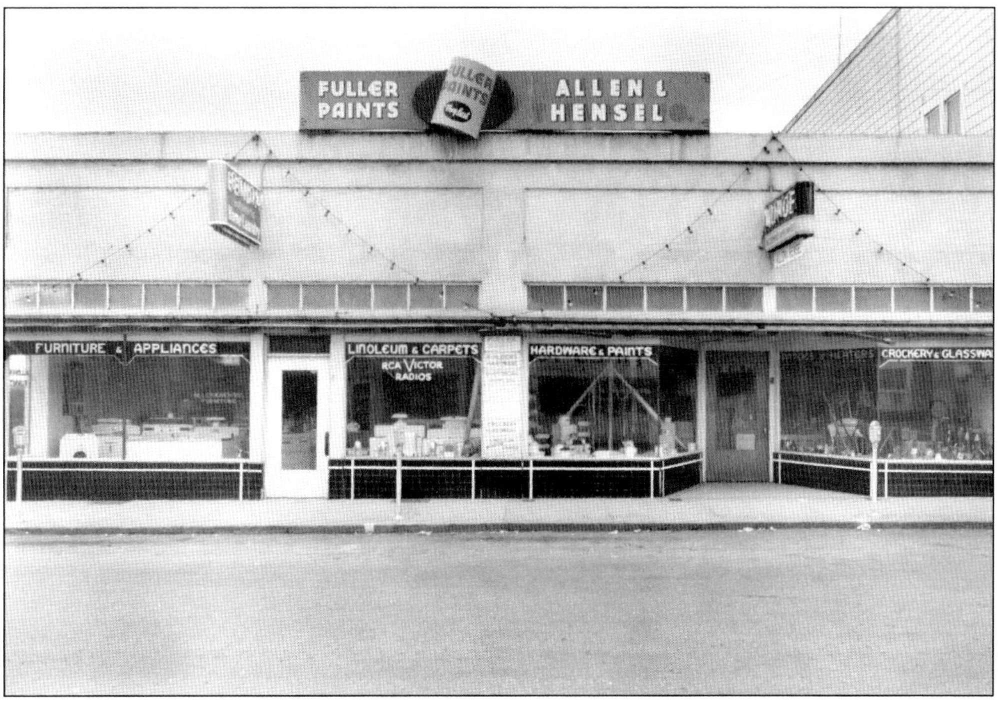

This image is of the Ninth Street Fuller Paint Store. (Courtesy of Peter Hess.)

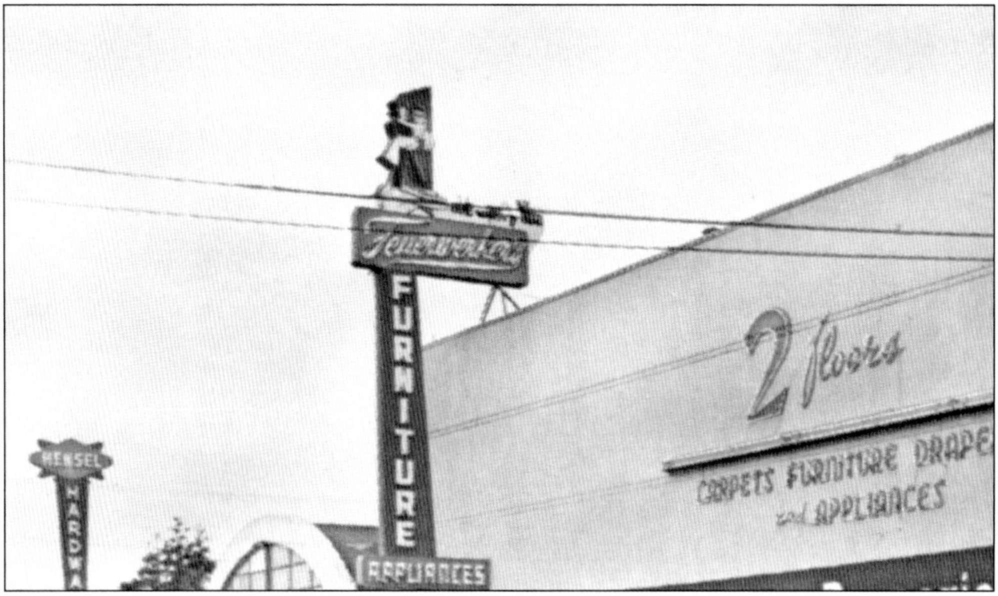

Feuerwerker's Furniture was a prominent fixture in the 800 block of Ninth Street in the 1950s and 1960s. (Courtesy of Peter Hess.)

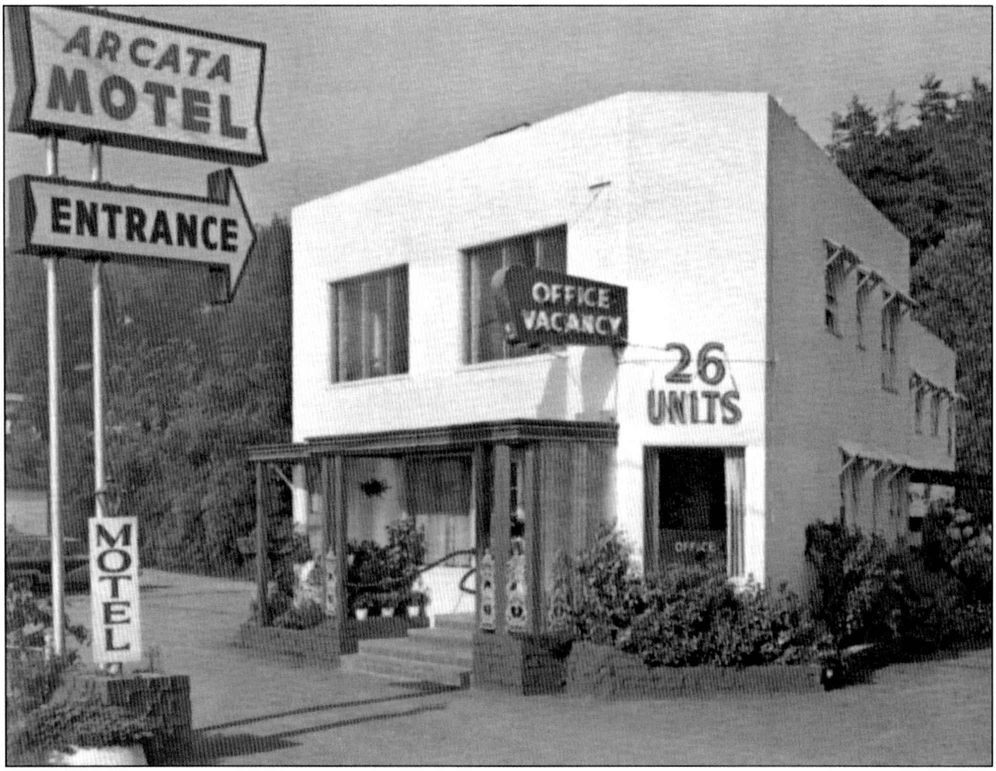

The Arcata Motel was one of the many structures that fell victim to progress when U.S. Highway 101 broadened its path through Arcata in the early 1970s. The motel advertised room-controlled heat, its prime location next to Scenic Redwood Highway, a café, and a service station. (Courtesy of Humboldt County Historical Society, Smith Collection.)

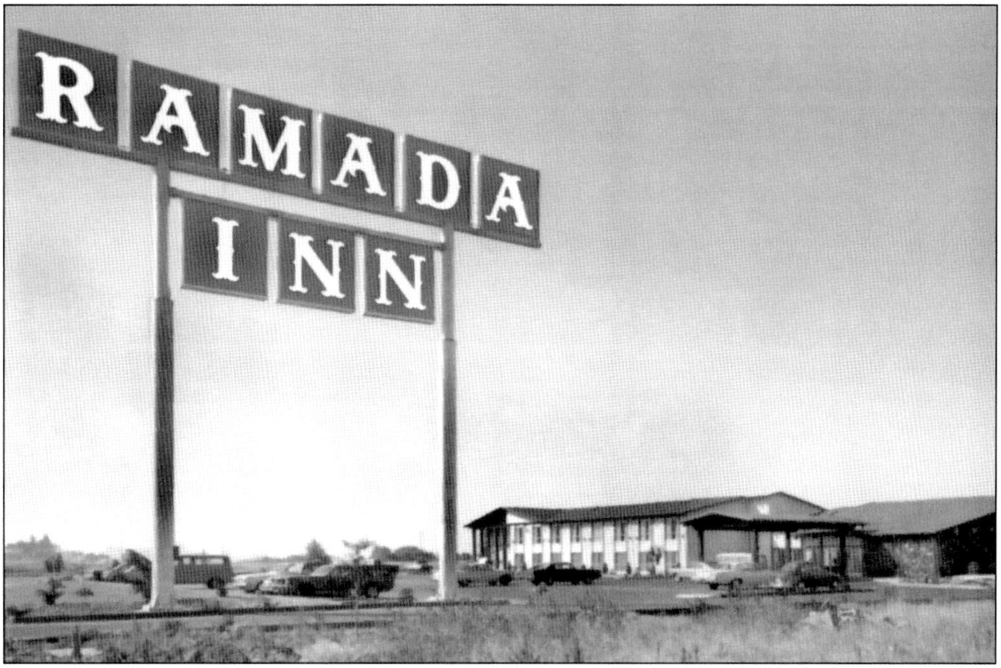

The Ramada Inn was the first nationwide motel/hotel enterprise to move into Arcata's Valley West, now home to several sources of overnight accommodation, all of which fill to capacity during Humboldt State University's graduation ceremonies each May. (Courtesy of Humboldt County Historical Society.)

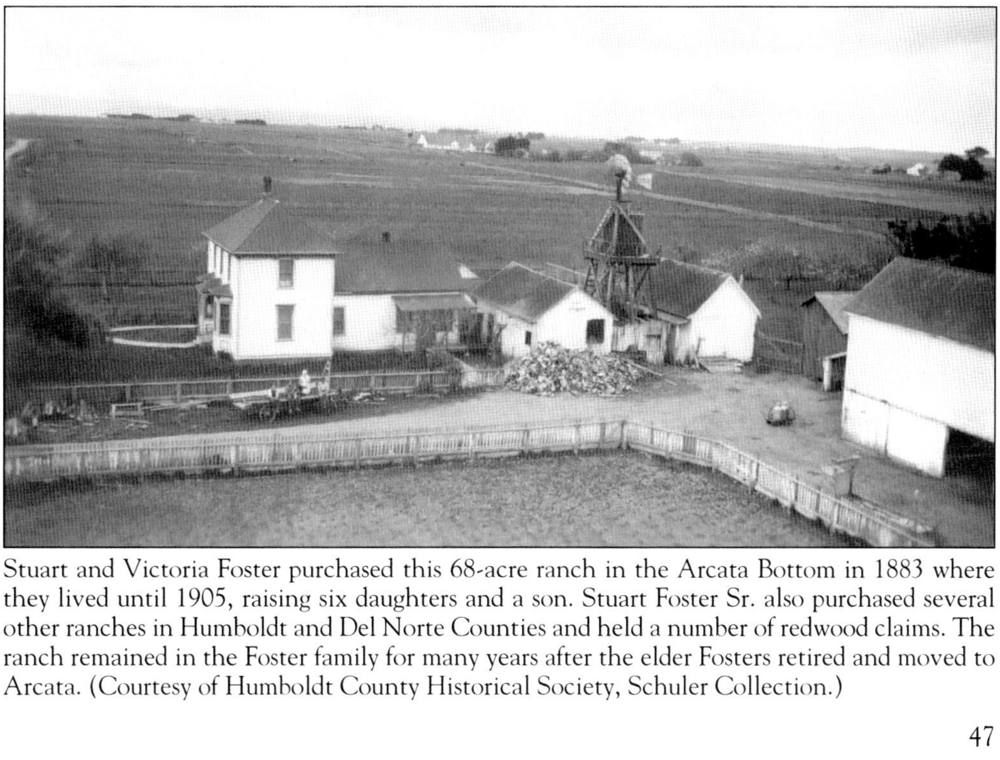

Stuart and Victoria Foster purchased this 68-acre ranch in the Arcata Bottom in 1883 where they lived until 1905, raising six daughters and a son. Stuart Foster Sr. also purchased several other ranches in Humboldt and Del Norte Counties and held a number of redwood claims. The ranch remained in the Foster family for many years after the elder Fosters retired and moved to Arcata. (Courtesy of Humboldt County Historical Society, Schuler Collection.)

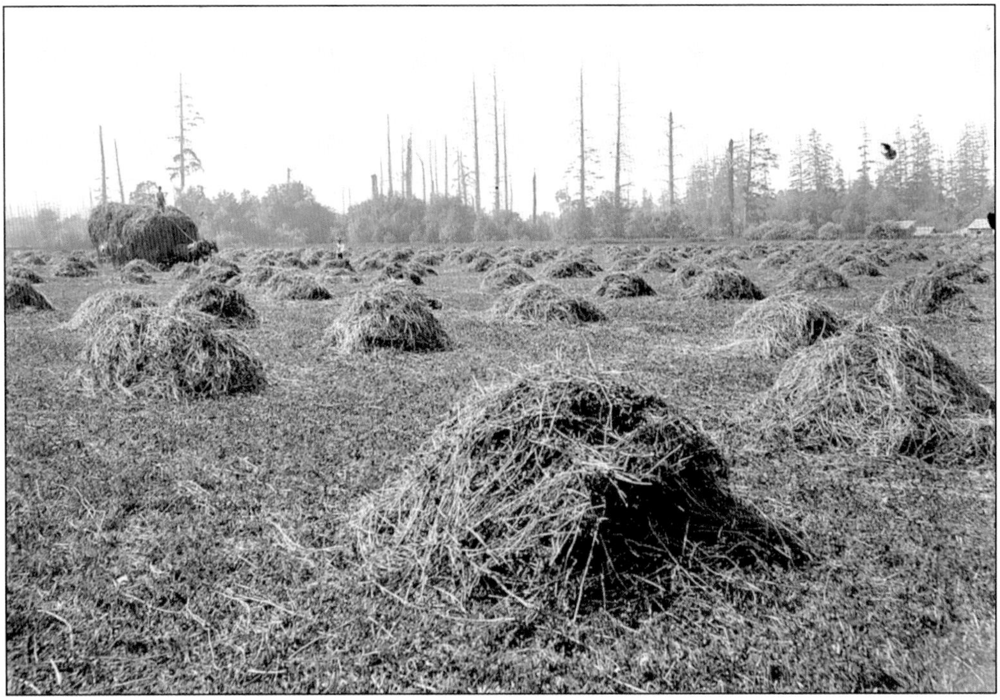

Shown here is one of the many hayfields present on the Arcata Bottom in the late 1800s and early 1900s. (Courtesy of Ericson Collection, Humboldt State University Library.)

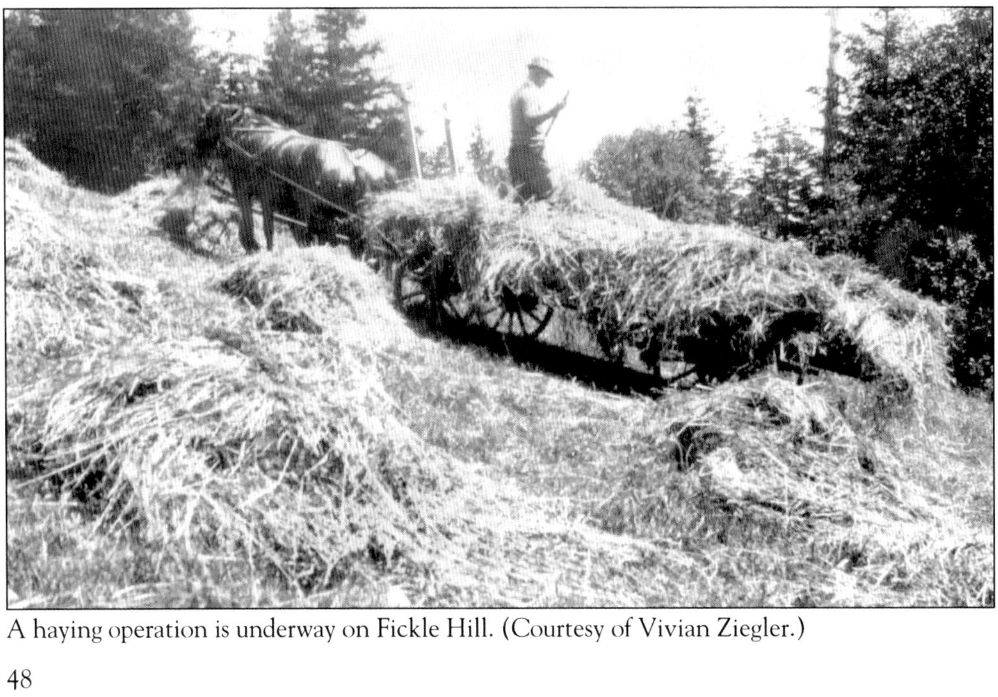

A haying operation is underway on Fickle Hill. (Courtesy of Vivian Ziegler.)

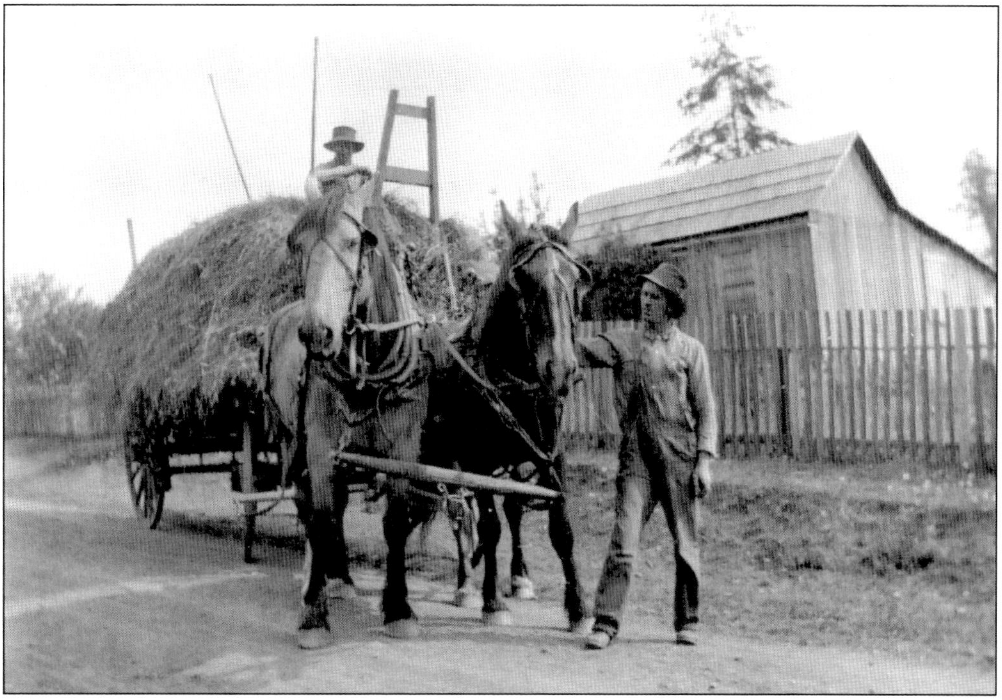

Desmond Donahue is keeping a careful eye on the horses pulling this hay wagon along Fickle Hill Road. The Wyatt home is seen in the background. (Courtesy of Vivian Ziegler.)

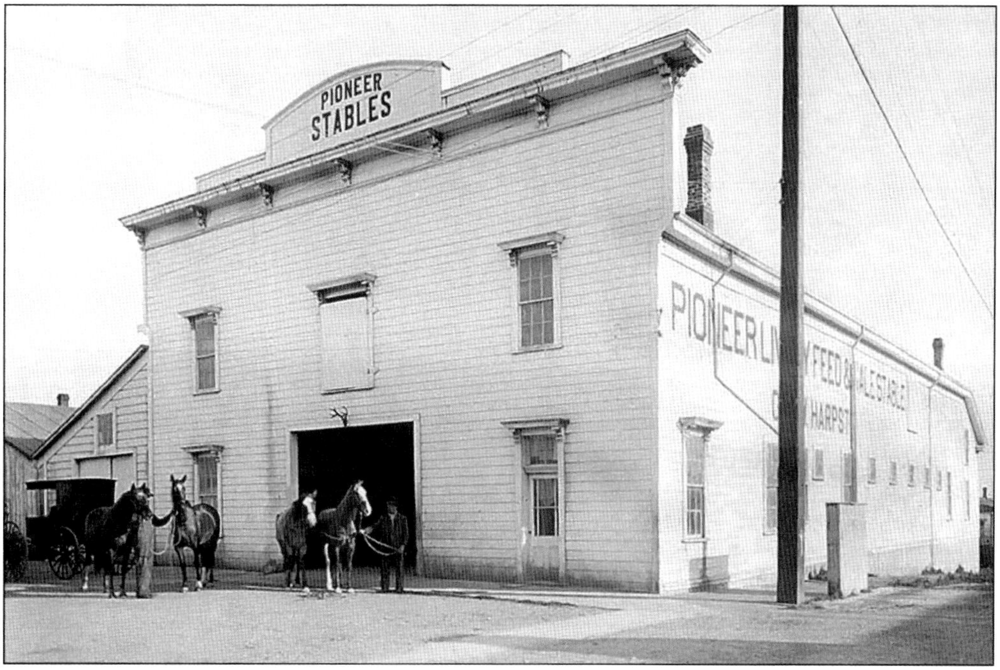

The Pioneer Stables site at the corner of Eighth and G Streets is now home to the Bank of America. Built around 1875, the Pioneer Stables offered special features for bicyclists in the 1890s, including a wheel room and a ladies' dressing room. (Courtesy of Ericson Collection, Humboldt State University Library.)

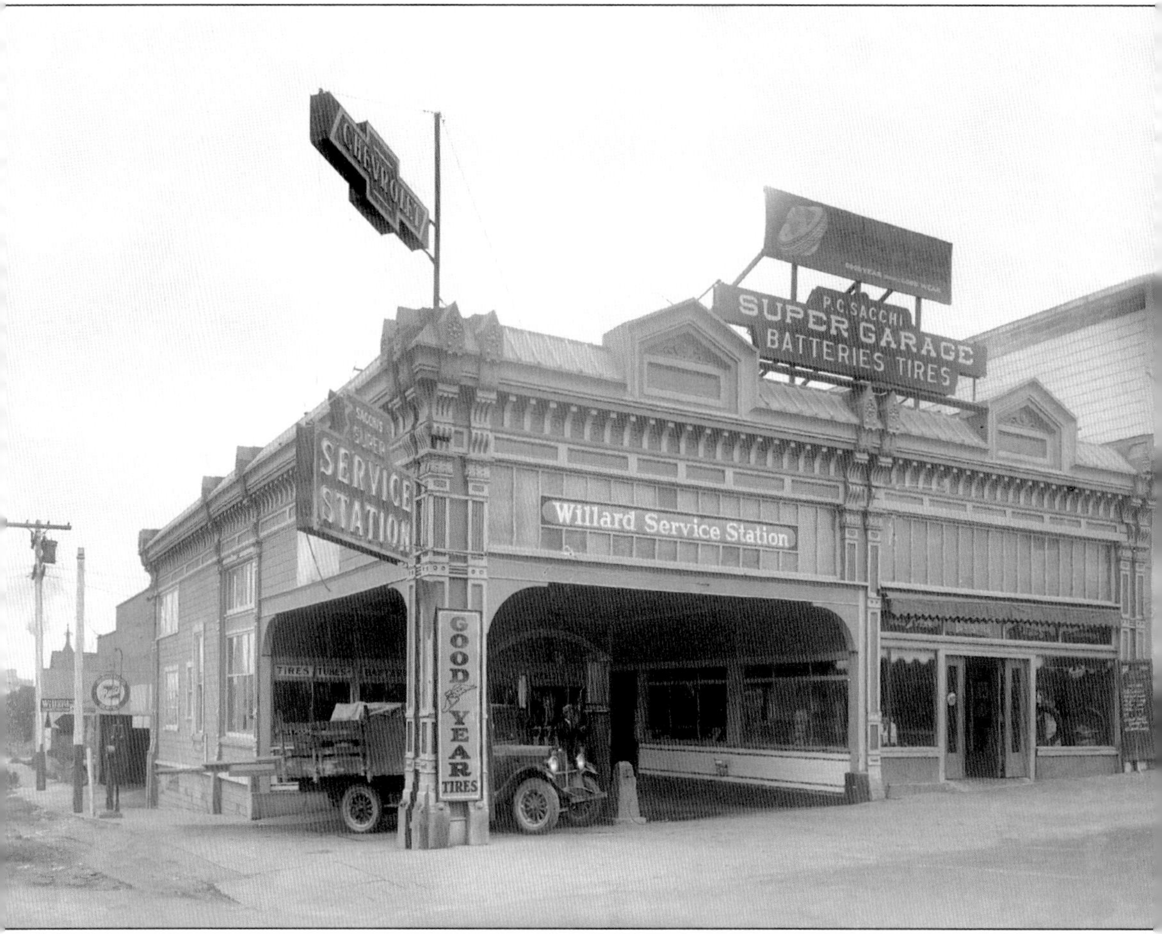

Shown here is the P.C. Sacchi Super Garage and Willard Service Station at Eighth and H Streets. Sacchi remodeled this 1885 building into his Super Garage and Vulcanizing Works in 1924. After 23 years a Ben Franklin store moved in. Today, a furniture store occupies this space. (Courtesy of Ericson Collection, Humboldt State University Library.)

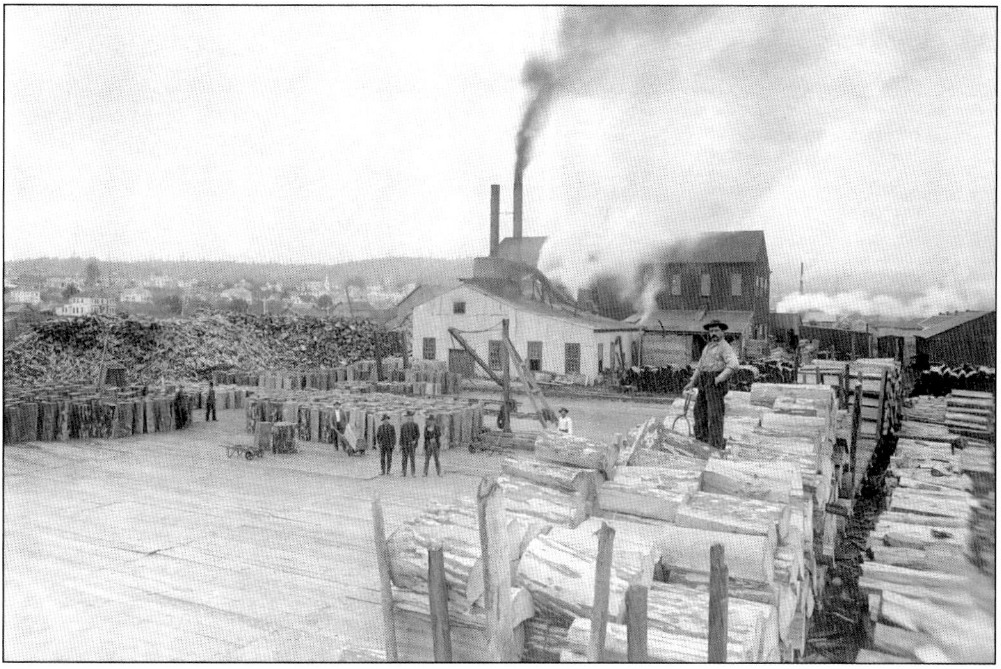

California Barrel Factory employed more than 1,100 people by the time it closed in 1956, and almost everyone in town either worked for them or knew someone who did. The plant stretched between Eighth Street and what was then Samoa Road. The railroad marked the eastern boundary. This image was likely taken not long after the San Francisco–based company opened its Arcata plant in 1902–1903; it was known as the Humboldt Cooperage Company for the first 16 years. The plant's workers made barrels, wire-bound boxes, and wooden containers. (Courtesy of Humboldt County Historical Society.)

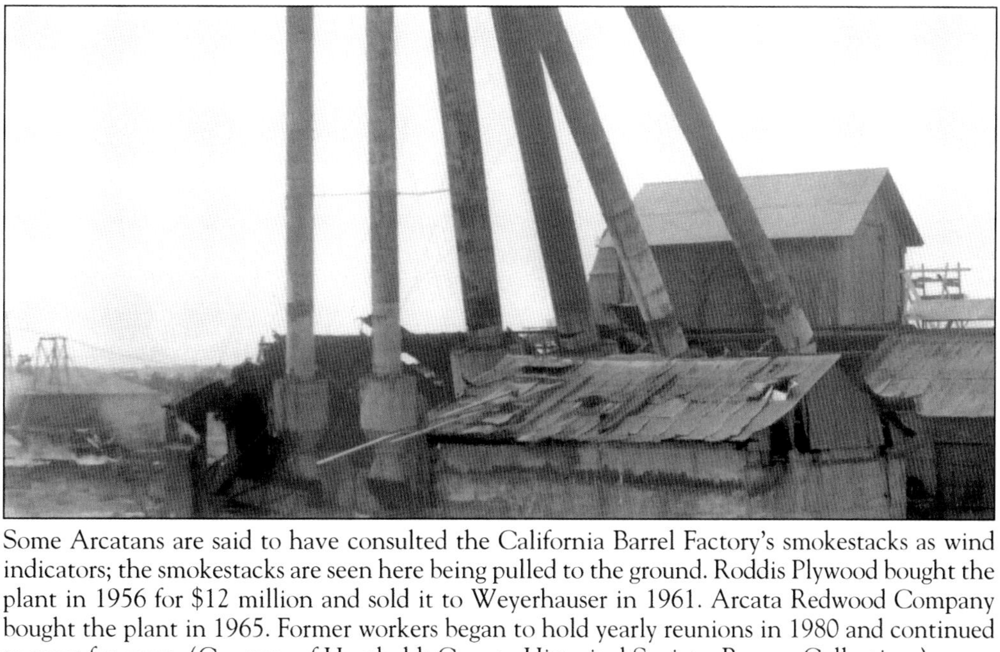

Some Arcatans are said to have consulted the California Barrel Factory's smokestacks as wind indicators; the smokestacks are seen here being pulled to the ground. Roddis Plywood bought the plant in 1956 for $12 million and sold it to Weyerhauser in 1961. Arcata Redwood Company bought the plant in 1965. Former workers began to hold yearly reunions in 1980 and continued to meet for years. (Courtesy of Humboldt County Historical Society, Roscoe Collection.)

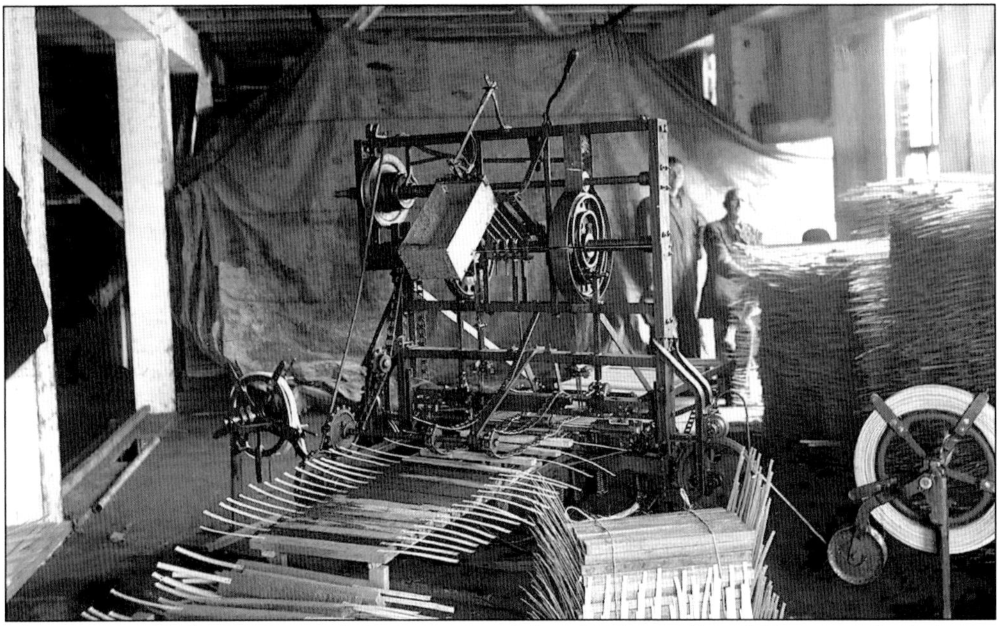

This is most likely an image of the interior of the California Barrel Factory, which began producing wire-bound boxes. The components are shown above in 1928. (Courtesy of Ericson Collection, Humboldt State University Library.)

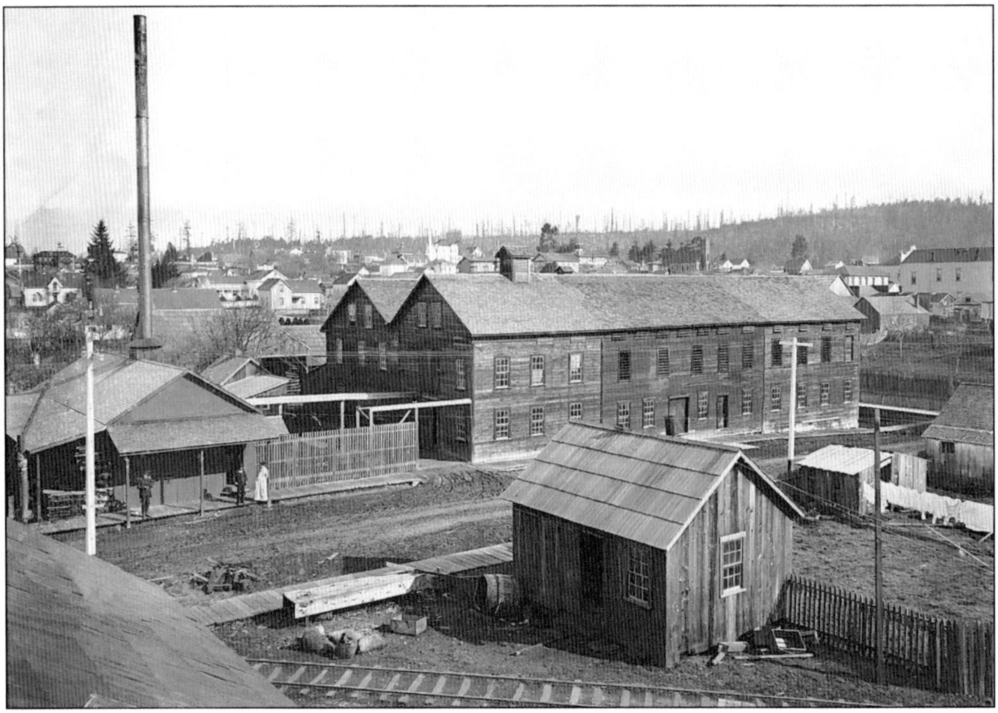

Thomas Devlin came to Arcata in 1866 and soon opened Thomas Devlin Tanning Company at Eighth and J Streets. Workers brought tanbark from the Fickle Hill area to process the leather, which won awards at the 1893 World's Fair in San Francisco. (Courtesy of Ericson Collection, Humboldt State University Library.)

Thomas Bair, like many early entrepreneurs, tried and succeeded at a variety of businesses. Orphaned as a young child, Bair immigrated to California from Madison County, Arkansas, with an uncle when he was 11. He came to Arcata in 1867 and at age 19 ran a mule-packing train for a local merchant. Over the years he was a storekeeper at Fort Gaston and a rancher, and he served as president of both the Redwood and Land Investment Company and the Bank of Arcata, the latter for 27 years. Bair and J.C. Bull Jr. landed the government contracts to build the Humboldt Bay jetties. (Courtesy of Humboldt County Historical Society, Woods Collection.)

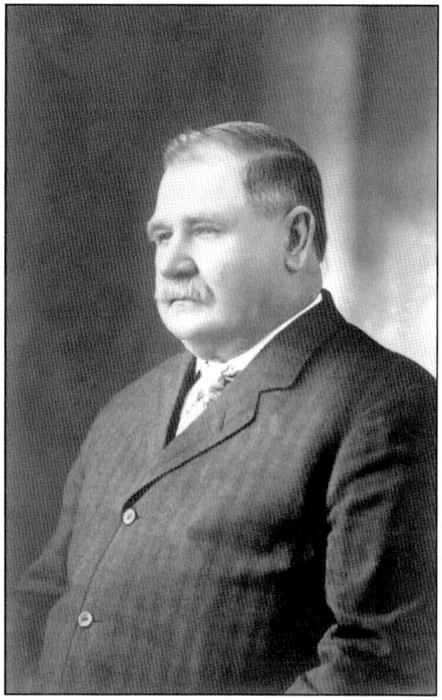

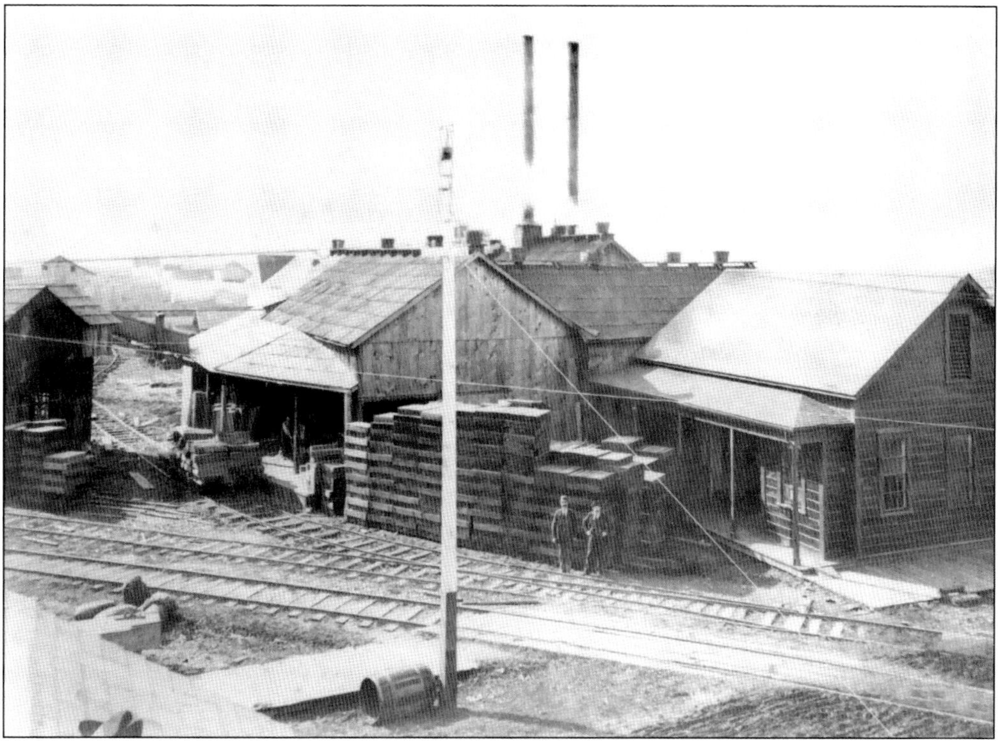

The Humboldt Manufacturing Company's Arcata Mill at Eighth and K Streets, seen here around 1896, began producing shingles two years earlier through the efforts of Isaac Cullberg, nephew of the storekeeper, and his partners. The mill burned in 1915. (Courtesy of Humboldt County Historical Society, Melendy Collection.)

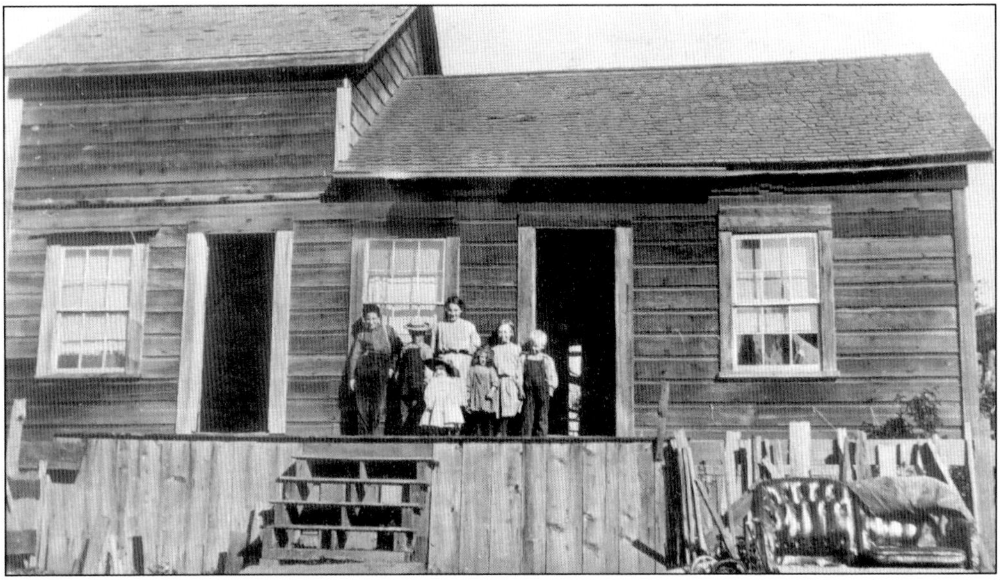

Fickle Hill, east of Arcata, was named for Ohio native Dr. William Young Fickle, who operated a small shingle mill on Fickle Hill Road. The Donahue and DeZordo children pose briefly on the porch of the mill's cookhouse. (Courtesy of Vivian Ziegler.)

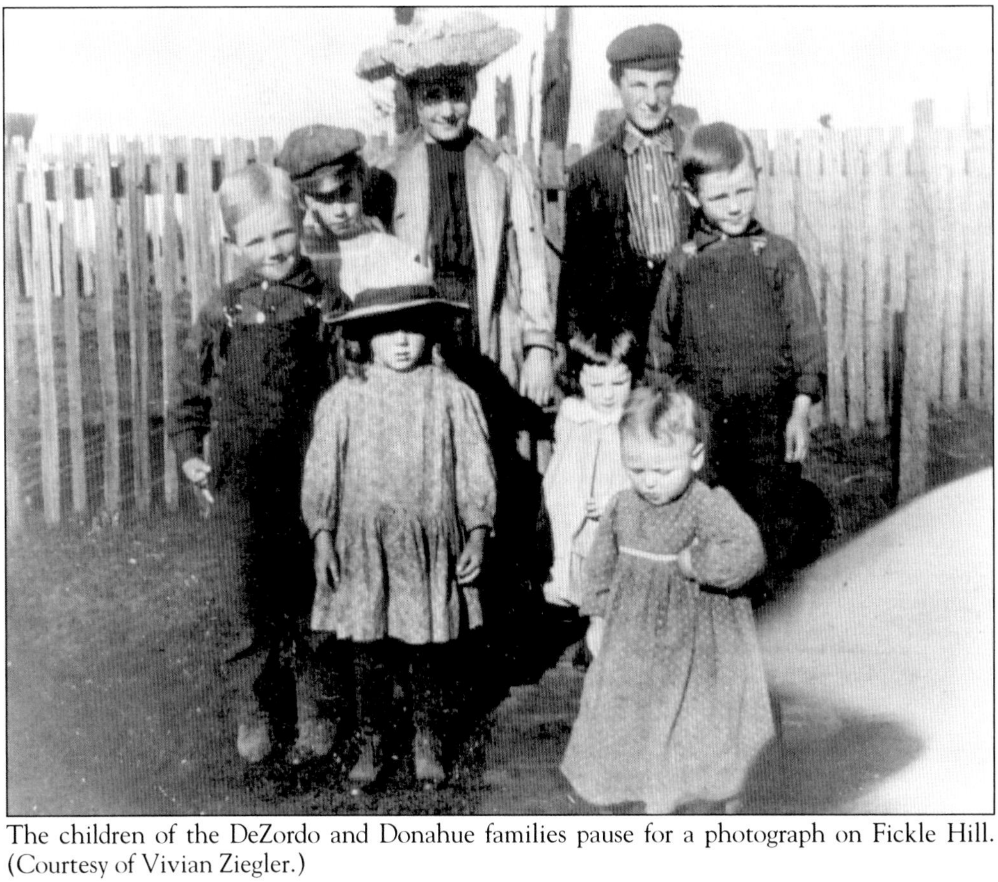

The children of the DeZordo and Donahue families pause for a photograph on Fickle Hill. (Courtesy of Vivian Ziegler.)

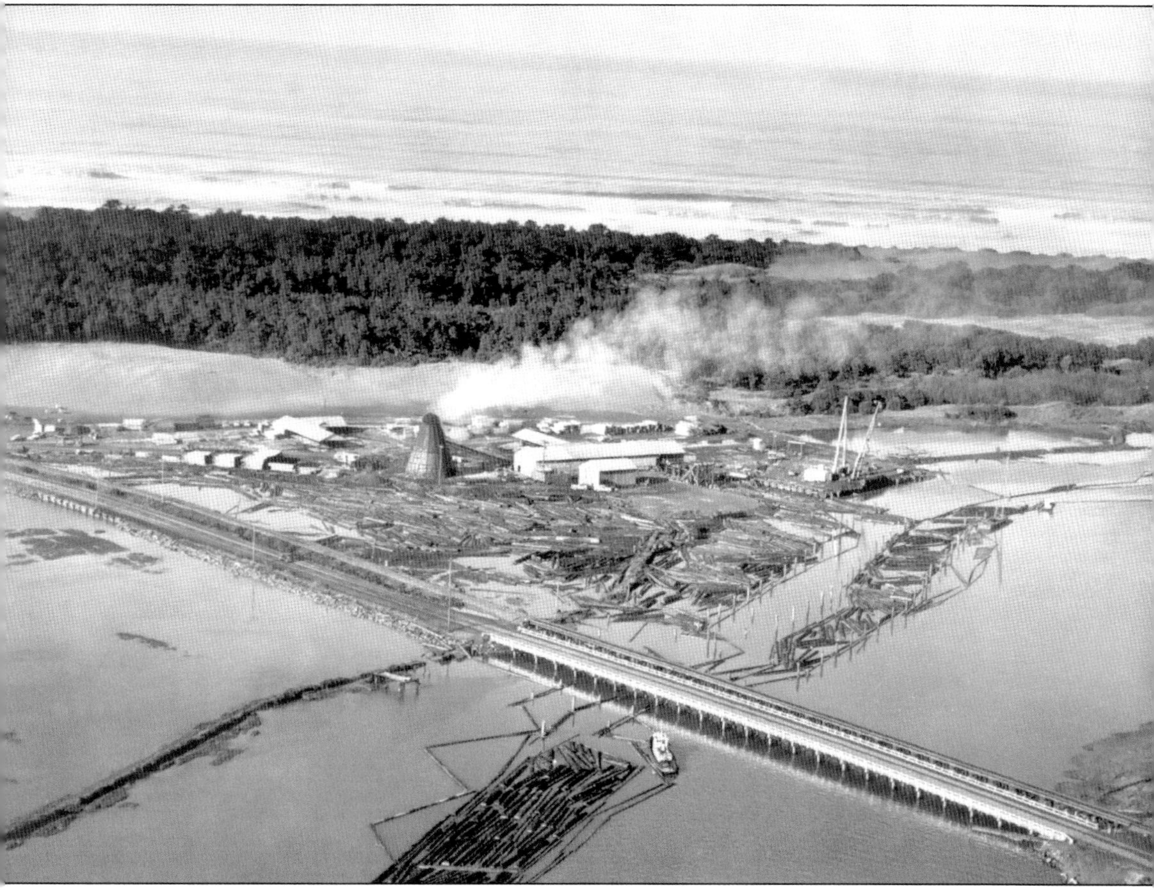

R.H. Emmerson & Son established the mill on the Mad River Slough southwest of Arcata in 1950. "Through efficient operation the firm of R.H. Emmerson & Son is able to produce an approximate 70 thousand board feet of fir lumber each day with a staff of some 35 mill workers and office personnel," according to an undated newspaper article. The planing mill was built first, and the sawmill followed in 1951. (Courtesy of Humboldt County Historical Society, Stine Collection.)

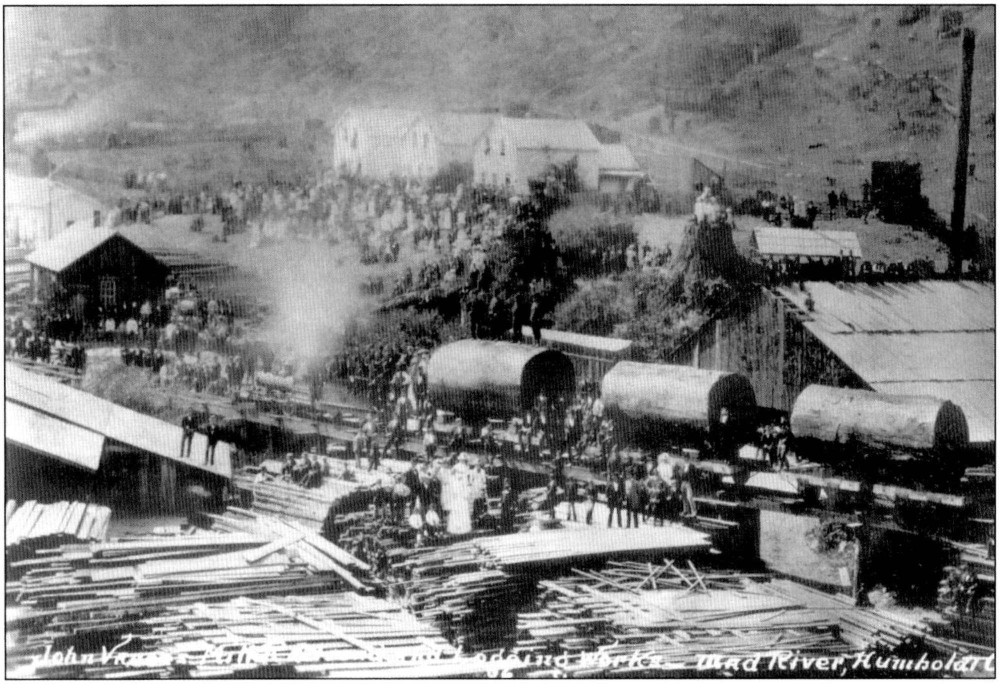

In its heyday, the Vance mill at Essex, northeast of Arcata, was handling these one-log-per-railroad-car size trees. (Courtesy of Humboldt County Historical Society, Melendy Collection.)

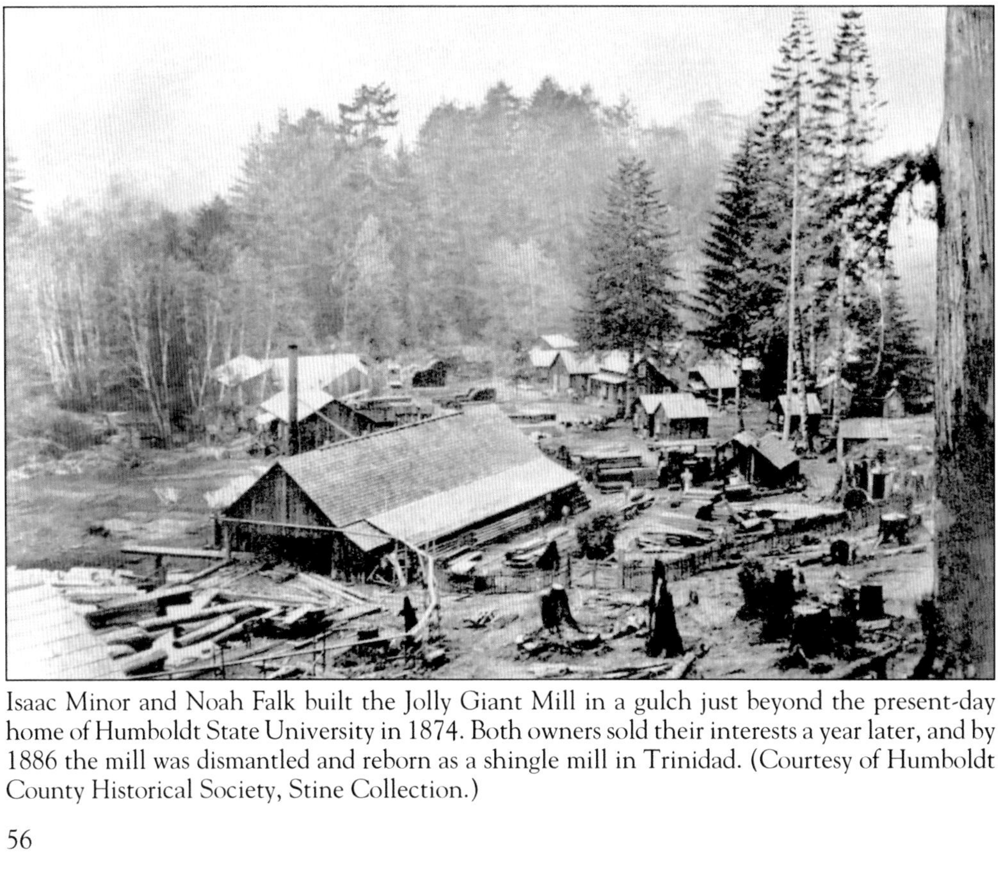

Isaac Minor and Noah Falk built the Jolly Giant Mill in a gulch just beyond the present-day home of Humboldt State University in 1874. Both owners sold their interests a year later, and by 1886 the mill was dismantled and reborn as a shingle mill in Trinidad. (Courtesy of Humboldt County Historical Society, Stine Collection.)

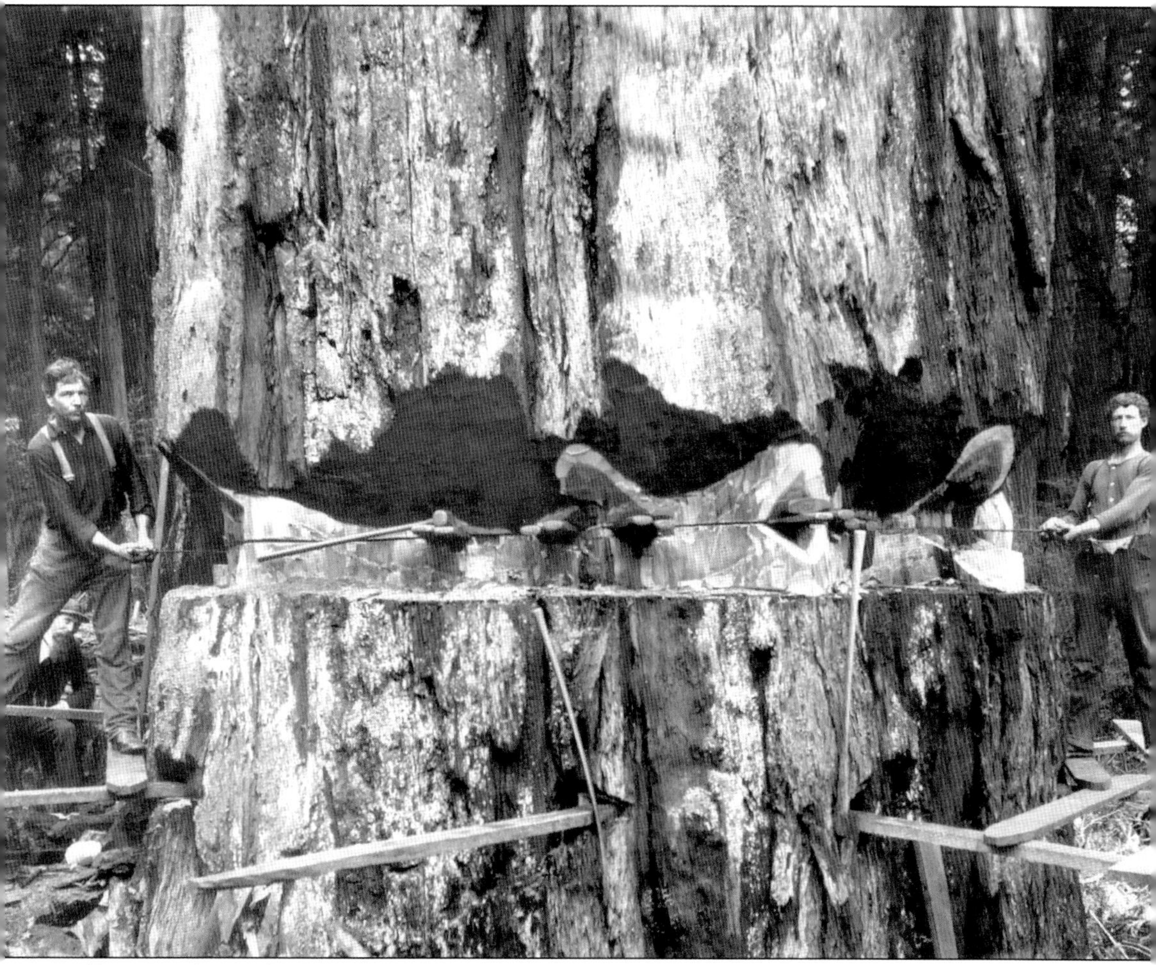

Fallers are shown here in the Vance Woods near Essex. (Courtesy of Humboldt County Historical Society, Melendy Collection.)

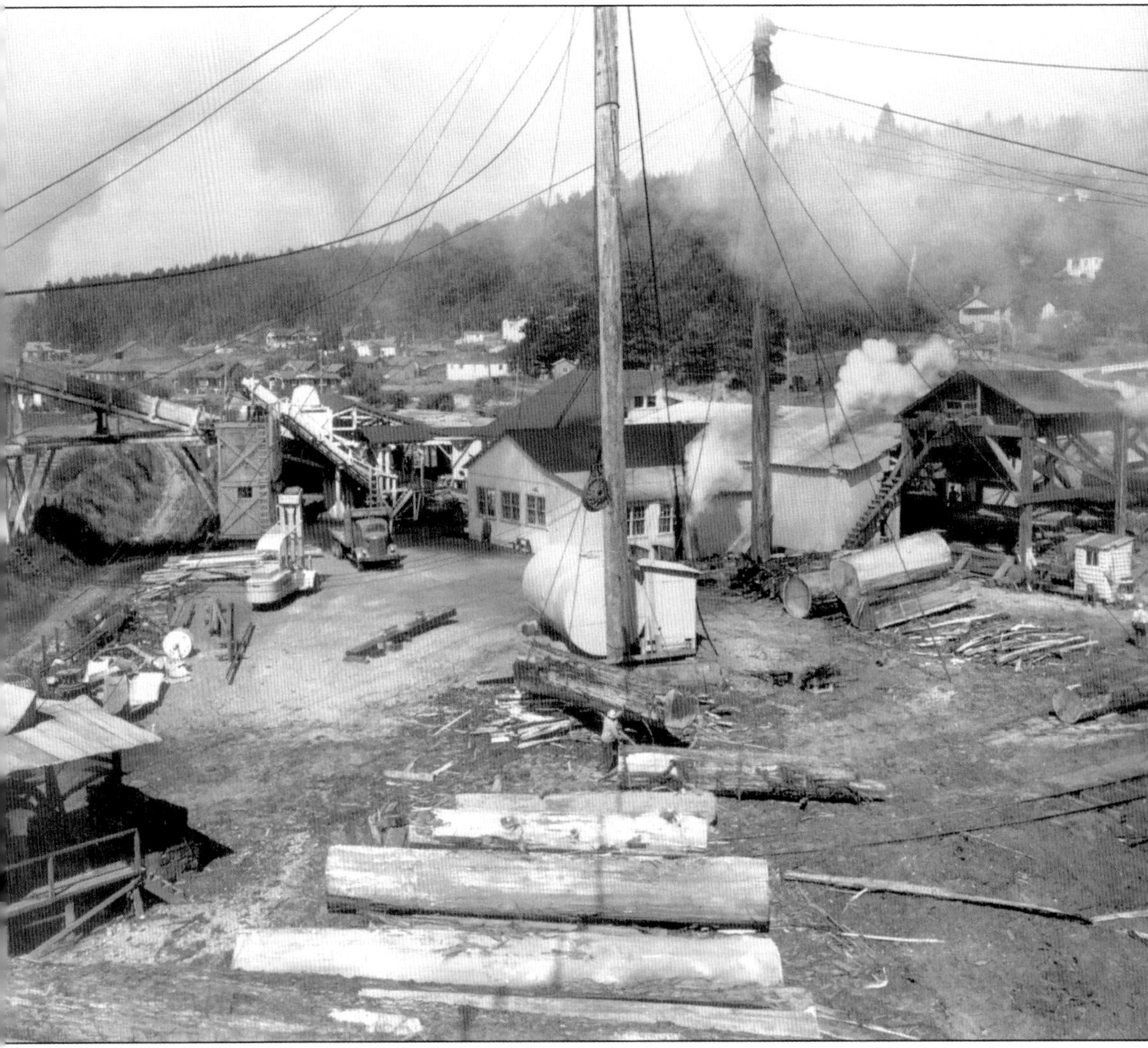

In the 1950s and 1960s, the heart of Arcata Redwood Company's operations lay north in Orick and at Brainard, midway between Eureka and Arcata, now home to the Simpson Timber Company mill. The site featured dry kilns, band mills, a planing mill, an end and edge glue plant, and storage, as well as an outdoor air-drying yard. (Courtesy of Humboldt County Historical Society, Melendy Collection.)

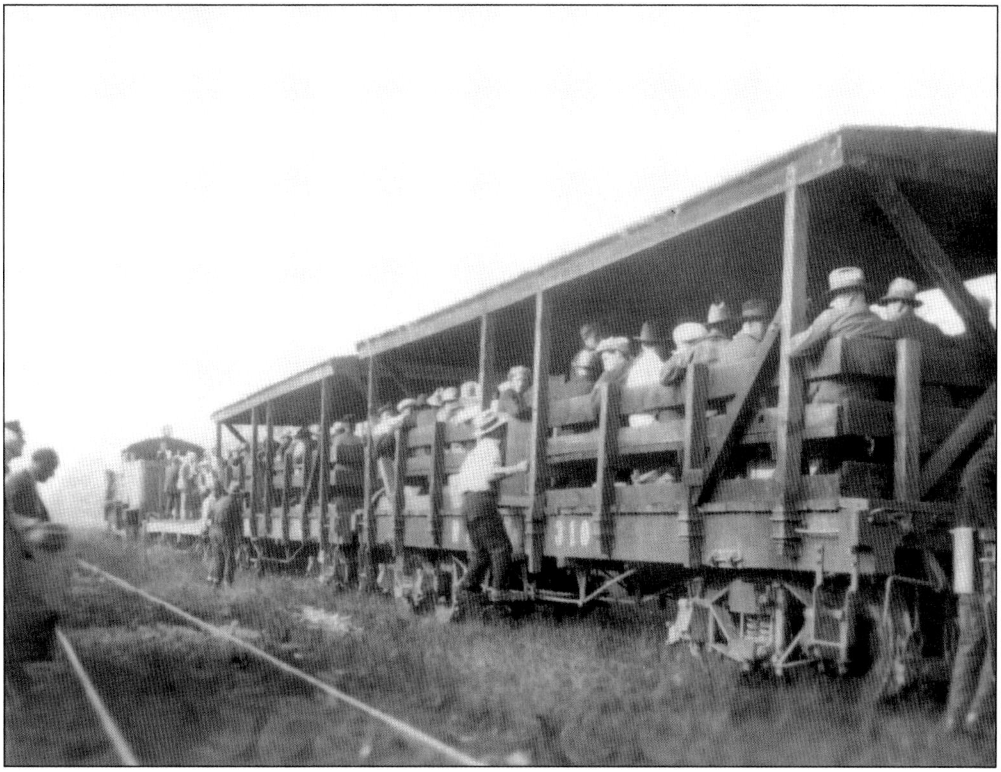

Hammond Lumber Company employees board a "Crummie" at Little River Junction to return to camp on Sunday evening. (Courtesy of Humboldt County Historical Society.)

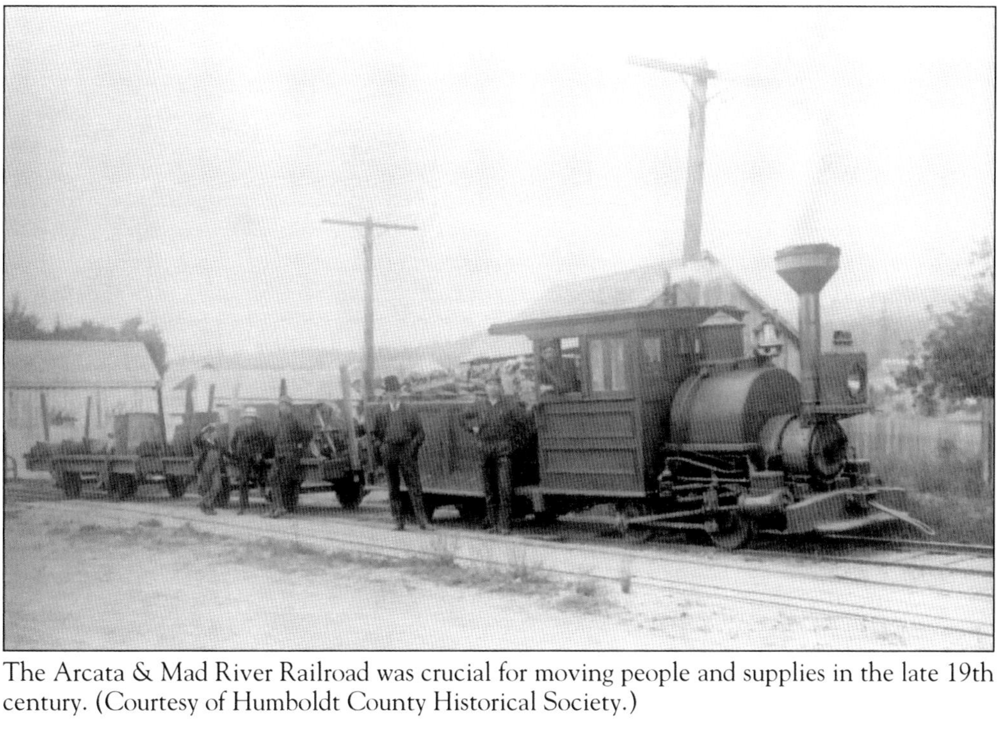

The Arcata & Mad River Railroad was crucial for moving people and supplies in the late 19th century. (Courtesy of Humboldt County Historical Society.)

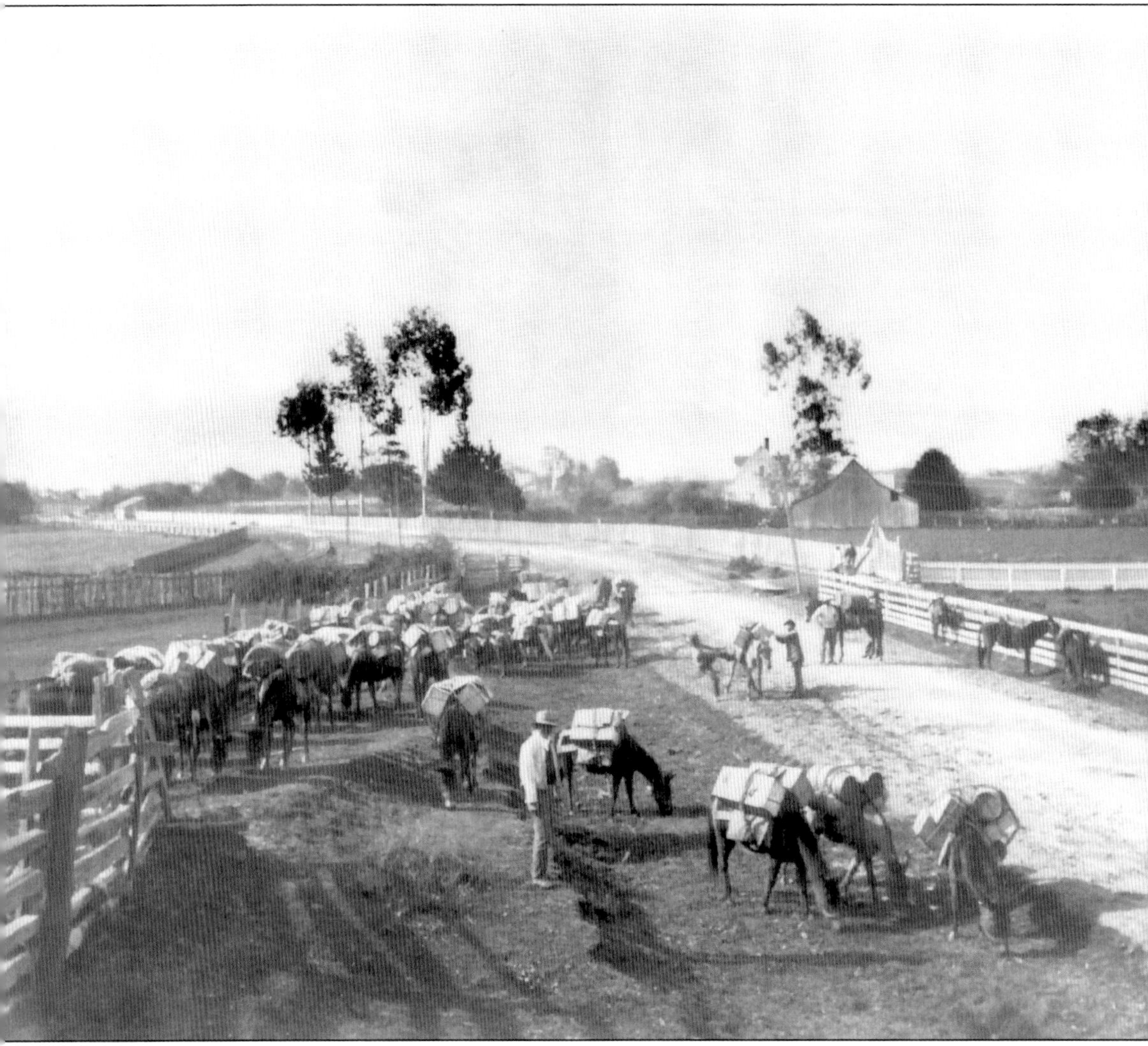

This c. 1885 image of men preparing a pack train for a trip to the inland mining camps near Hoopa may be one of Arcata photographer A.W. Ericson's best-known images. Pictured at Alliance in northwest Arcata, the pack train of 55 mules was soon en route east with goods that had been delivered to Arcata by sailing ships and steamers. (Courtesy of Humboldt County Historical Society, Stine Collection.)

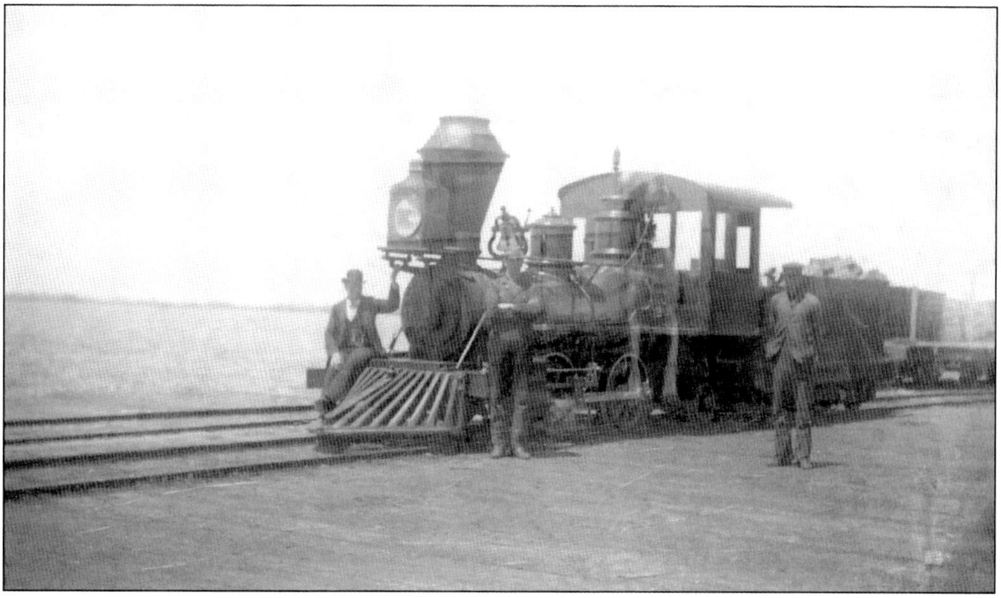

In its heyday, the Arcata wharf was linked to the tracks to simplify the movement of incoming supplies and passengers from the water to the plaza. (Courtesy of Humboldt County Historical Society.)

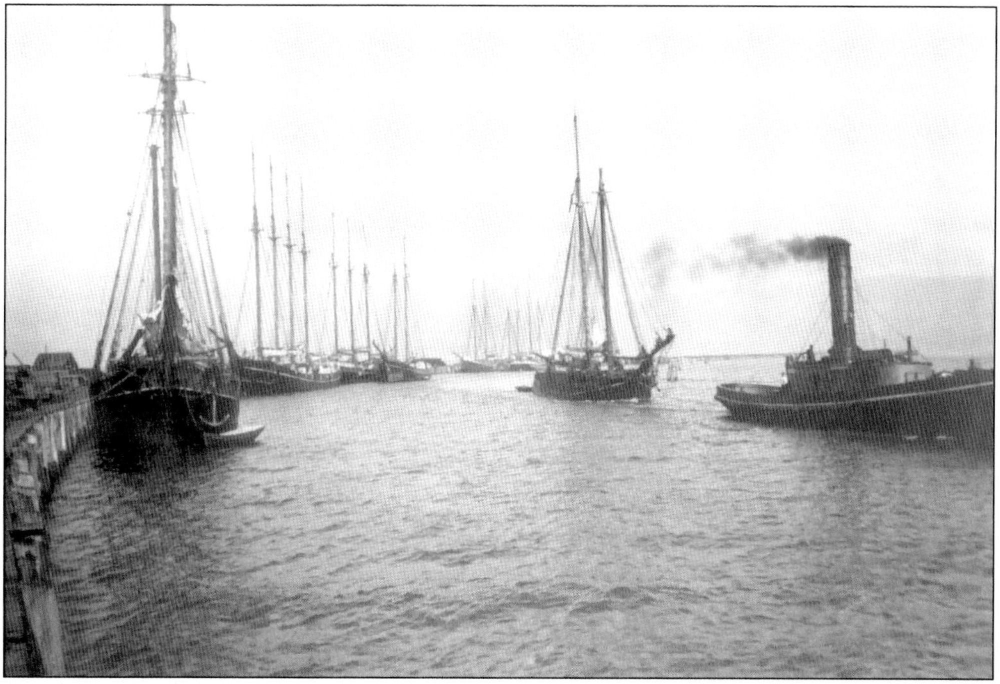

Merchants supplying the clamoring miners of eastern Humboldt quickly took action to ease the delivery by ship. A pier measuring nearly two miles in length was completed in 1855 by the Union Plank Walk and Railroad Company, later incorporated as the Arcata & Mad River Railroad Company. A railroad track from the southwest corner of the plaza to the wharf, with cars initially drawn by horses, was claimed as the first railroad built in California. (Courtesy of Humboldt County Historical Society.)

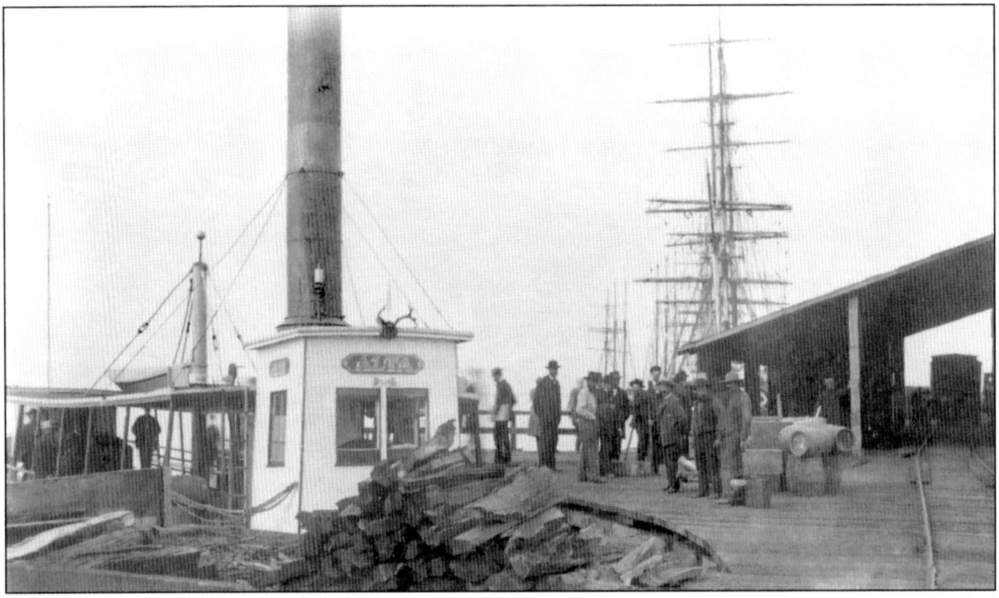

The steamer *Alta*, shown here at the Arcata Wharf around 1883, was one of three stern-wheeled ferries providing service to towns, landings, and mills on Humboldt Bay. (Courtesy of California State Library, Humboldt County Historical Society.)

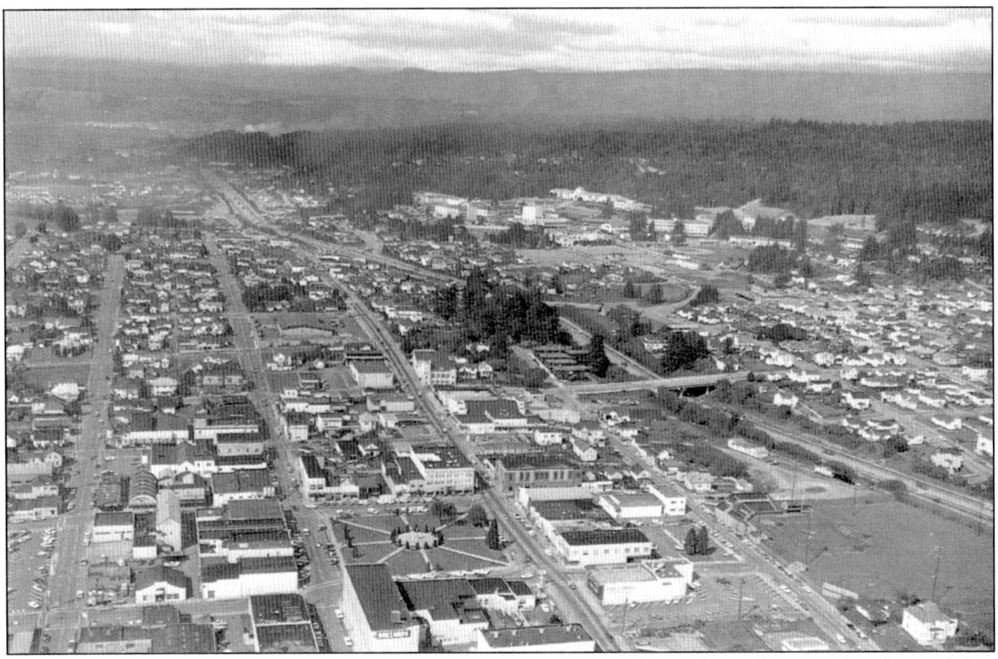

Looking north, the configuration of U.S. Highway 101 on the right indicates the date of this photo to be sometime in the 1950s and 1960s. (Courtesy of Humboldt County Historical Society, Stine Collection.)

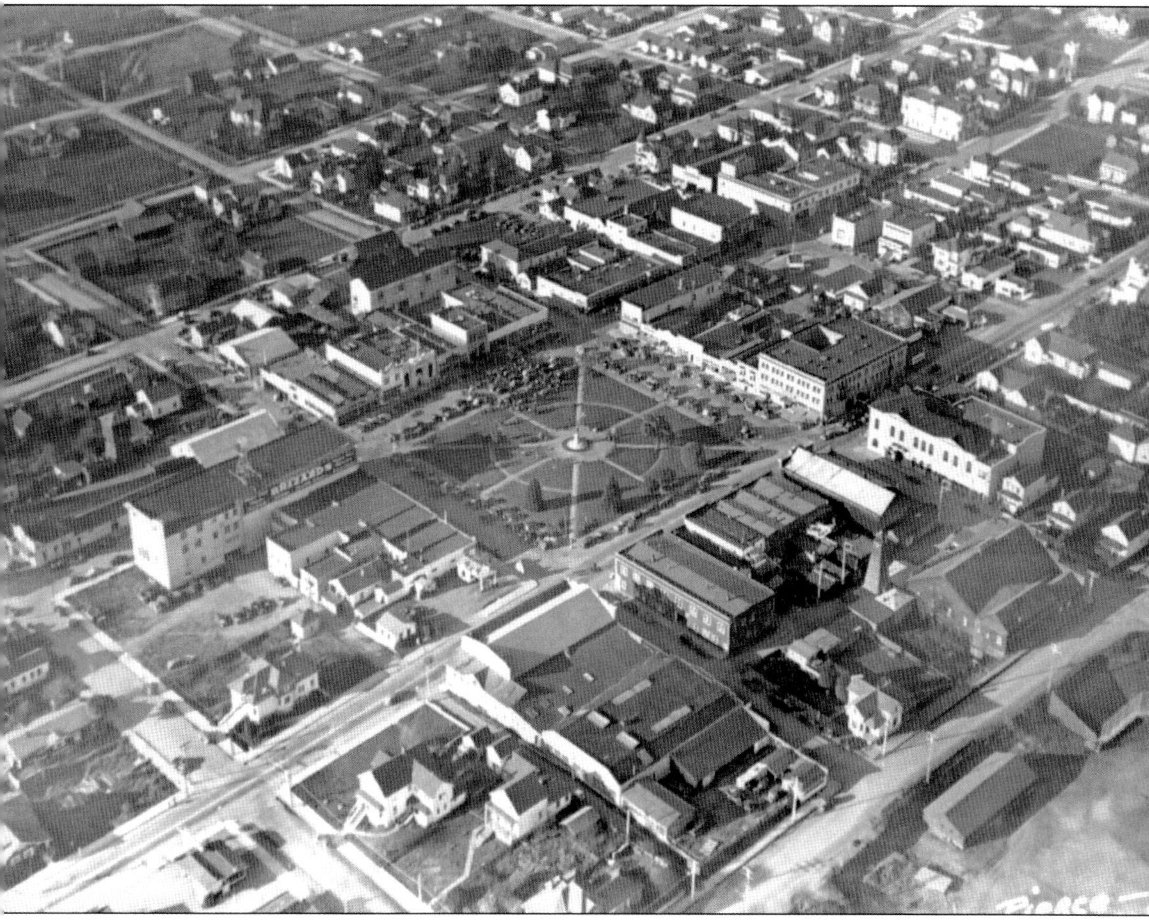

Looking like a compass, the Arcata Plaza stands out in this view taken from the southeast. (Courtesy of Humboldt County Historical Society.)

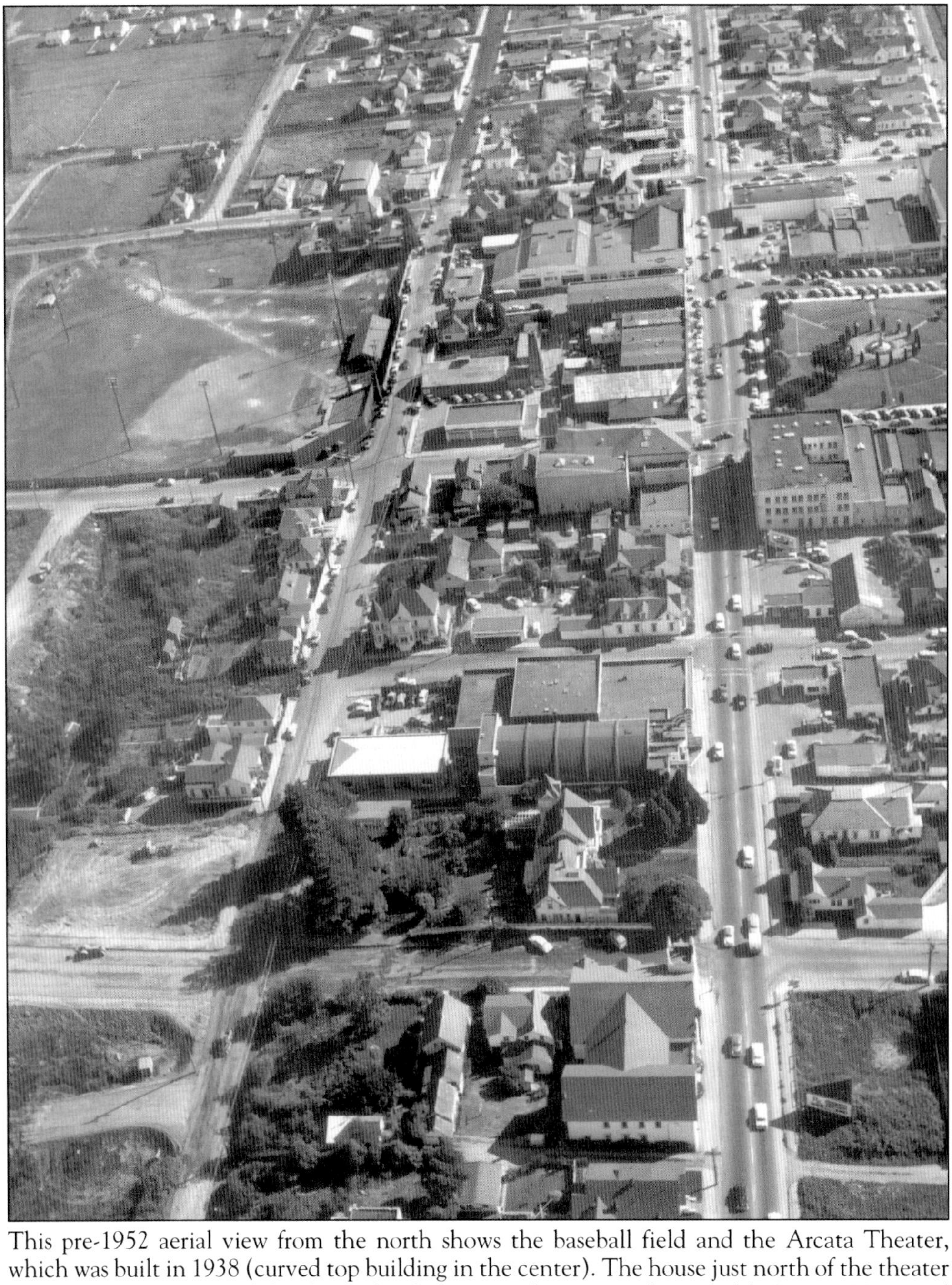

This pre-1952 aerial view from the north shows the baseball field and the Arcata Theater, which was built in 1938 (curved top building in the center). The house just north of the theater was owned by the Brizard family until at least 1949. (Courtesy of Humboldt County Historical Society, Chamber of Commerce Collection.)

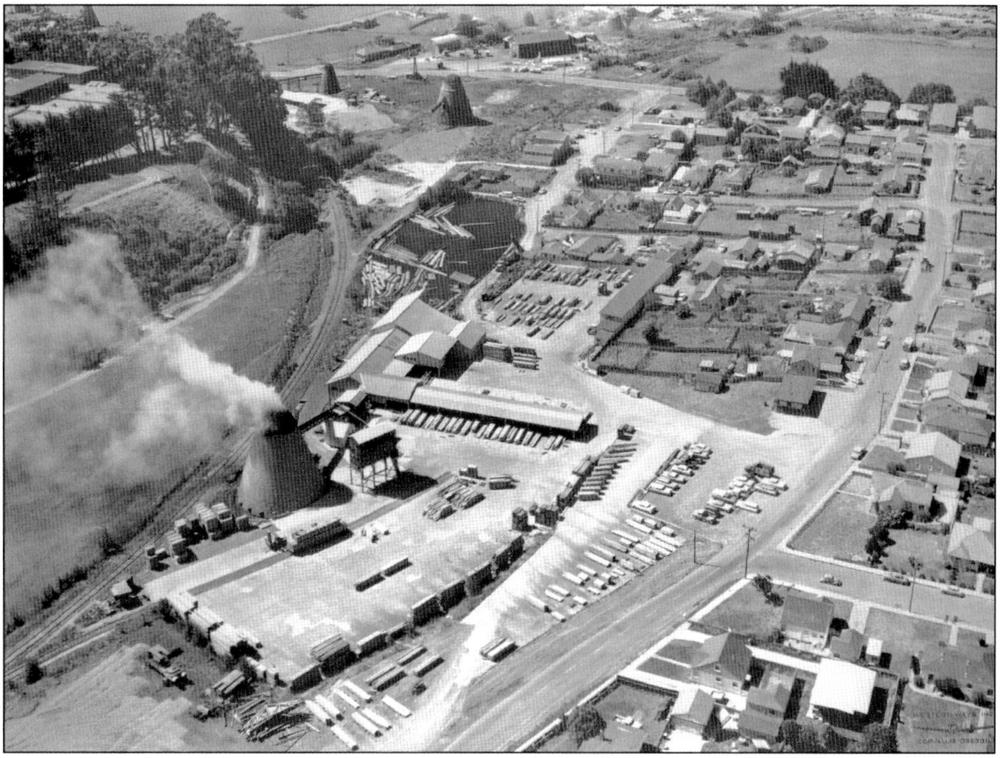

Shown here are two aerial views of the Twin Parks Mill. (Courtesy of Peter Hess.)

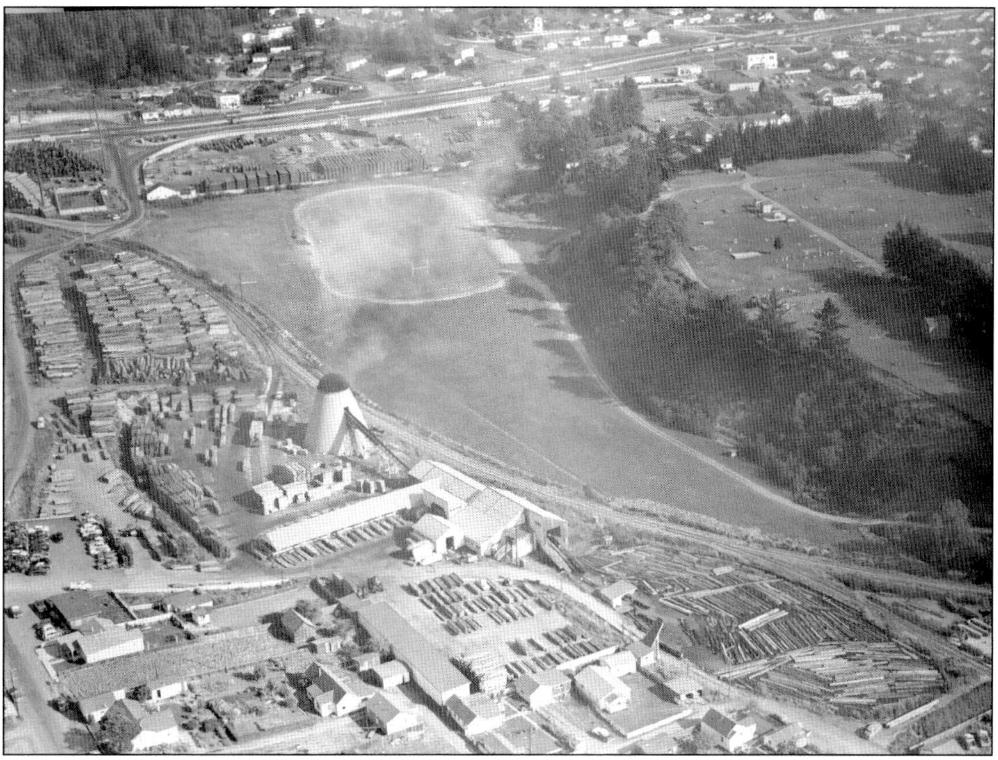

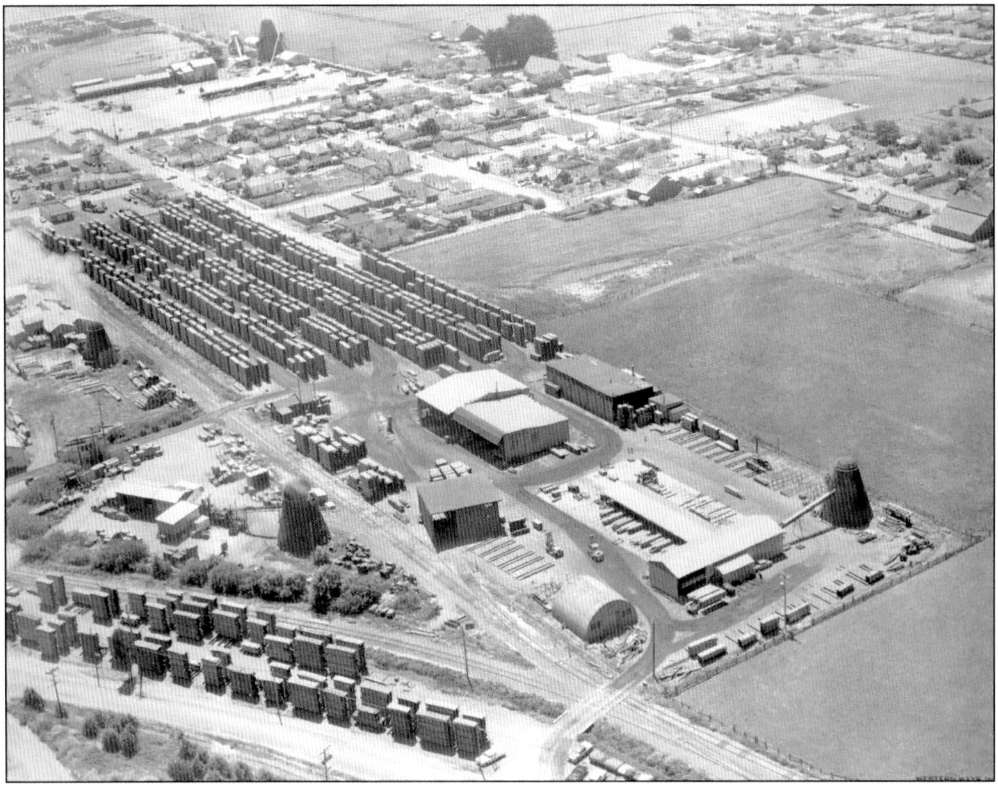

Jim Franke and James Berry owned James Redwood Sales, which operated in west Arcata from the late 1960s to early 1970s. Note the four teepee burners captured in this image. (Courtesy of Peter Hess.)

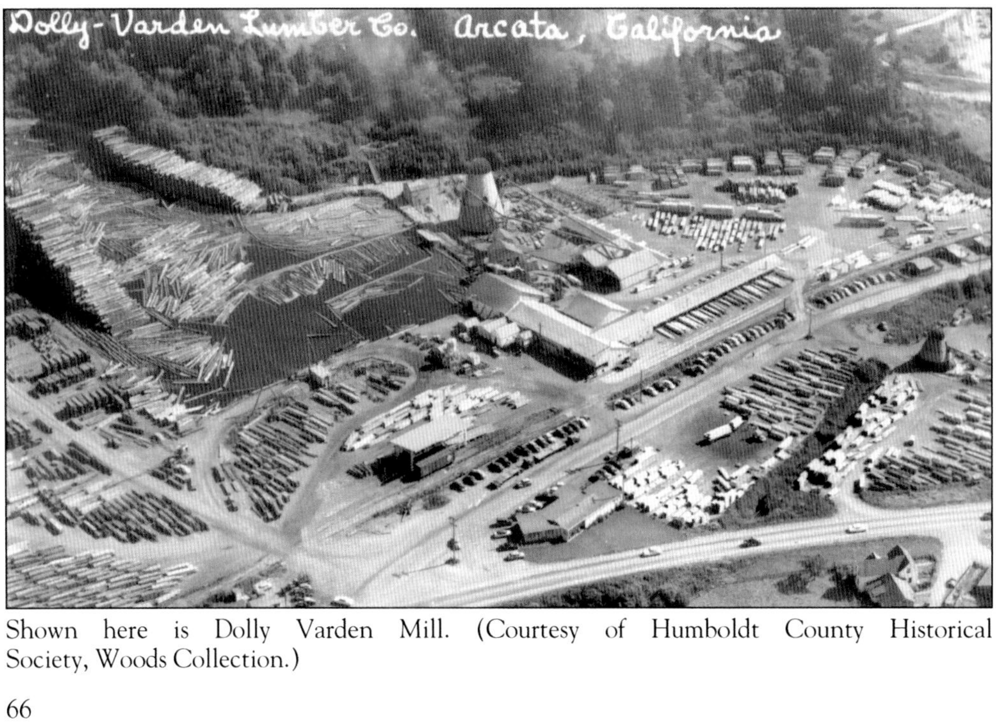

Shown here is Dolly Varden Mill. (Courtesy of Humboldt County Historical Society, Woods Collection.)

Three

Education

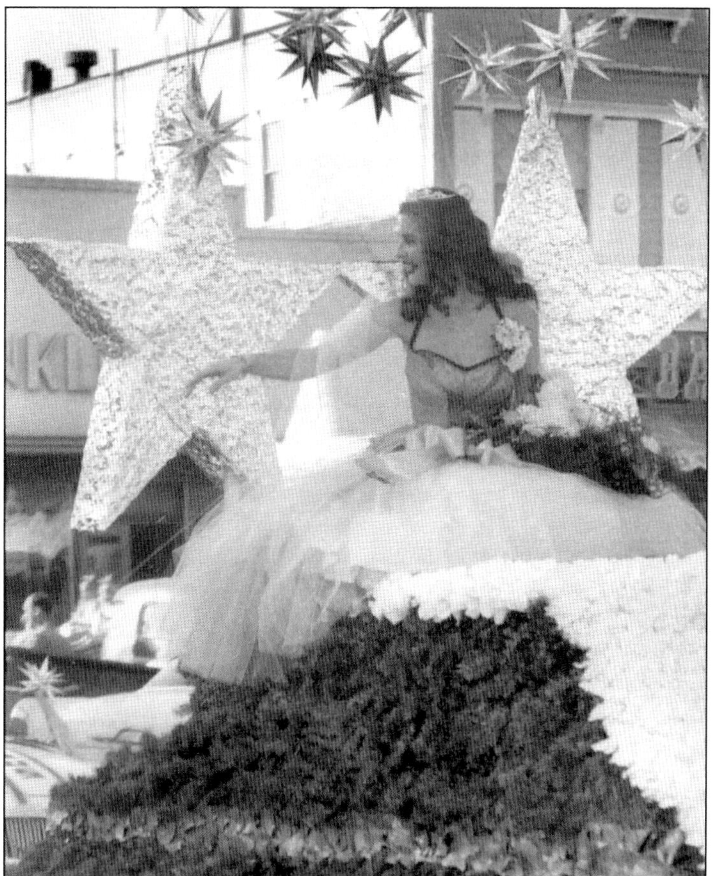

Homecoming Queen Mrs. Kris Church, also known as the Stardust Queen, rode in the October 1957 Humboldt State College's Homecoming Parade around the plaza. She was a junior majoring in physical education. (Courtesy of Humboldt County Historical Society, Roscoe Collection.)

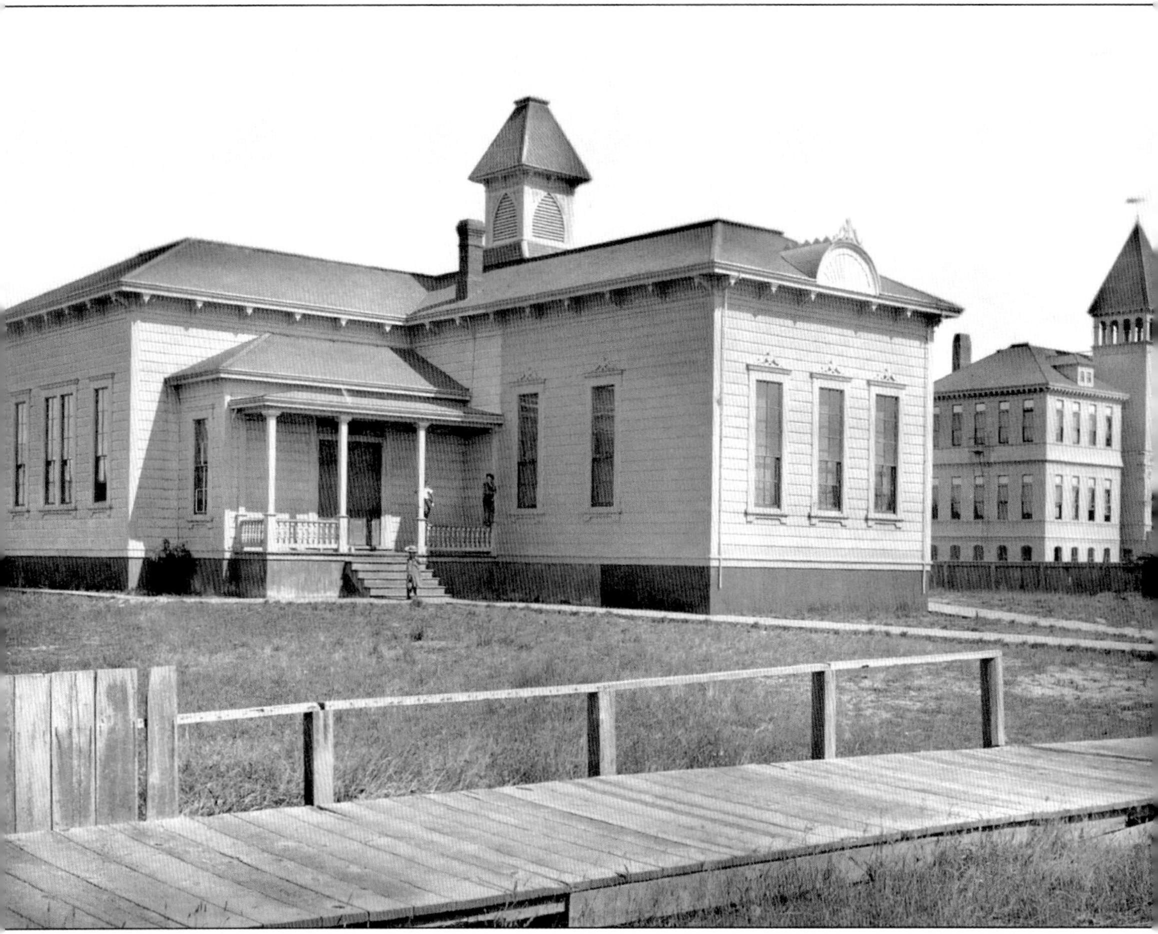

The State of California leased this building on Eleventh Street in the spring of 1914 from the Arcata Grammar School (on right) as the first home of the Humboldt Normal School. The school's first president was Nelson Blieau Van Matré, who led the college until 1924. After acquiring 51 acres on a hilltop east of Arcata from William Preston and the stockholders of the Union Water Company, the Normal School moved to its present site in January 1916. (Courtesy of Historic Sites Society of Arcata, Ruth Horel Collection.)

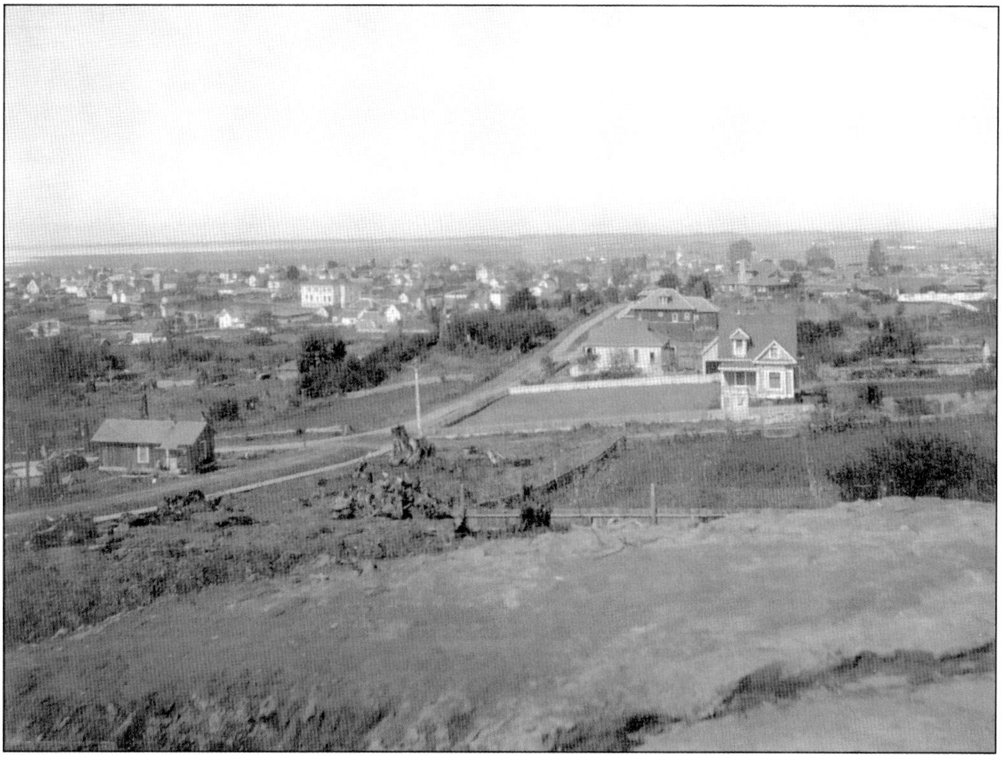

This early view of Arcata looks west from the south end of the campus of Humboldt Normal School. (Courtesy of Humboldt State University Library.)

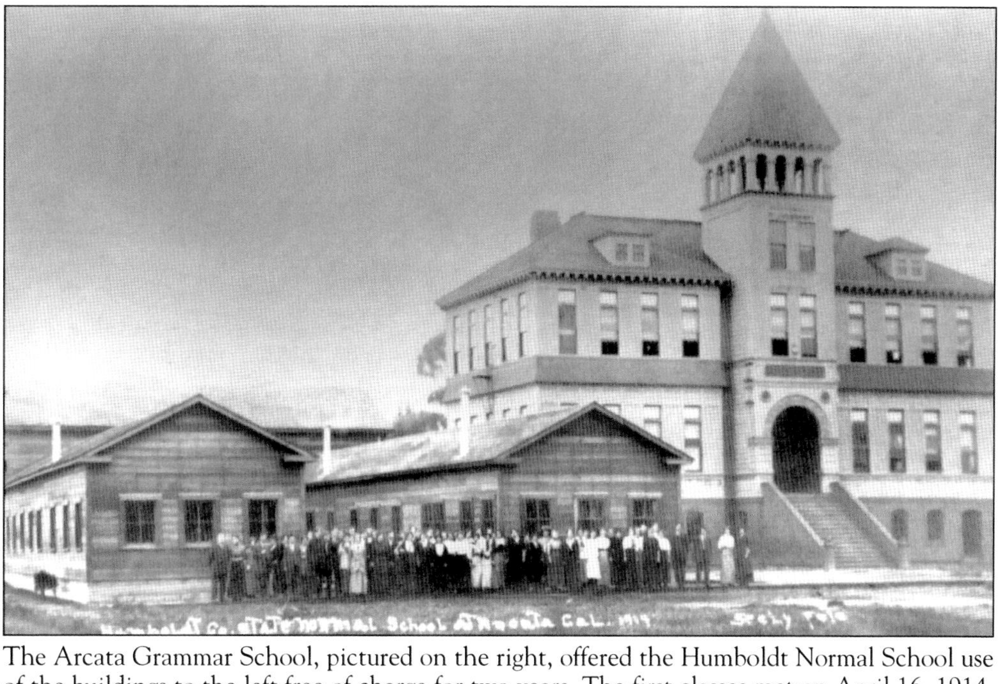

The Arcata Grammar School, pictured on the right, offered the Humboldt Normal School use of the buildings to the left free of charge for two years. The first classes met on April 16, 1914. (Courtesy of Humboldt County Historical Society, Woods Collection.)

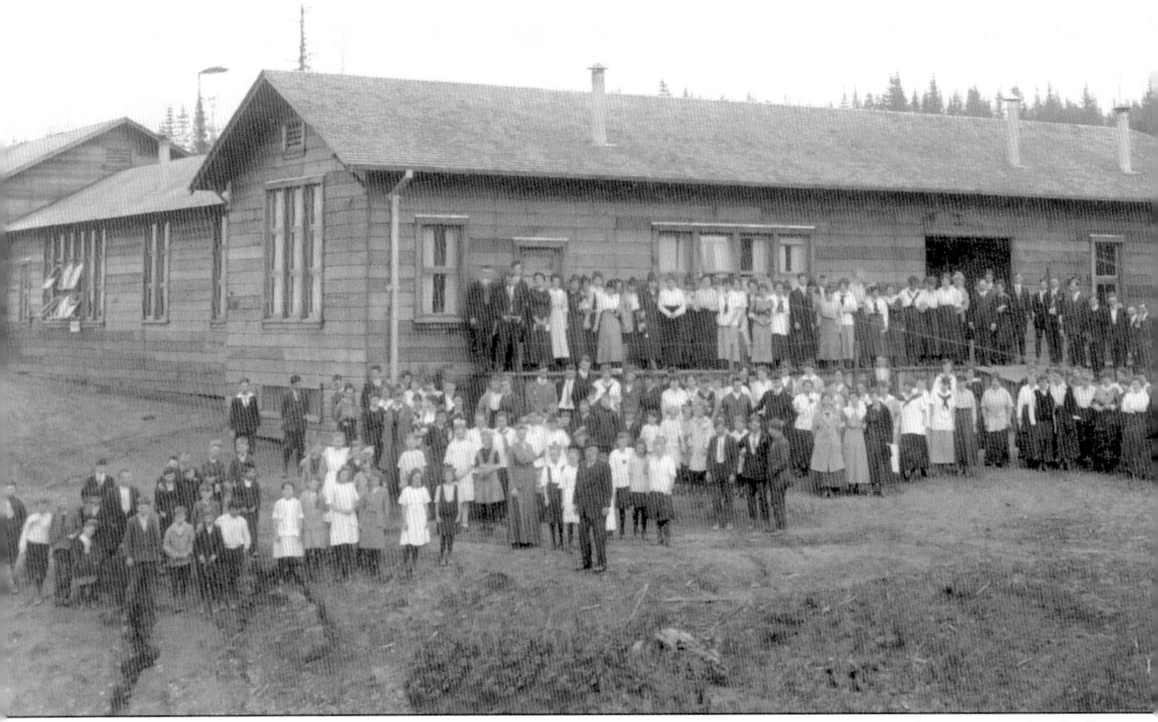

Shown here are Humboldt Normal School's temporary buildings at its new home on the hill due east of town. (Courtesy of Humboldt County Historical Society, Roscoe Collection.)

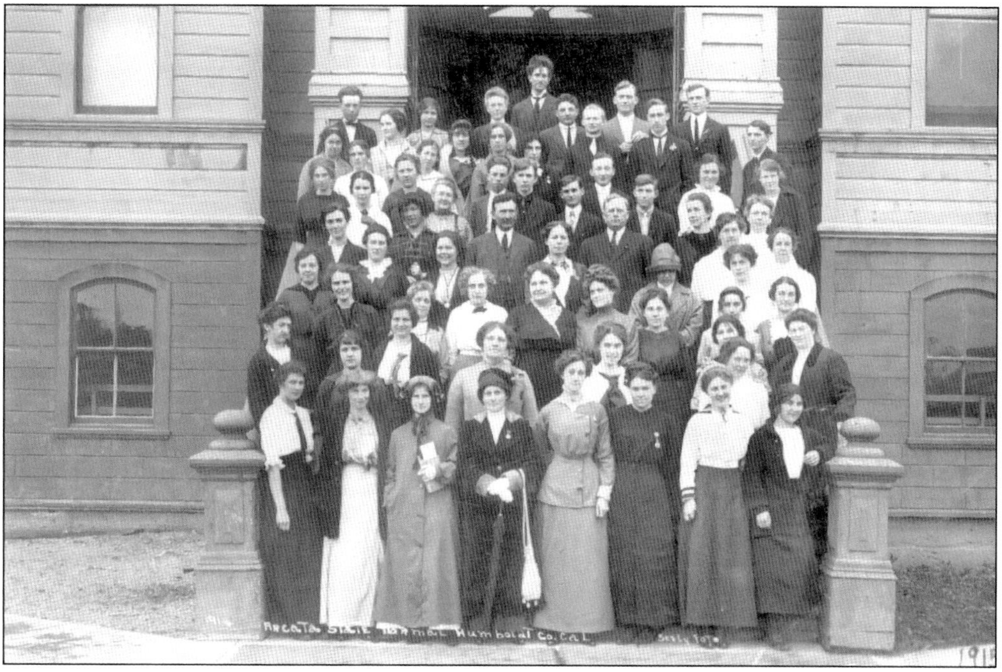

The First Humboldt Normal School class poses for a picture. Susie Baker Fountain (front row, third from the left) was the teacher college's very first graduate. She went on to become a devoted collector and chronicler of North Coast history. (Courtesy of Humboldt State University Library.)

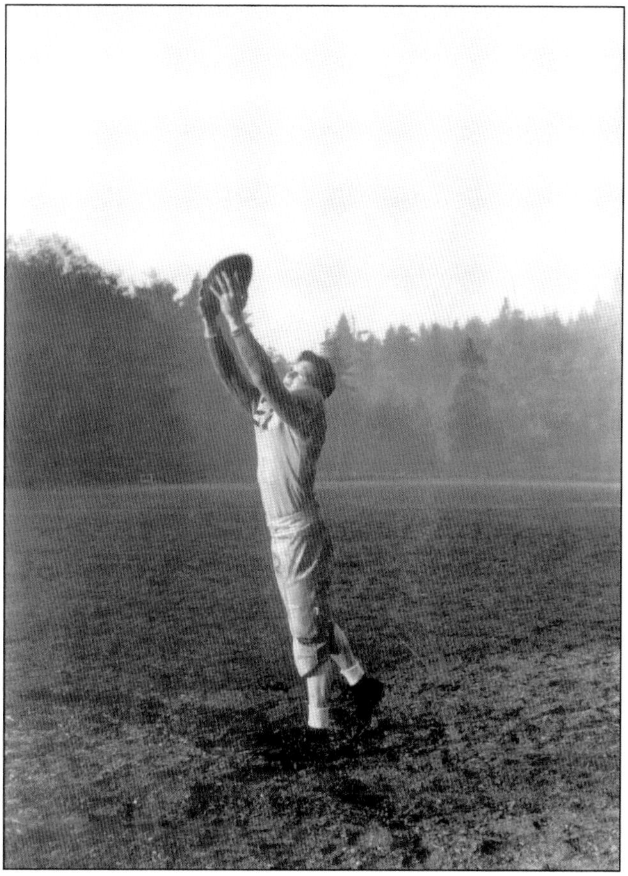

A Humboldt State College graduate in 1940, Franny Givins went on to coach the college's basketball teams from 1953 to 1964 and was named to the university's Athletics Hall of Fame in football, basketball, and track in 1968. (Courtesy of Humboldt County Historical Society, Givins Collection.)

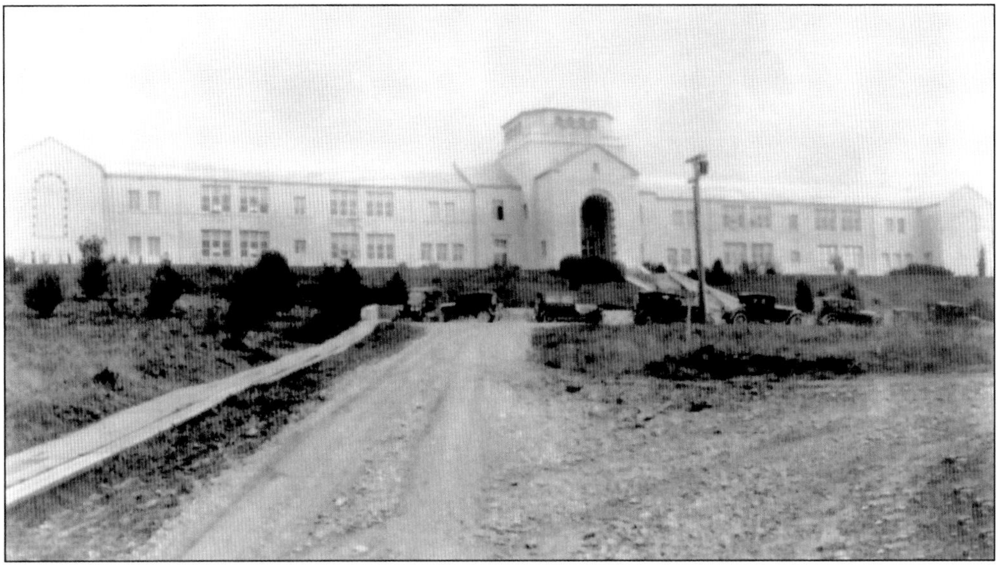

The walk from their vehicles to Founders Hall on the Humboldt Normal School campus was considerably shorter in 1925 and 1926 than the walk facing today's Humboldt State University students. (Courtesy of Humboldt County Historical Society, Woods Collection.)

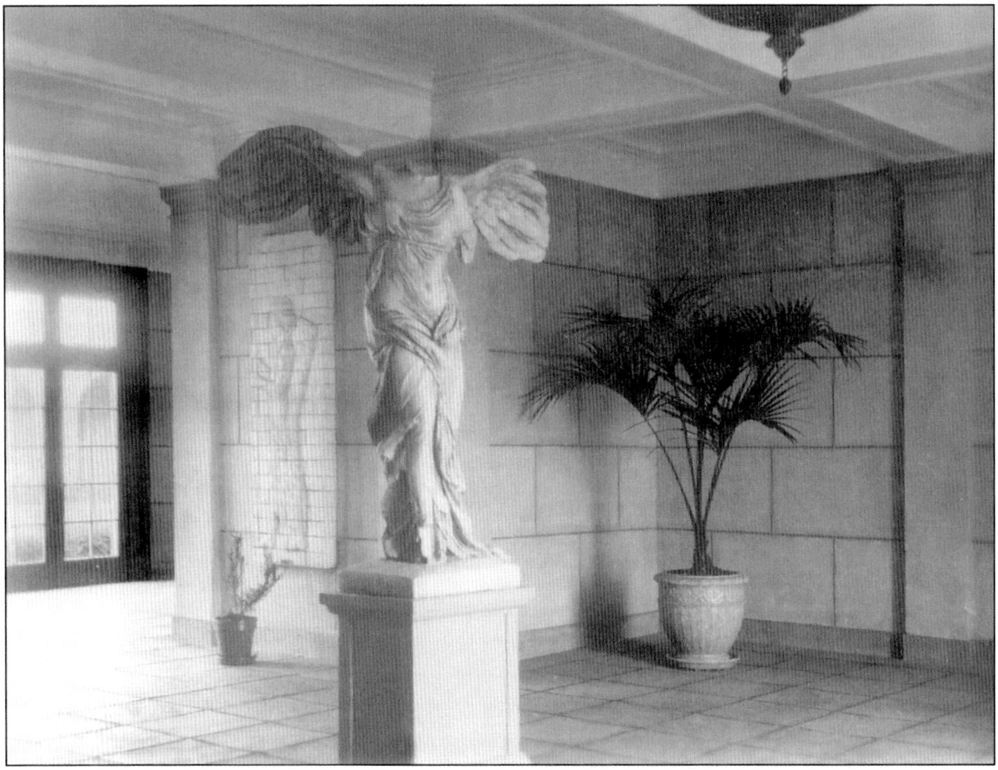

A replica of the Greek sculpture *Winged Victory of Samothrace* once greeted students entering Founders Hall lobby. The original sculpture depicting the Greek goddess Nike is on display at Paris's Musee du Louvre and was found on the island of Samothrace. Scholars date the sculpture from between 190 and 250 B.C. (Courtesy of Humboldt State University Library.)

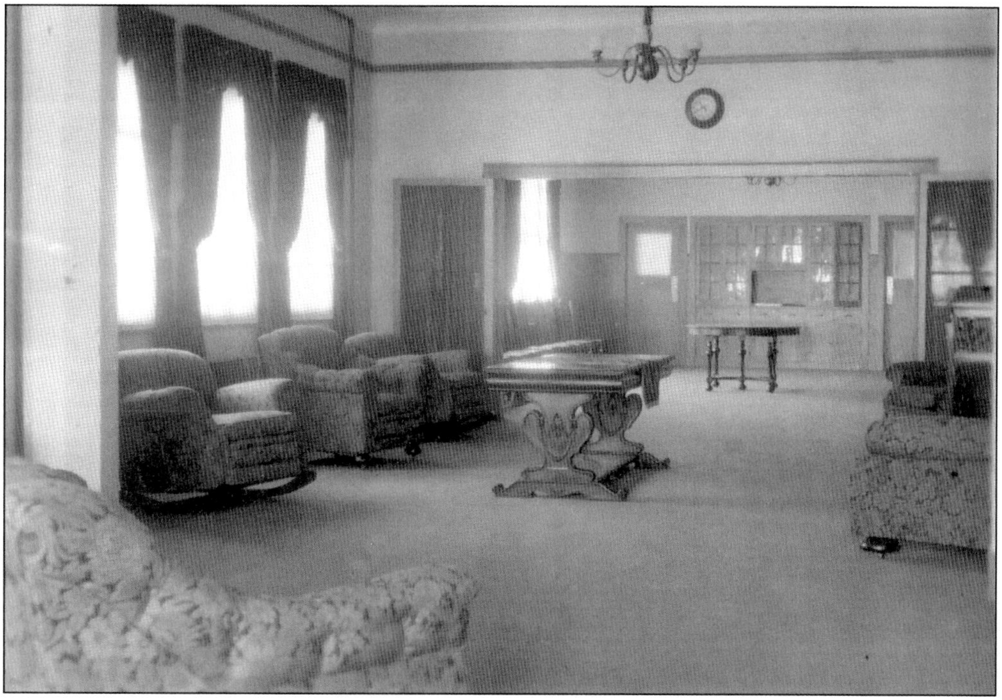

Many philosophies were likely discussed in the elegant lobby of Founders Hall in the 1920s and 1930s. (Courtesy of Humboldt State University Library.)

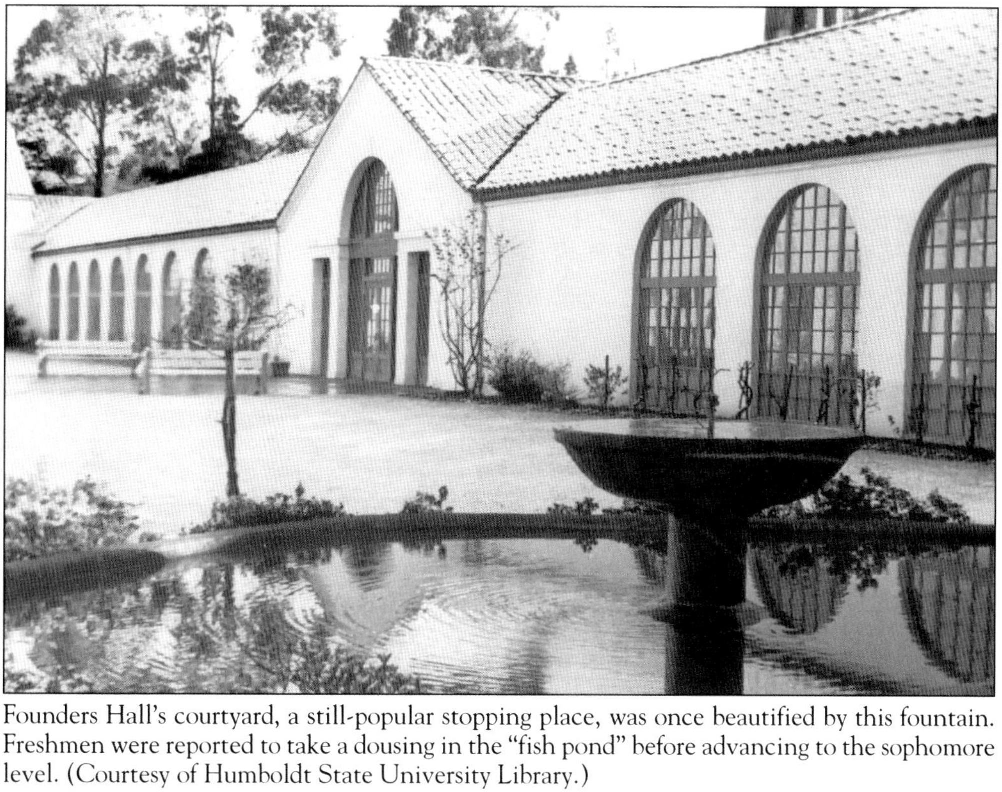

Founders Hall's courtyard, a still-popular stopping place, was once beautified by this fountain. Freshmen were reported to take a dousing in the "fish pond" before advancing to the sophomore level. (Courtesy of Humboldt State University Library.)

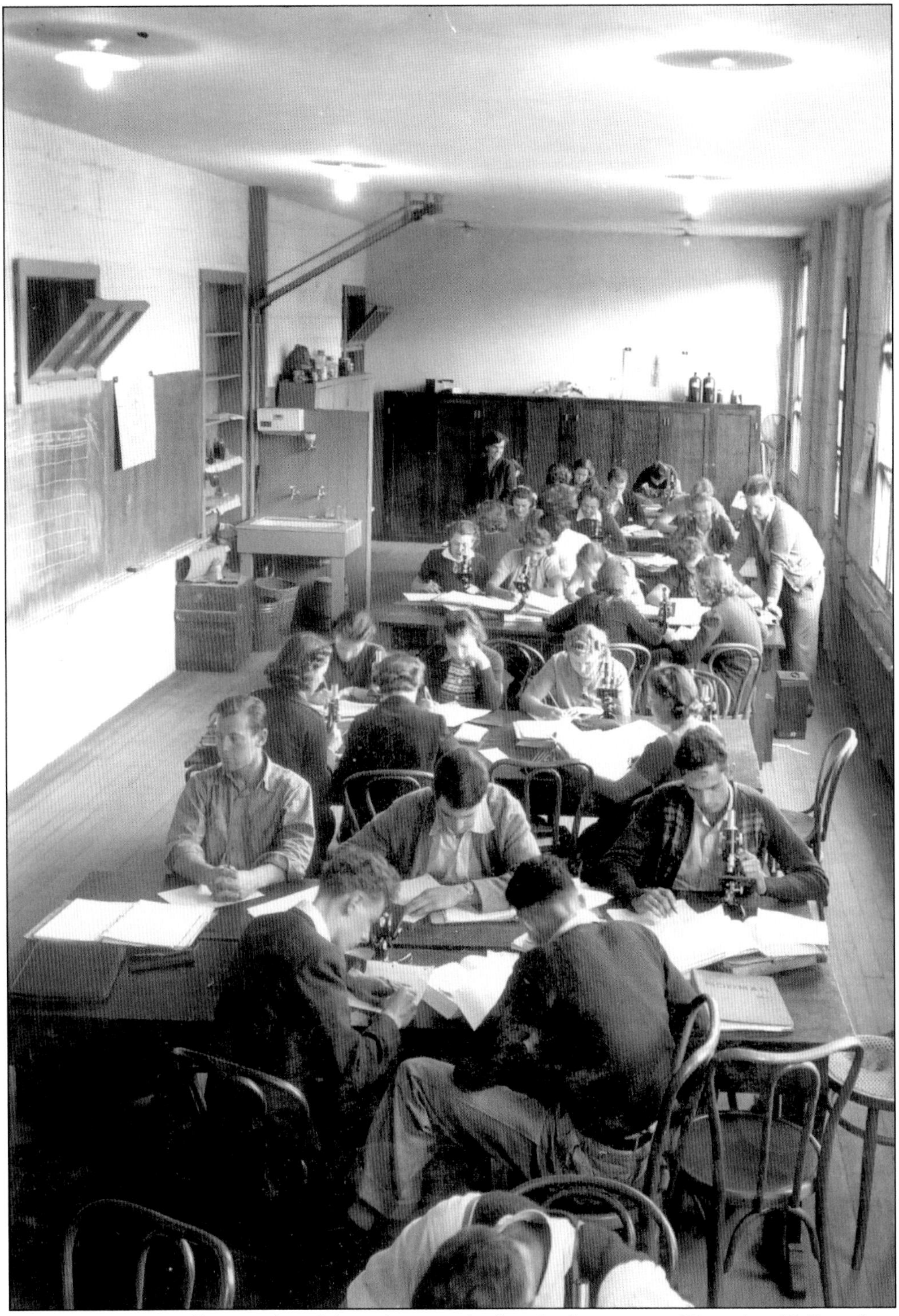

Humboldt State College zoology lab students studied in the basement of Founders Hall in the 1938 class shown here. (Courtesy of Humboldt State University Library.)

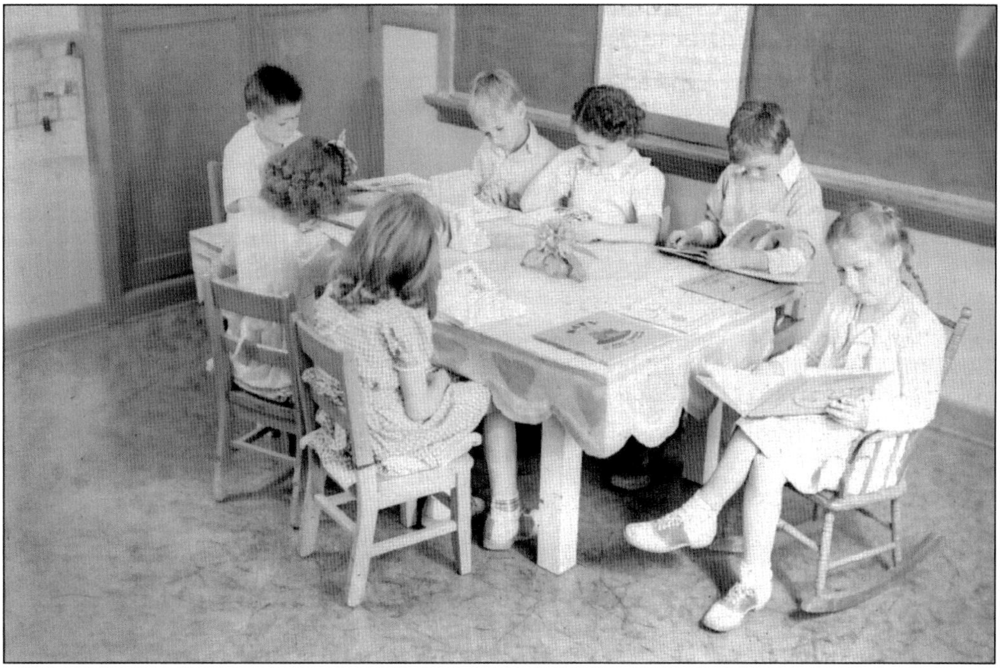

These focused students were among the children who attended Humboldt's College Elementary School, known informally as C.E.S, an on-campus grammar school for the children of staff and students, as well as the community. (Courtesy of Humboldt State University Library.)

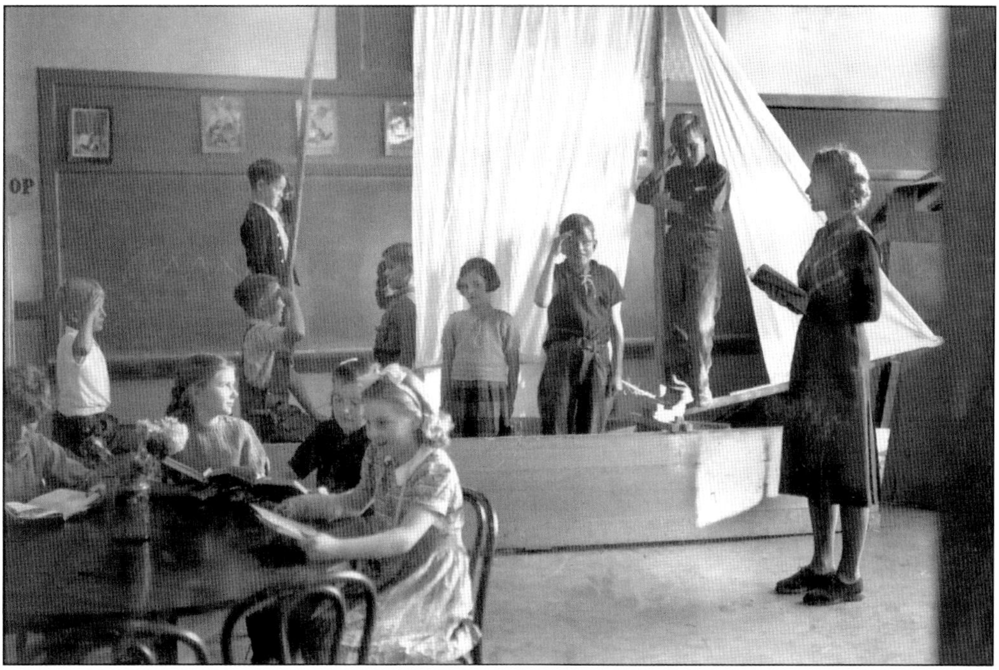

Esther "Bess" Ritola completed her student teaching requirements in 1939 while teaching this fourth-grade class at College Elementary School, Humboldt State College's on-campus lab school. Here the students are re-enacting an early sea voyage. (Courtesy of Humboldt County Historical Society, Givins Collection.)

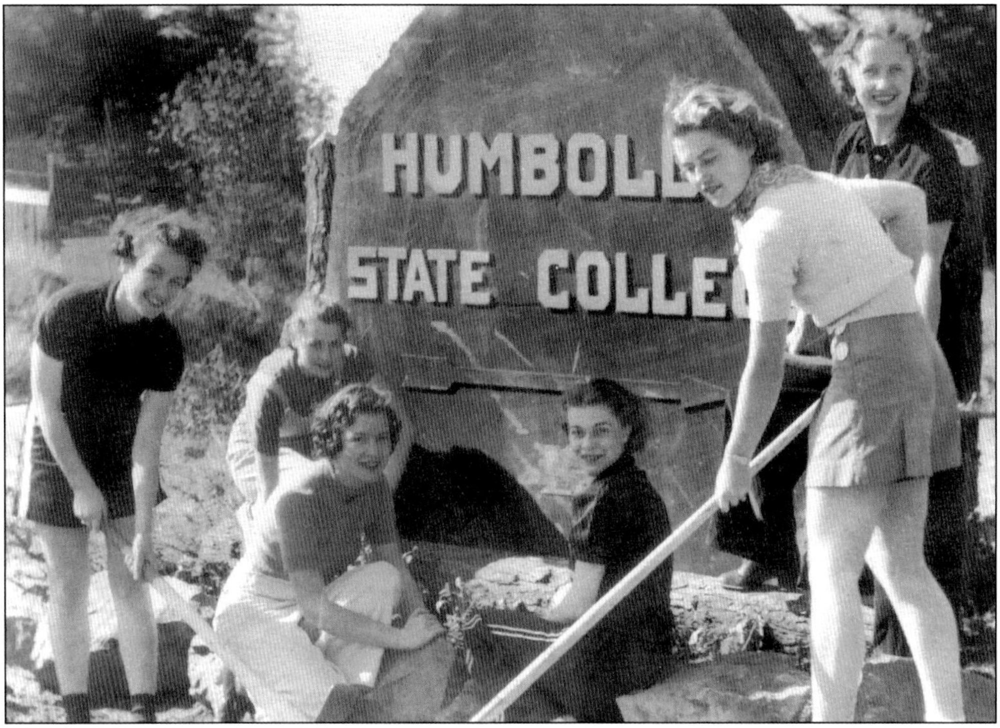

In the latter 1920s and 1930s, Humboldt State College students and faculty took part in the annual Work Day, established in 1925, to clean up the grounds and buildings. Excused from class for the day, the workers would gather at 8 a.m. for a Faculty Show to inspire them with such entertainment as all-male faculty hula dances, mock operas, and the annual solo by Vice President Dr. Homer Balbanis, a former president of the Humboldt County Historical Society. "In 1947, the school called two consecutive Work Days in order to construct the east stands of Redwood Bowl," William Tanner wrote in his 1993 book, *A View from the Hill: A History of Humboldt State University*. (Courtesy of Humboldt County Historical Society, Givins Collection.)

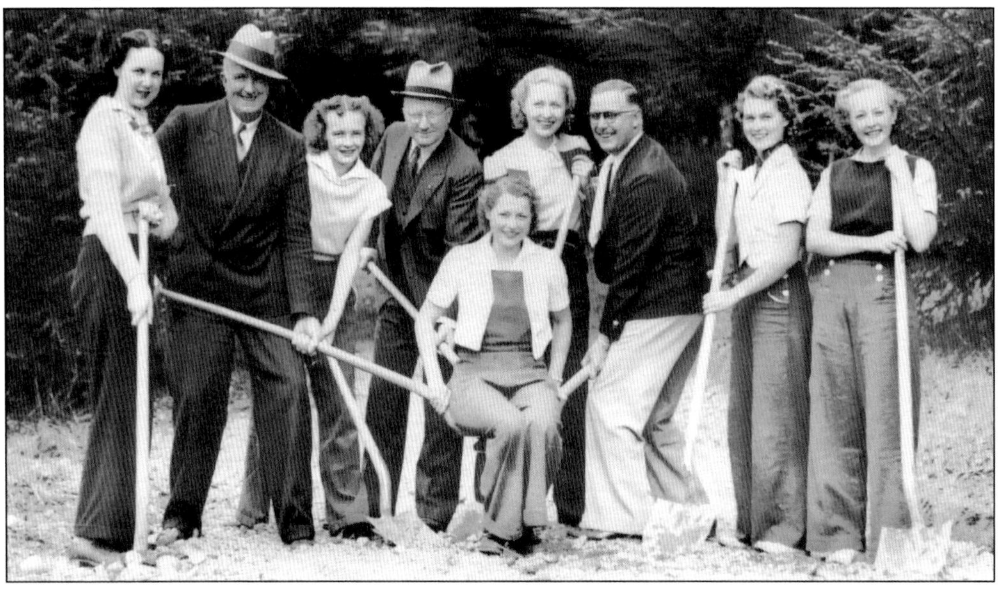

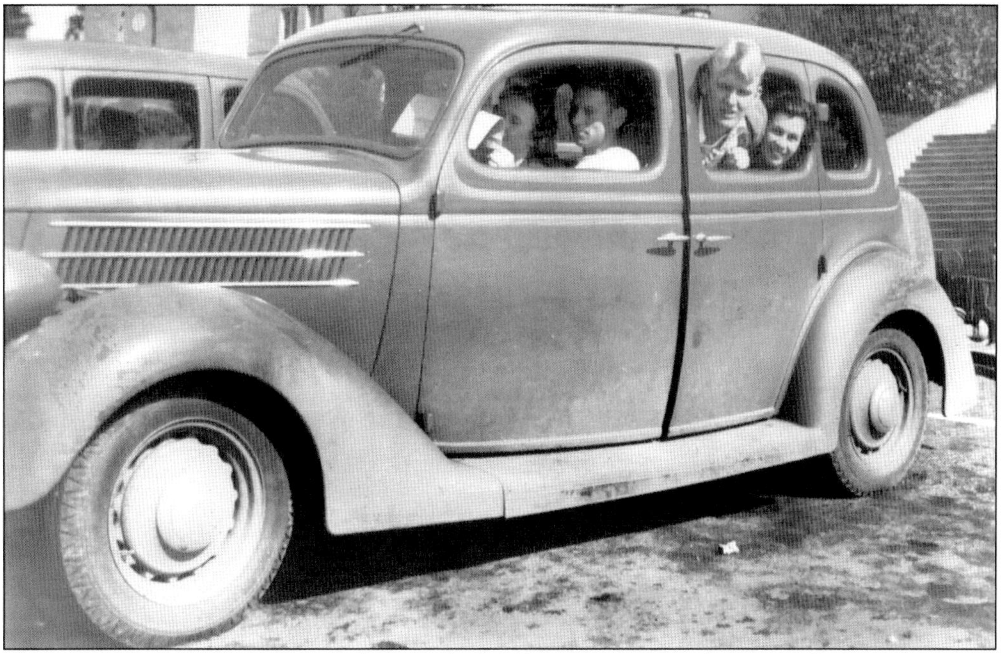

Affectionally named Henrietta, this car faithfully transports students enrolled at Humboldt State College in the 1936–1937 school year. (Courtesy of Humboldt County Historical Society, Givins Collection.)

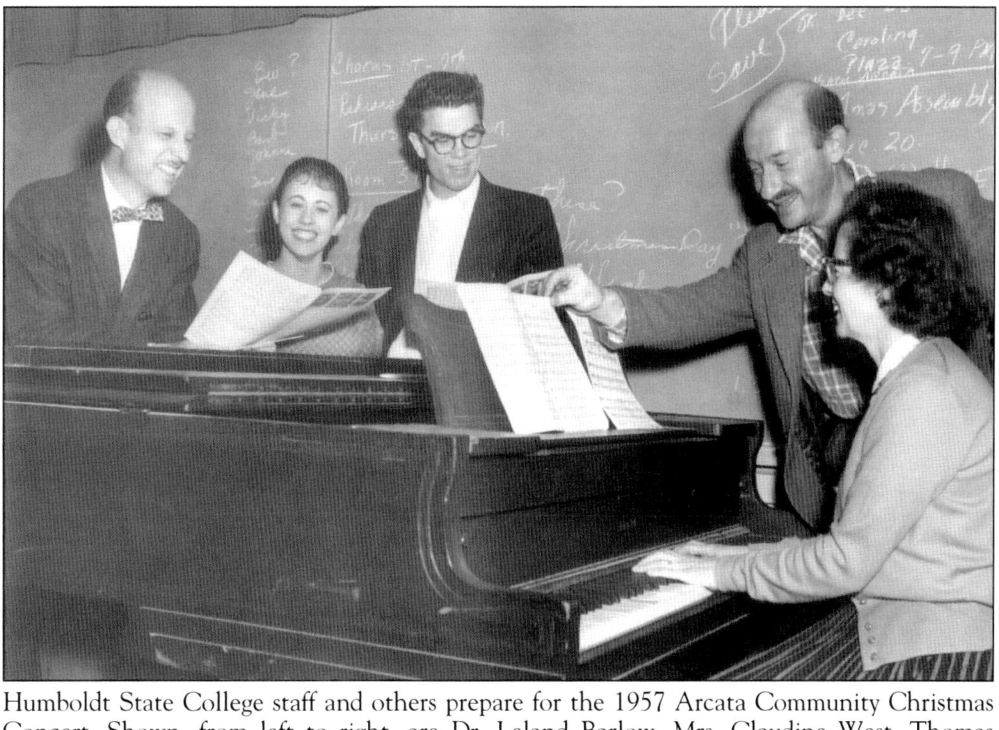

Humboldt State College staff and others prepare for the 1957 Arcata Community Christmas Concert. Shown, from left to right, are Dr. Leland Barlow, Mrs. Claudine West, Thomas Hibdon, Dr. Leon Wagner, and Mrs. Earl Smith. (Courtesy of Humboldt County Historical Society, Roscoe Collection.)

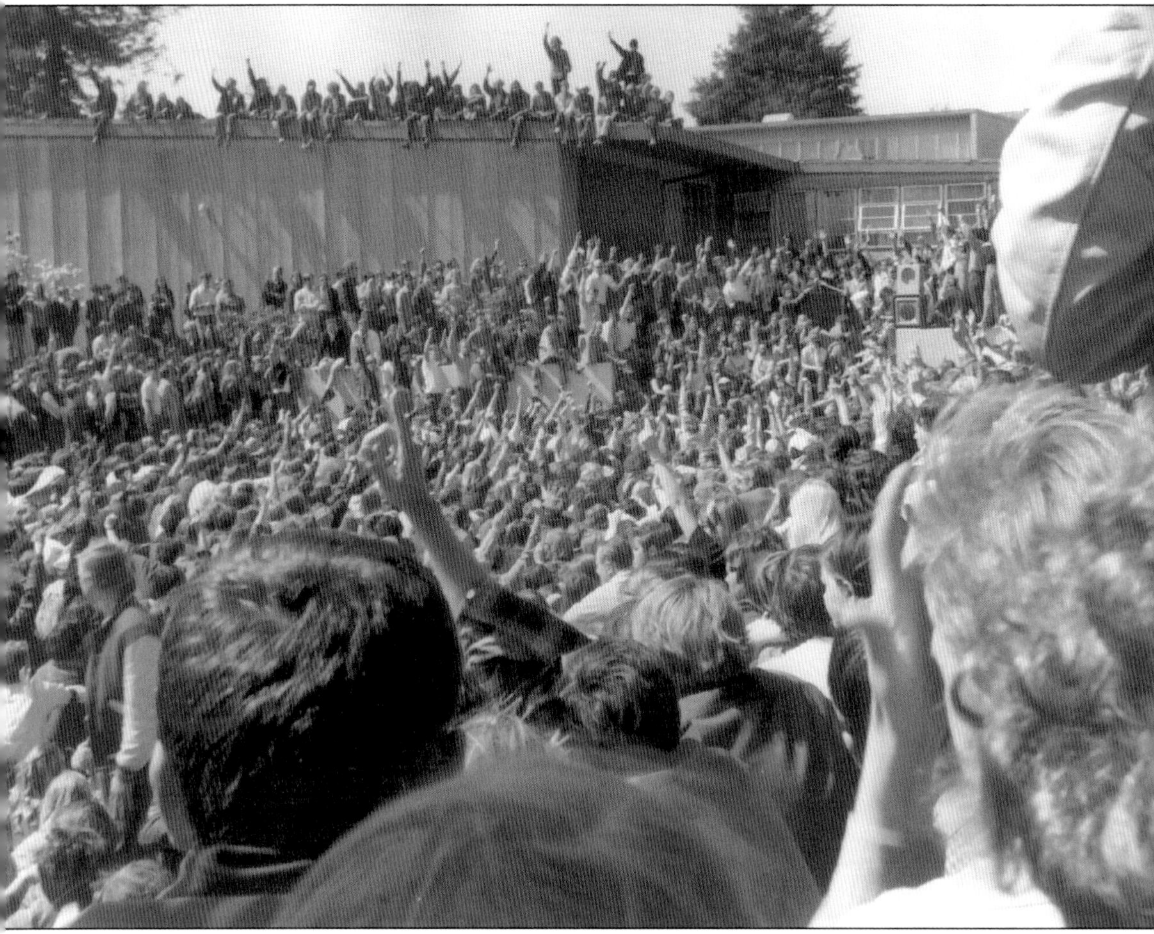

Humboldt State College students joined thousands nationwide in their opposition to the Vietnam War. After four years of increasingly serious conflict and the invasion and bombing of Cambodia, the Humboldt Student Legislative Council voted to take steps to make the students' opposition to all war and violence known, as shown in this May 6, 1970 photograph. On May 11, some 3,000 students and staff gathered to vote for a voluntary, peaceful, one-day strike. "They then canvassed door-to-door in Arcata and held a teach-in at Arcata High to gain community support," author William Tanner reported in his 1993 history of Humboldt State. "President Siemens called for abolition of the draft system and condemned the Cambodian incursion." Gov. Ronald Reagan closed the state colleges and universities. (Courtesy of Humboldt State University Library.)

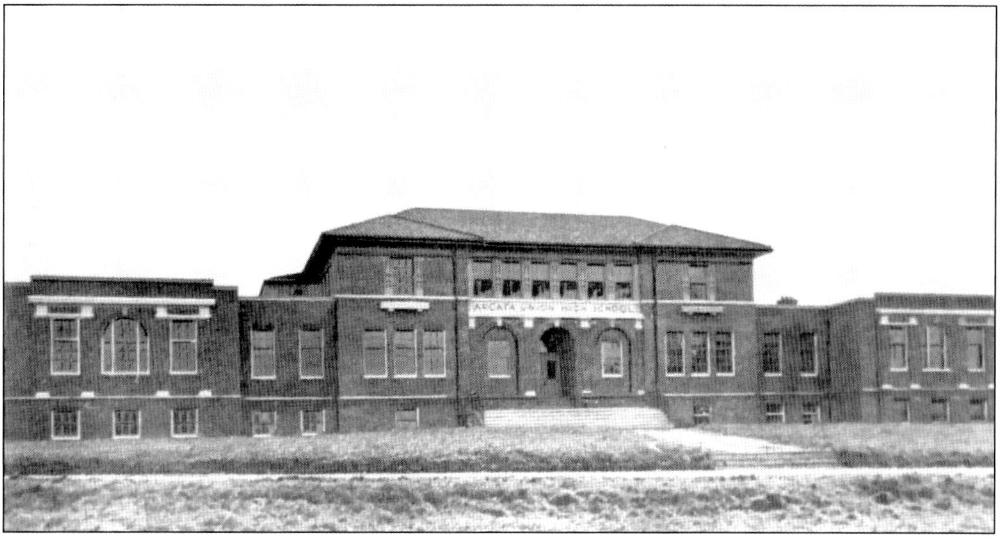

The second Arcata High School was built in 1918 and was ready for occupancy in 1919, thanks to a $60,000 bond approved by the voters on October 12, 1917. Around the same time, the high school extended its reach to 14 elementary districts from beyond Trinidad in the north to the crest of the mountains in the east. Many students took the Arcata & Mad River Railroad to school. (Courtesy of Humboldt County Historical Society, Woods Collection.)

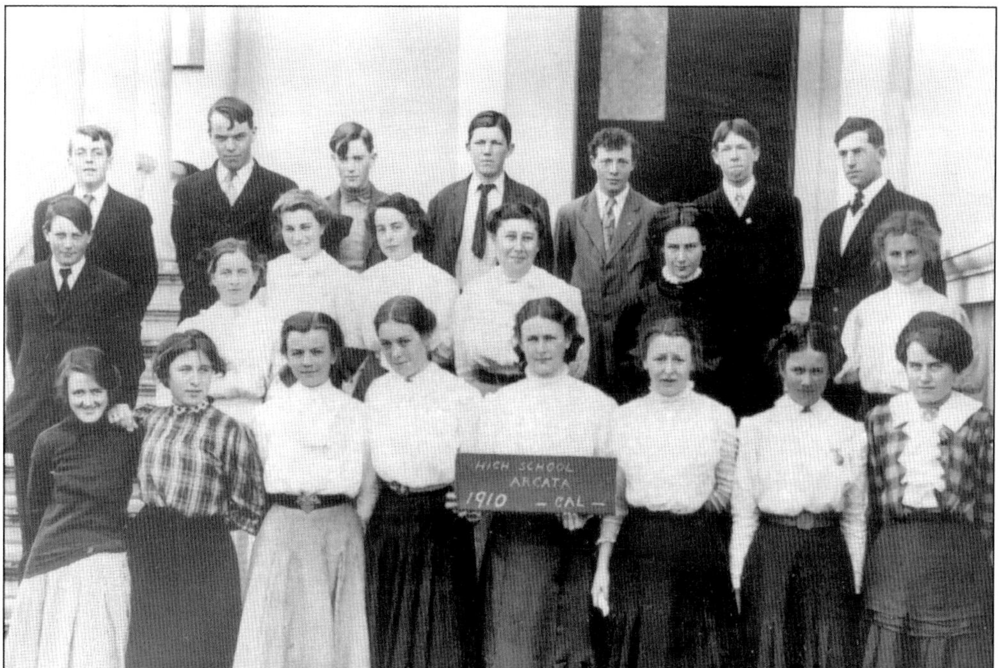

Students from Arcata High School in 1910 gather for their annual photo. Eight students graduated that year: Yetta Bull, Pearl Garcelon, Zelia Vaissade, Everett Quear, Lydia Blake, Lettie Dunham, Atlant Roberts, and Ernest Sweet. The school was located on the southeast corner of Fifteenth and G Streets. (Courtesy of Humboldt County Historical Society.)

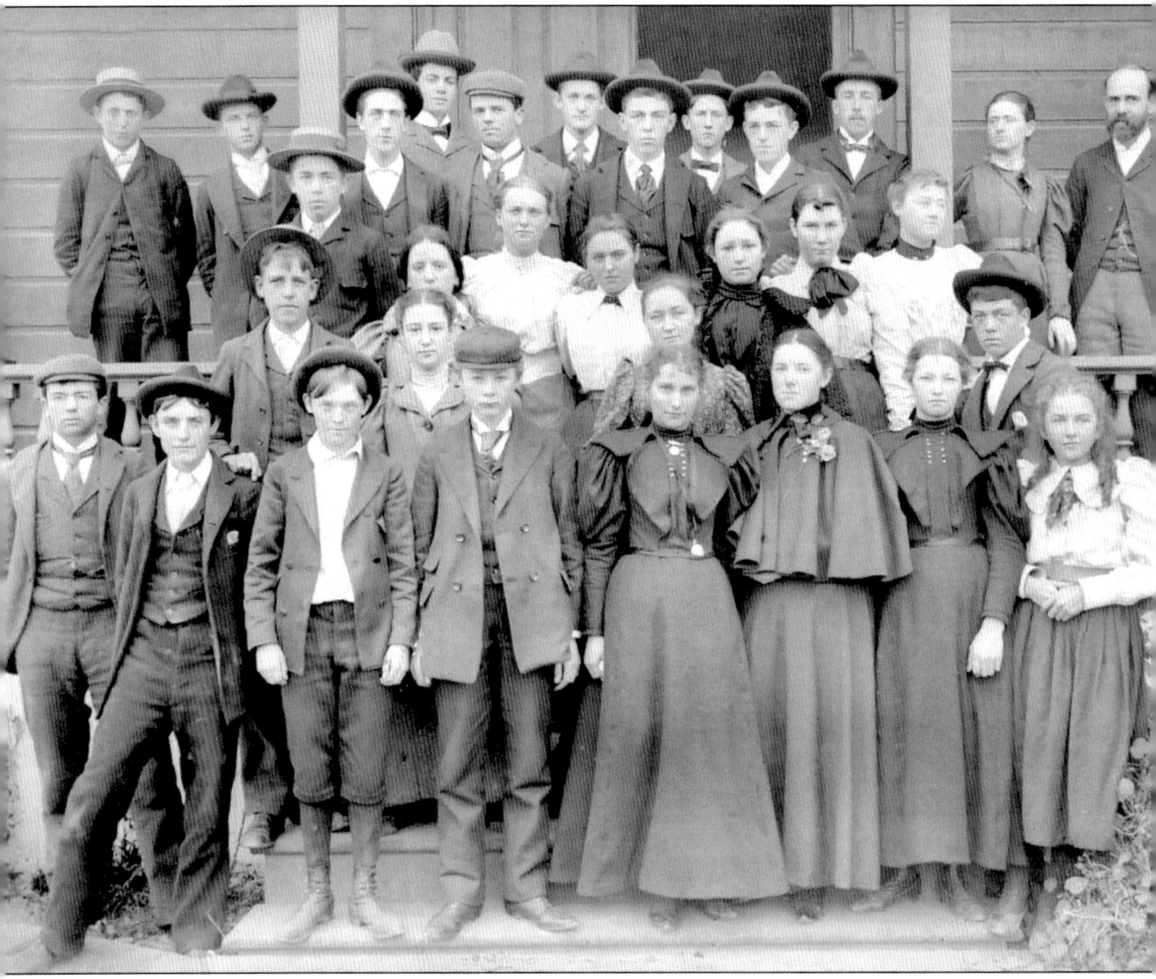

The Arcata High School students of 1898 are shown here, just three years after the school's opening. Voters approved the establishment of the high school for Arcata, Janes, Bay, and Jacoby Creek School Districts on August 11, 1894. The class of 1898 had three graduates: Frank Tripp, Ben Lord, and Gwen Hansen. The early high school was on Eleventh and M Streets. A.D. Tenney, teacher and principal, and his assistant, Miss Atkinson, are on the porch to the far right. (Courtesy of Humboldt County Historical Society.)

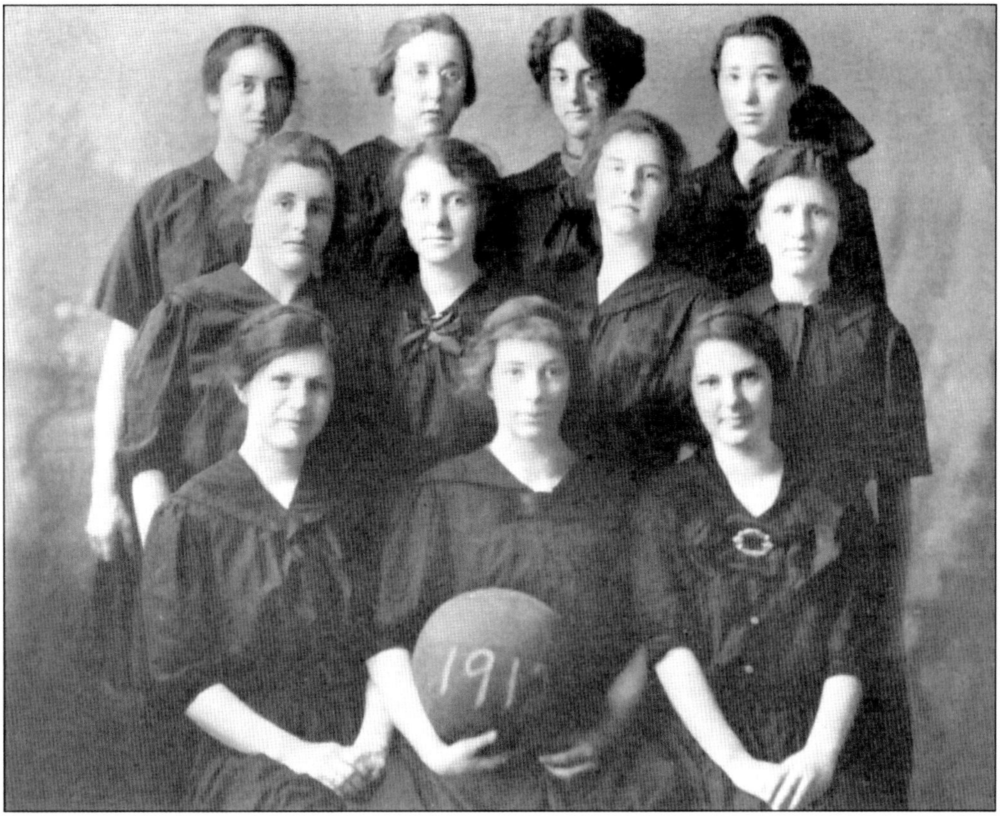

Arcata High School's 1910 girls basketball team paused briefly for this photograph. (Courtesy of Peter Hess.)

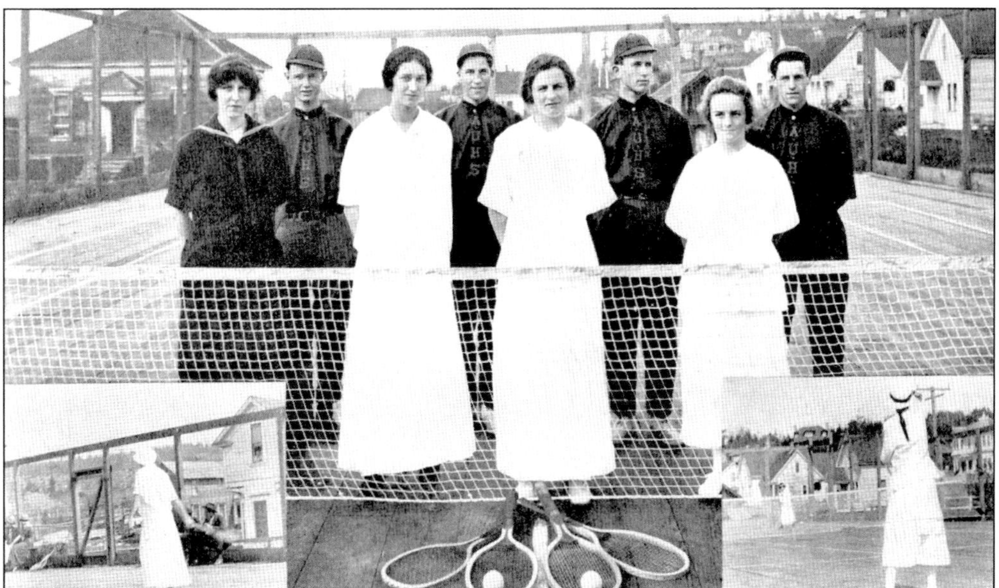

Shown here is Arcata High School's 1914 tennis team. (Courtesy of Humboldt County Historical Society, Arcata Advance.)

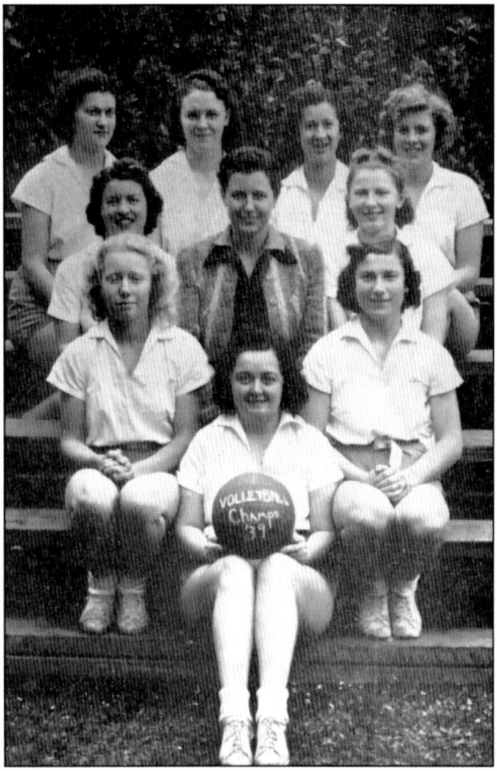

Nine girls volleyball teams competed to be declared the 1939 champs, but the seniors managed to prevail with a perfect season, despite some close calls. Clockwise, beginning at the bottom, are Betty Sue Wilson, D. Nielsen, Lois Hufford, Marie R. Canclini, L. Caprile, Betty Jane Atwood, J. Underwood, Ruth E. Sequist, and Jean M. Schussman. Miss Fielding, the coach, sits in the middle. (Courtesy of Humboldt County Historical Society, 1939 Advance.)

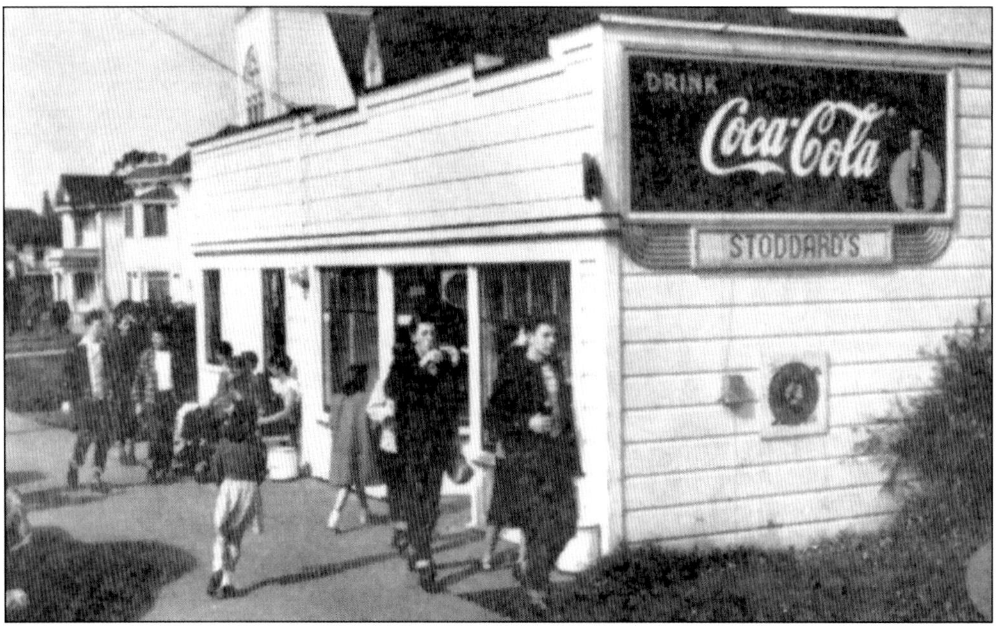

Stoddard's, which stood close to Arcata High School and across Sixteenth Street from Stewart Elementary, was a popular destination for students. Shown here in 1948, the business was owned by teacher Harry D. Stoddard and was listed alternately as a confectionery, grocery, and restaurant. A portion of St. Mary's Catholic Church across the alley can be seen in the background. (Courtesy Humboldt County Historical Society, 1948 Advance.)

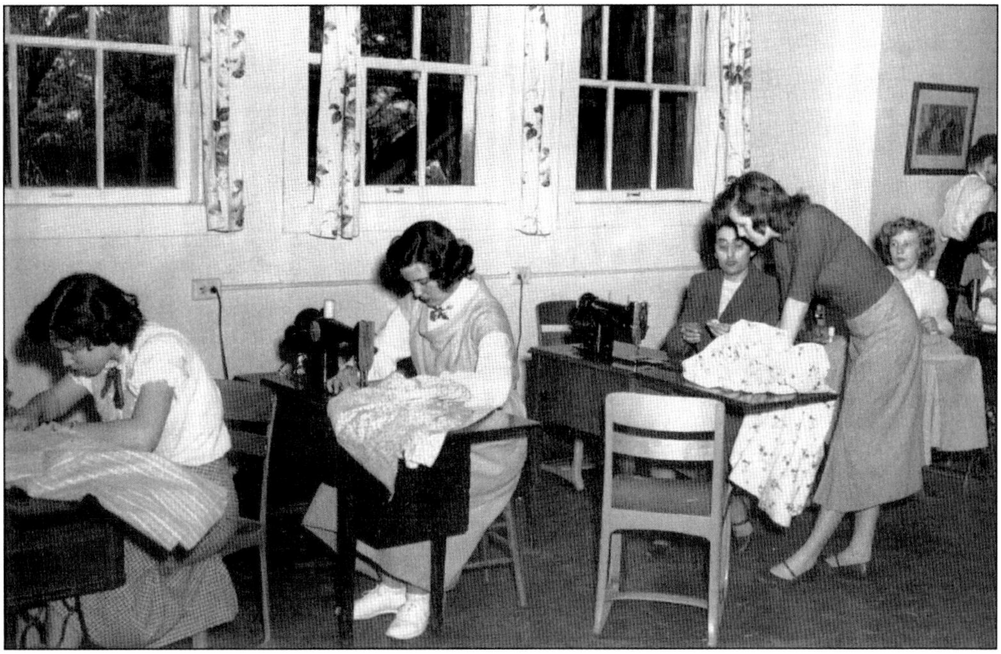

Arcata High School homemaking students Faye Smart and Cleon Teery prepare summer outfits in 1954 while Miss Rose helps Jerri Smith. (Courtesy of Humboldt County Historical Society, 1954 Advance.)

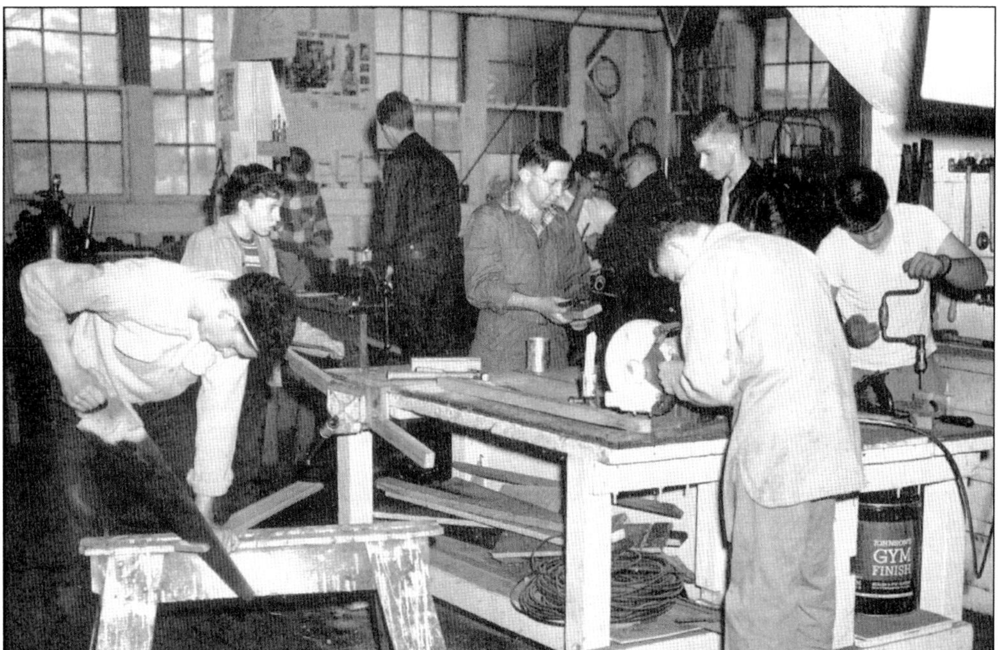

Meanwhile, the boys are busy in the Arcata High School woodshop. This 1954 class includes Johnny Avila (sawing on the left) and Larry Getz behind him. (Courtesy of Humboldt County Historical Society, 1954 Advance.)

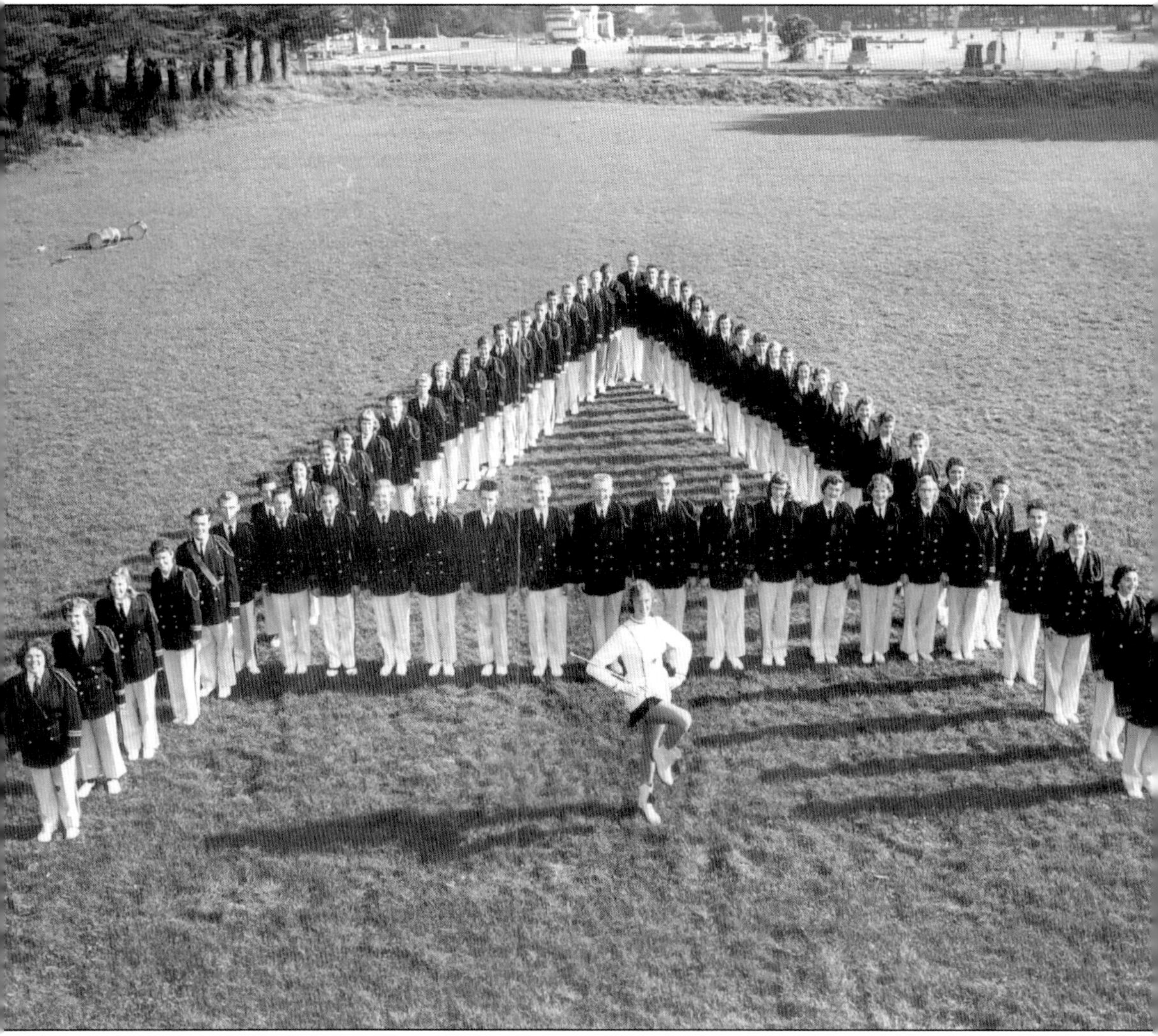

The 1957 Arcata High School Band shows off its alphabetic formation. The Greenwood Cemetery is visible in the background. (Courtesy of Humboldt County Historical Society, Roscoe Collection.)

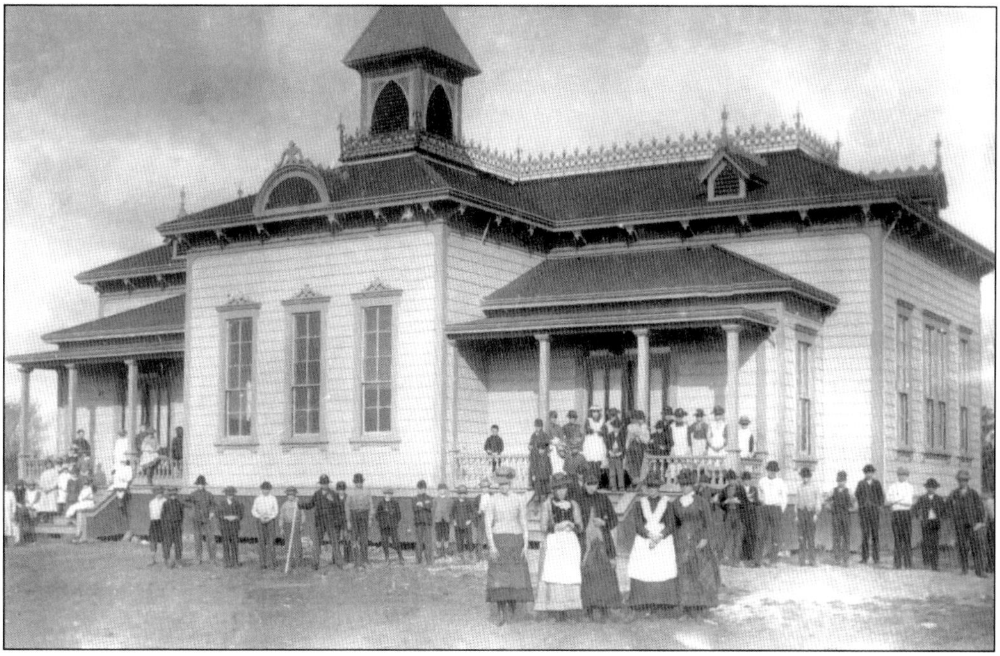

The Arcata Grammar School is shown here c. 1884. (Courtesy of Humboldt County Historical Society, Woods Collection.)

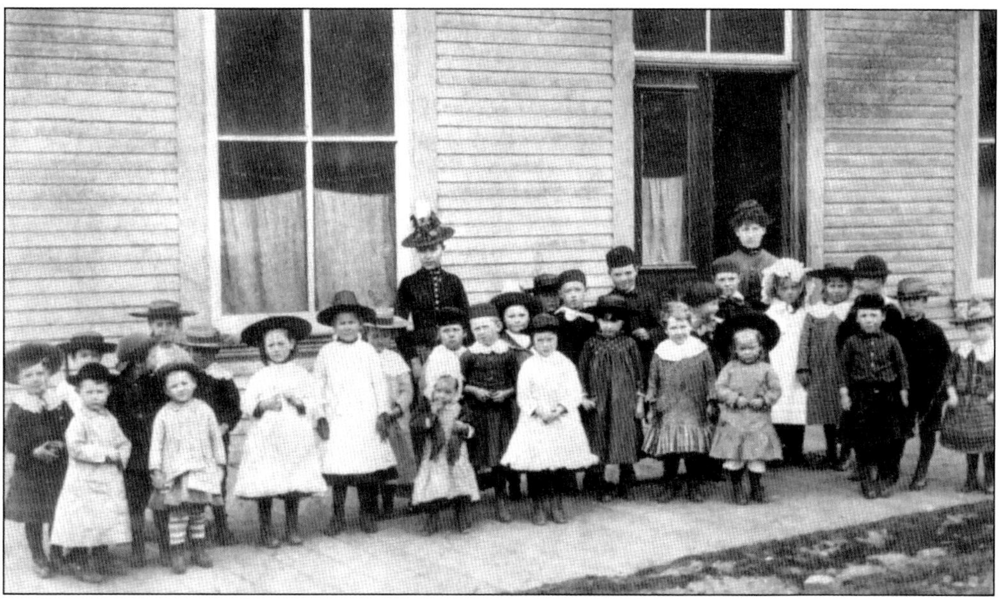

The Knights of Pythias Hall was home to the first kindergarten class in Arcata, established in the late 1850s. Teacher Mamie Cutler and her assistant, Lula Smith, oversaw this later class, which included nearly 30 students of varying ages. (Courtesy of Humboldt County Historical Society, Gustafson Collection.)

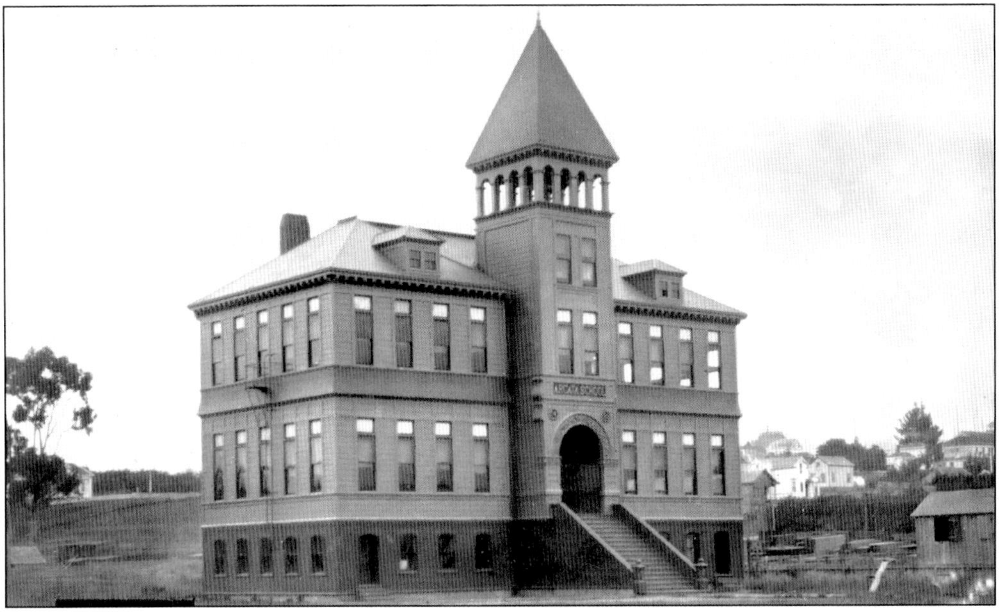

Arcata Grammar School, a majestic place of learning at Eleventh and M Streets, was built in 1892 and served the community's children until 1925. (Courtesy of Humboldt County Historical Society.)

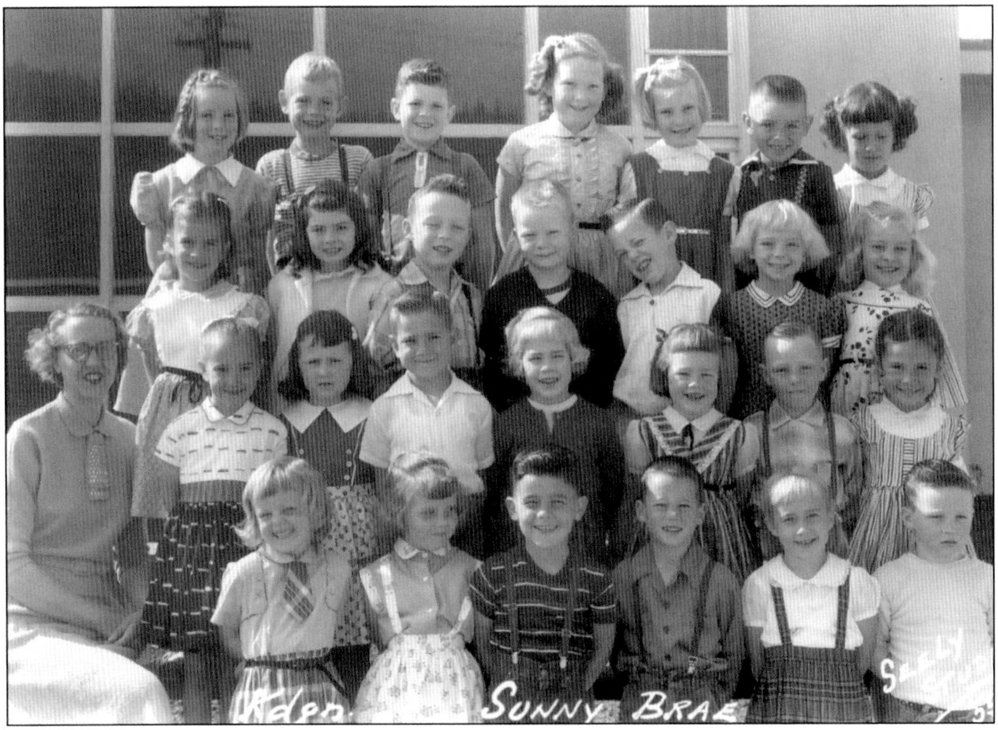

Shown here in 1955 are Sunny Brae School kindergarten students. (Courtesy of Humboldt County Historical Society, Goss Collection.)

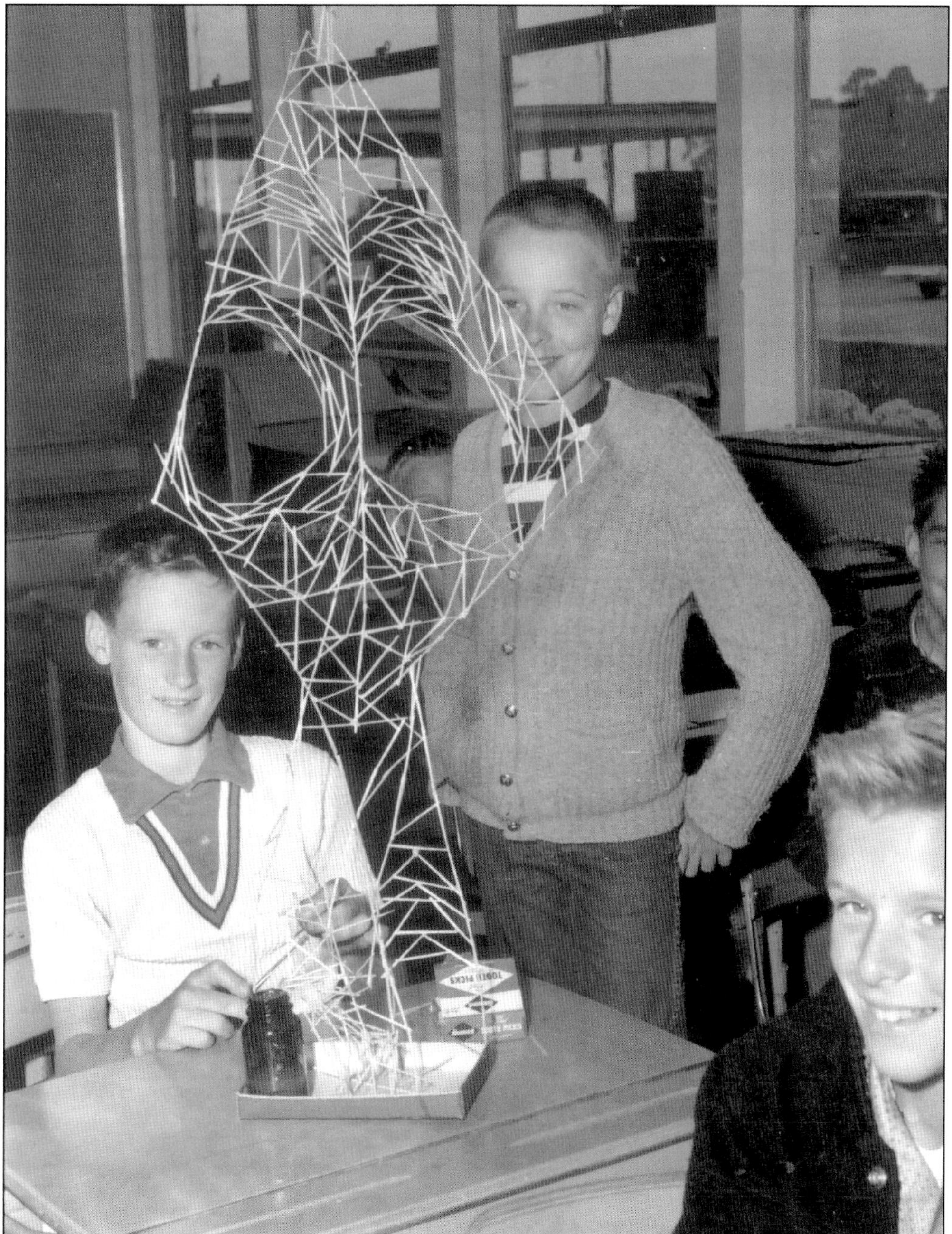

These sculptors were likely among the first students of the Sunny Brae School, which was built in 1955. The school's February 2, 1955 dedication drew state senator Arthur W. Way, assemblyman Frank Belotti, and fifth district supervisor Sam Merryman to admire the 13-classroom building with a $375,000 price tag. The new school was designed to accommodate 350 kindergarten through sixth-grade students. (Courtesy of Humboldt County Historical Society, Goss Collection.)

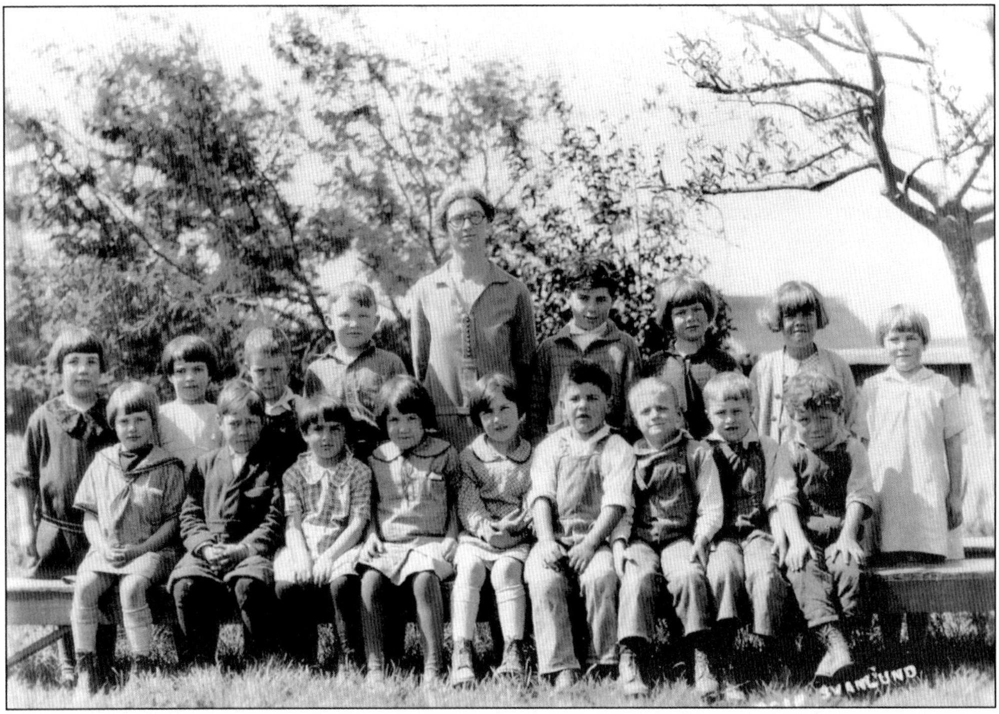

An unidentified but cheerful Arcata class is shown here around the 1920s. (Courtesy of Humboldt County Historical Society.)

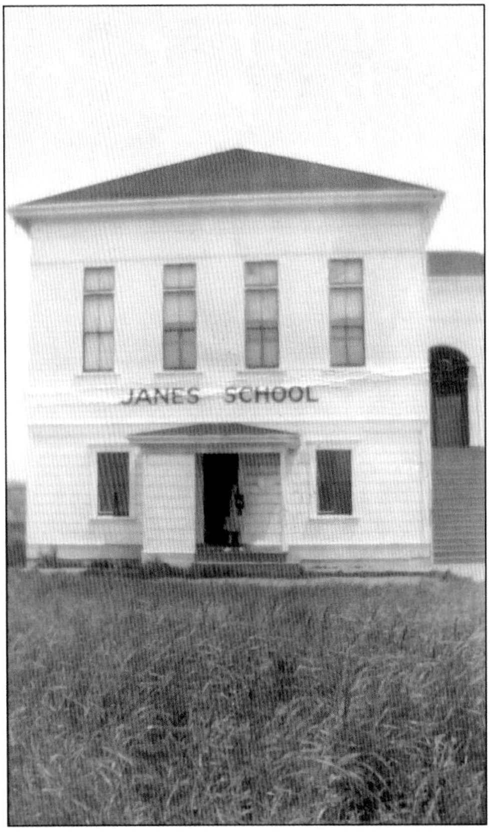

Both Janes School, Janes Road, and Janes Creek were named after Henry Janes, who was one of the first Arcata Bottom ranchers making a claim in November 1850. The Janes Creek School District was established in 1873; the first school burned in 1906. The second school, shown here, was built in 1907 and was used for more than 50 years until 1959, when it was torn down to make way for Pacific Union School. (Courtesy of Humboldt County Historical Society, Woods Collection.)

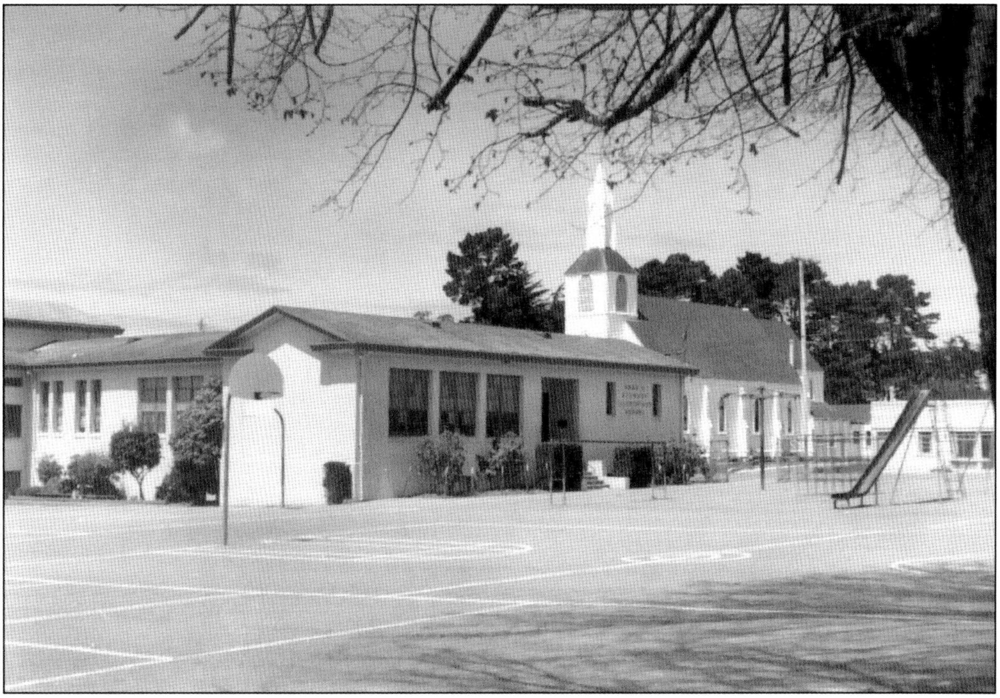

Stewart School on Sixteenth and J Streets was dedicated in 1925 and rededicated in 1952 in honor of teacher, principal, and superintendent Hugh Stewart, who spent 41 years in the school district. Initially the building was constructed for less that $70,000 with 10 classrooms, a lunchroom, and an auditorium. In 1976, after failing to meet state seismic standards, the building was abandoned. (Courtesy of Humboldt County Historical Society, Goss Collection.)

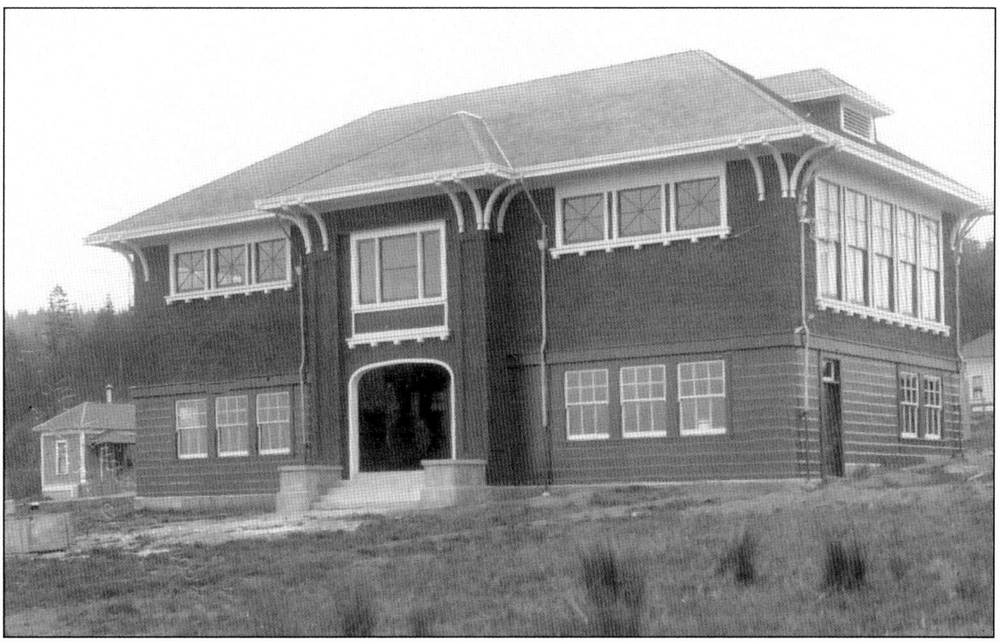

Pleasant Hill School was built in 1912 on Eleventh Street between Union and A Streets. (Courtesy of Humboldt County Historical Society.)

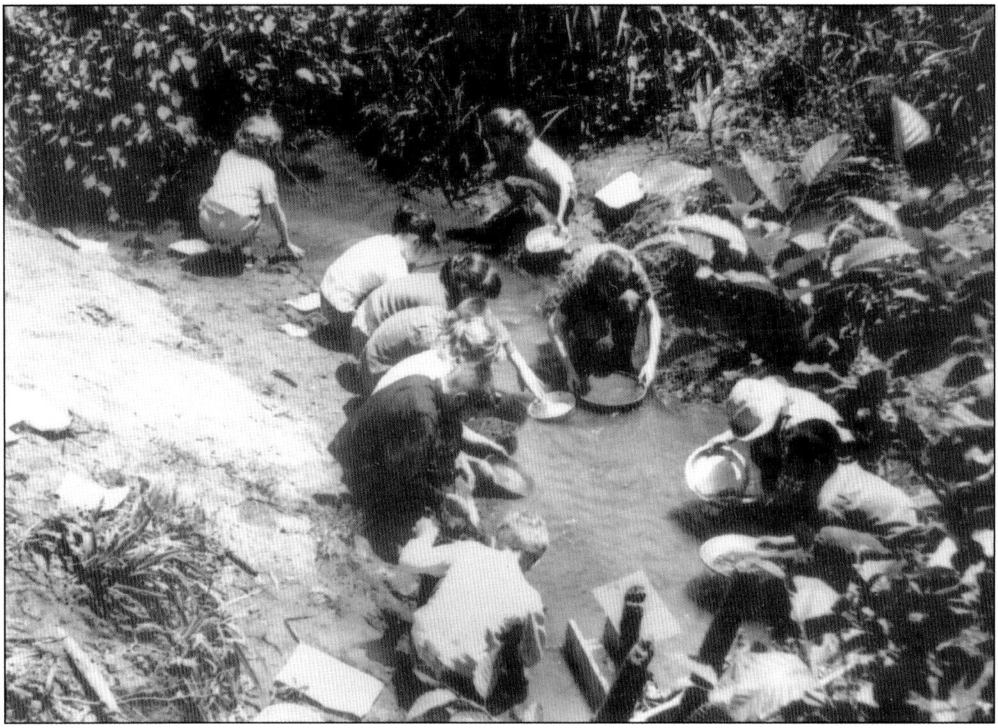

Sunny Brae Elementary School students try their hand at gold panning in 1956. (Courtesy of Humboldt County Historical Society, Goss Collection.)

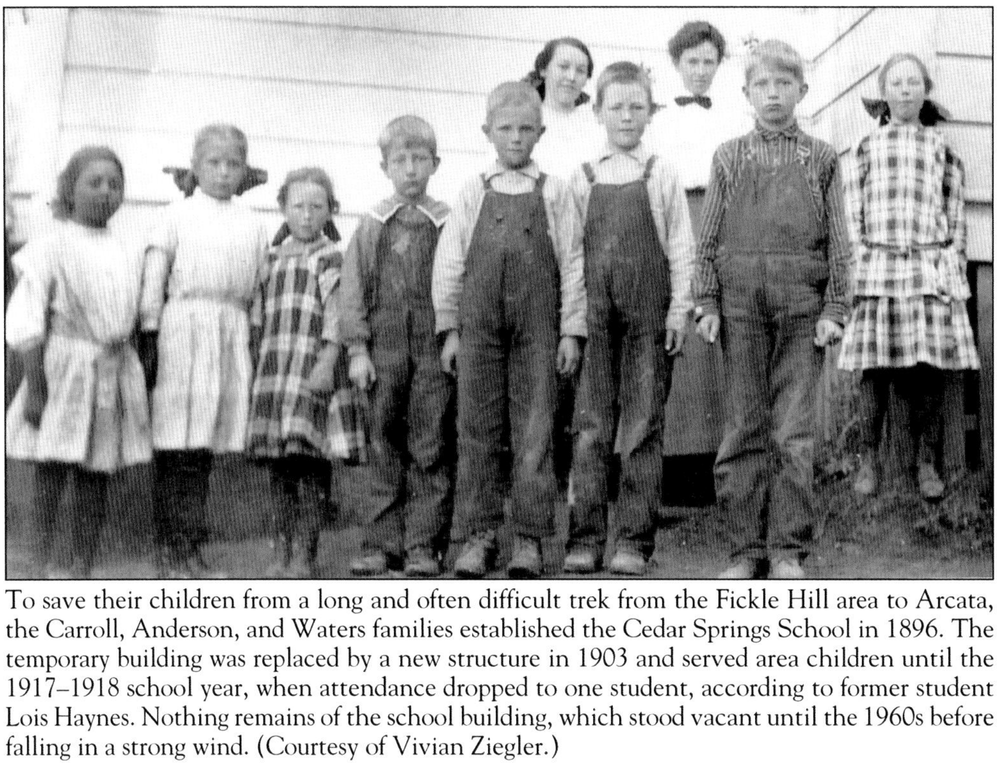

To save their children from a long and often difficult trek from the Fickle Hill area to Arcata, the Carroll, Anderson, and Waters families established the Cedar Springs School in 1896. The temporary building was replaced by a new structure in 1903 and served area children until the 1917–1918 school year, when attendance dropped to one student, according to former student Lois Haynes. Nothing remains of the school building, which stood vacant until the 1960s before falling in a strong wind. (Courtesy of Vivian Ziegler.)

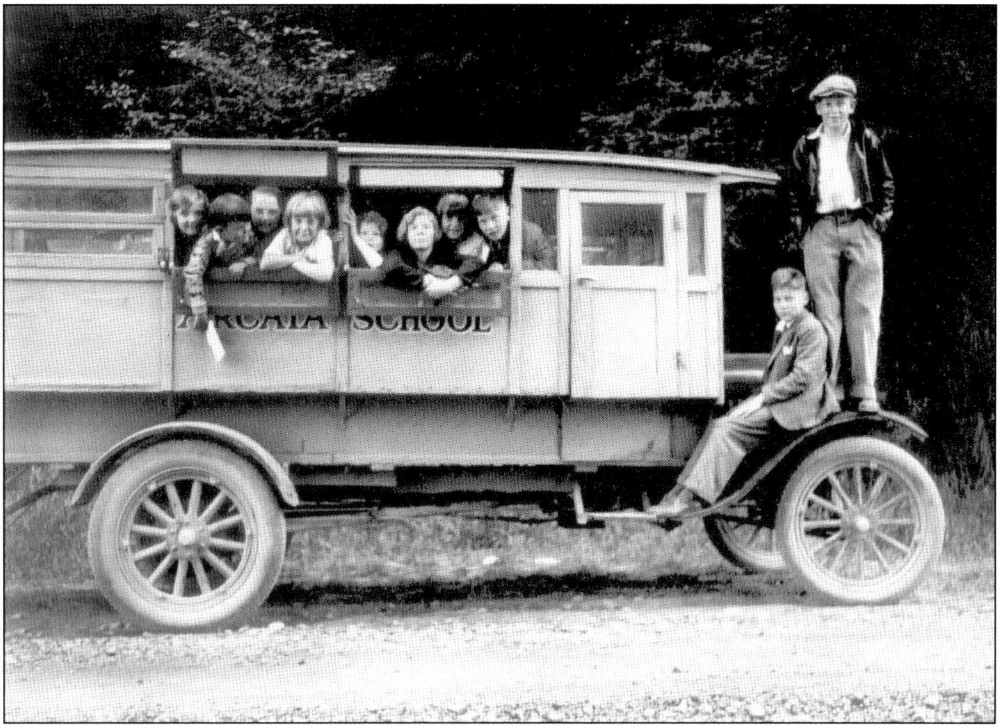

The children of Fickle Hill clamber inside the school bus that served the east Arcata area. Many of the families of the area either worked in Fickle's sawmill or were farmers. Among those shown are Vivian Larson, Alta Sequist, Viola Jensen, Aileen Knighton, and Jud Knighton. (Courtesy of Vivian Ziegler.)

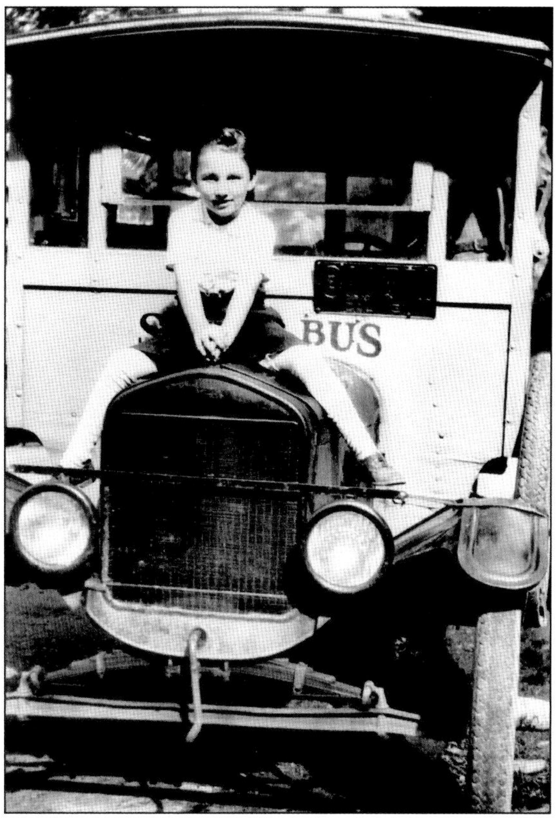

In this photograph from the early 1930s, an unidentified Fickle Hill student holds on dearly to the Arcata school bus that carried the hill's children to and from class. (Courtesy of Vivian Ziegler.)

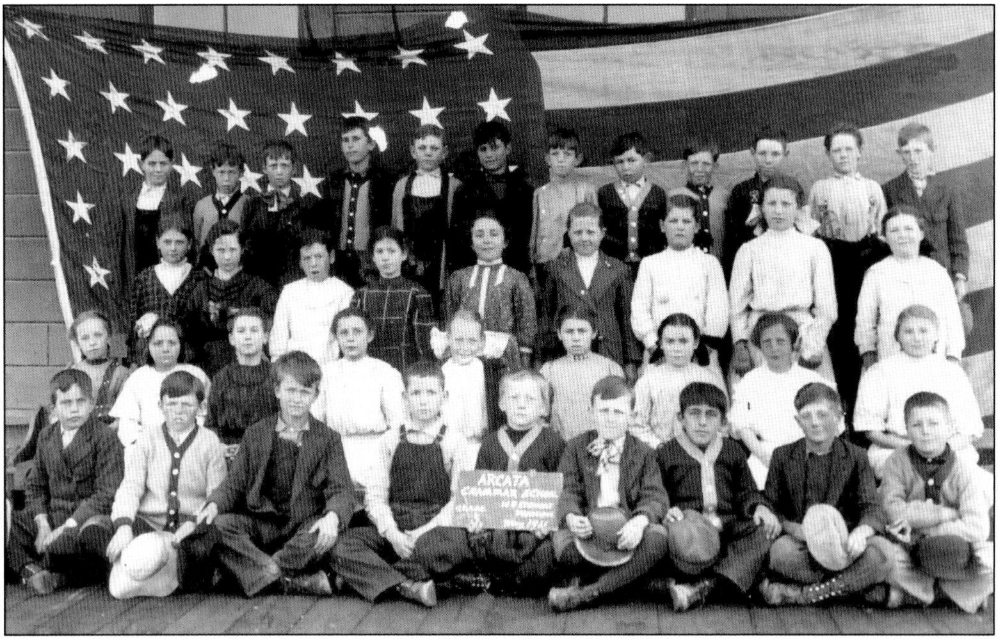

Arcata Grammar School is pictured above in 1911 and below in 1913. (Both courtesy of Humboldt County Historical Society.)

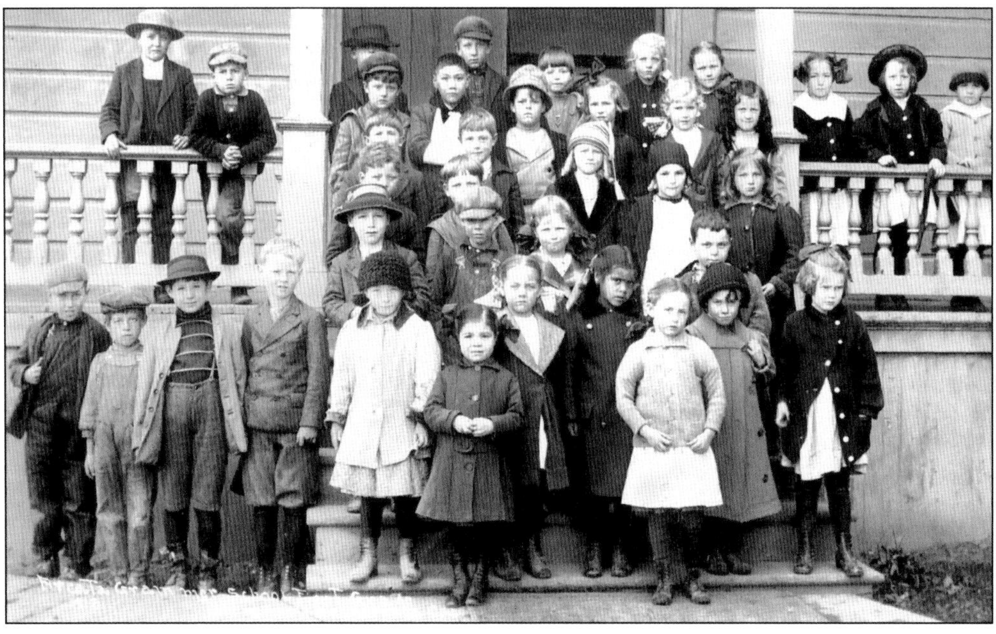

Four

In Our Service

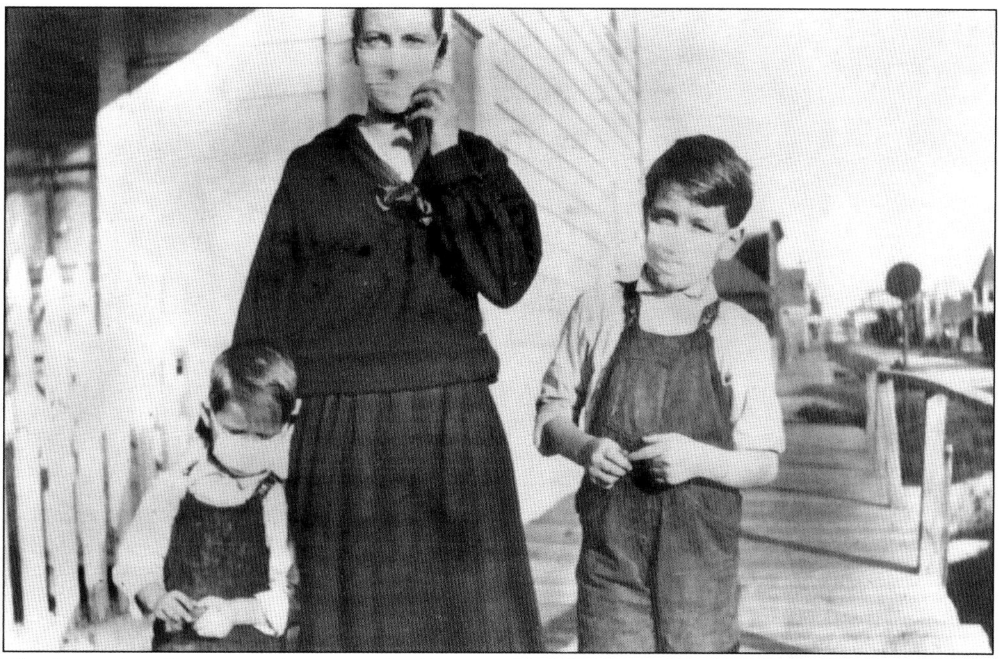

The Spanish influenza epidemic reached Humboldt County in 1918 as part of the third wave of the illness that swept the country after the end of World War I, but Arcatans took precautions. Elmer Evans, age 4 (left), and Nathaniel Evans, age 10 (right), the sons of Nat and Martha Evans, are cared for by their cousin Essie Van Deventer, age 16 (center). The City of Arcata established the first mask ordinance of Humboldt County on October 23, 1918, requiring residents to wear masks in public. (Courtesy of Humboldt County Historical Society.)

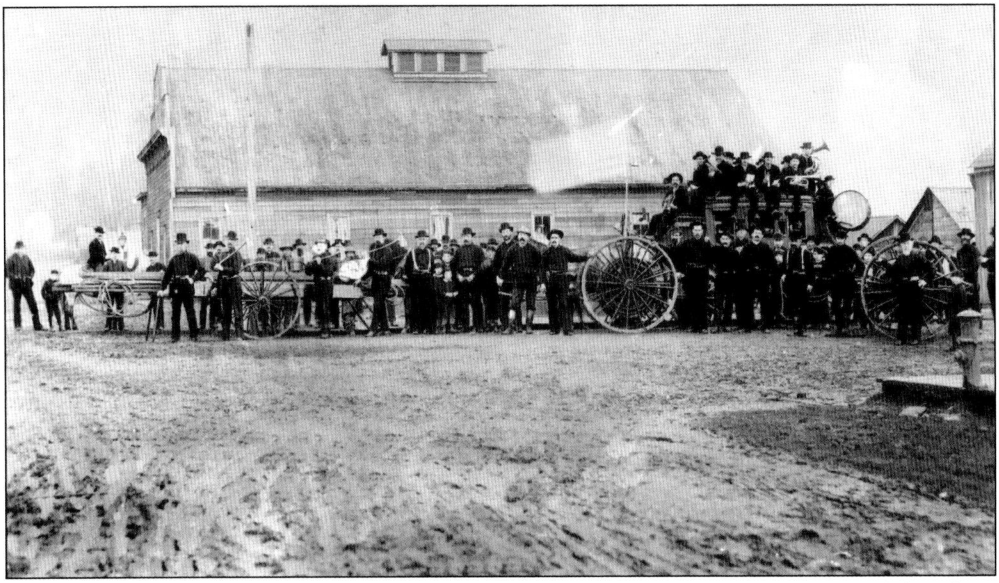

In 1875 a quick-moving blaze destroyed three blocks on the north and east sides of the plaza. Another 10 years would pass before Arcata Fire Company No. 1 was formed in January 1884. For the next 60 years, an 800-pound fire bell would call the volunteers who pulled and pushed hand-powered carts to the fires until 1925. Sometimes they responded to their own station—on July 30, 1945, the fire house burned down for the second time in its history. (Courtesy Humboldt County Historical Society, Stine Collection.)

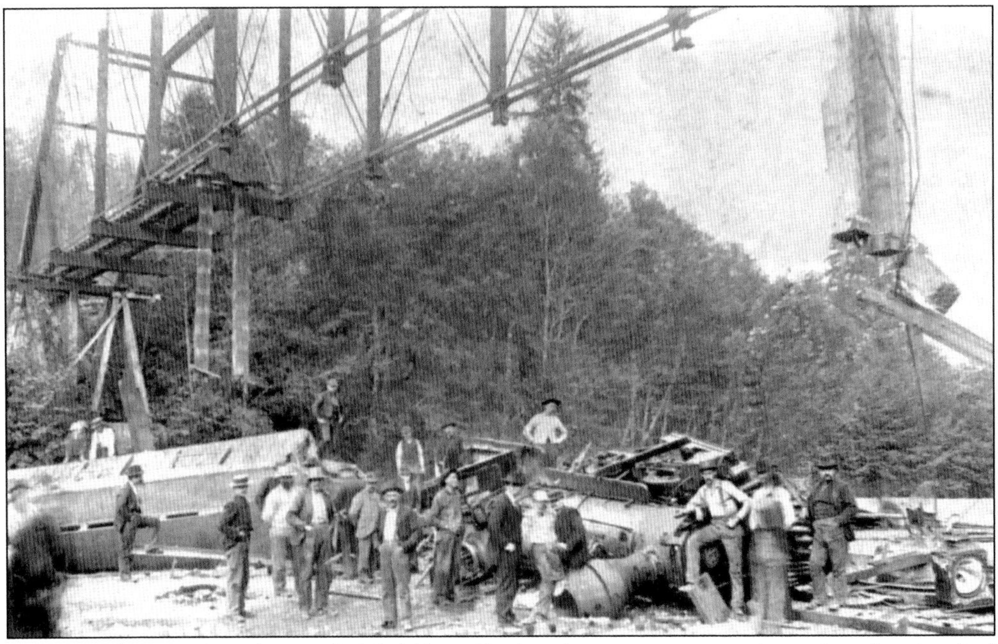

In September 1896 an Arcata & Mad River Railroad passenger train plunged to the riverbed below when the trestle's planks gave way. Of the 33 passengers on their way back to Arcata after spending a Sunday in Korbel, 7 would die ranging in age from 8 months to 34 years. Many others were seriously injured. The train's impact was said to be audible a mile away. (Courtesy of Humboldt County Historical Society, DeLong Collection.)

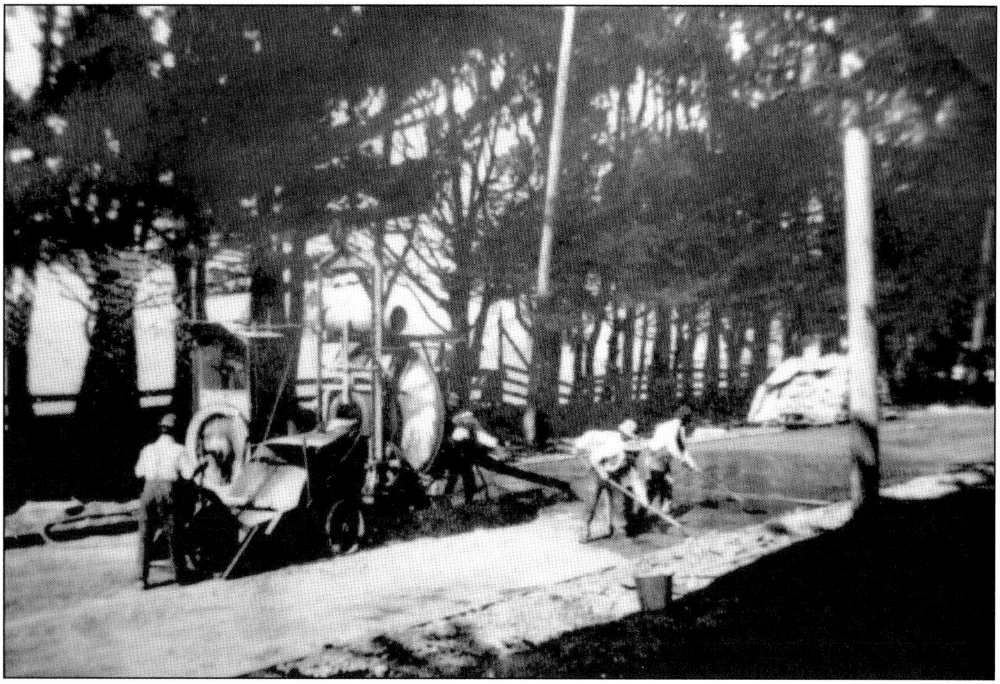

Construction of the road from Arcata to Eureka is underway. (Courtesy of Humboldt County Historical Society, Nielson Collection.)

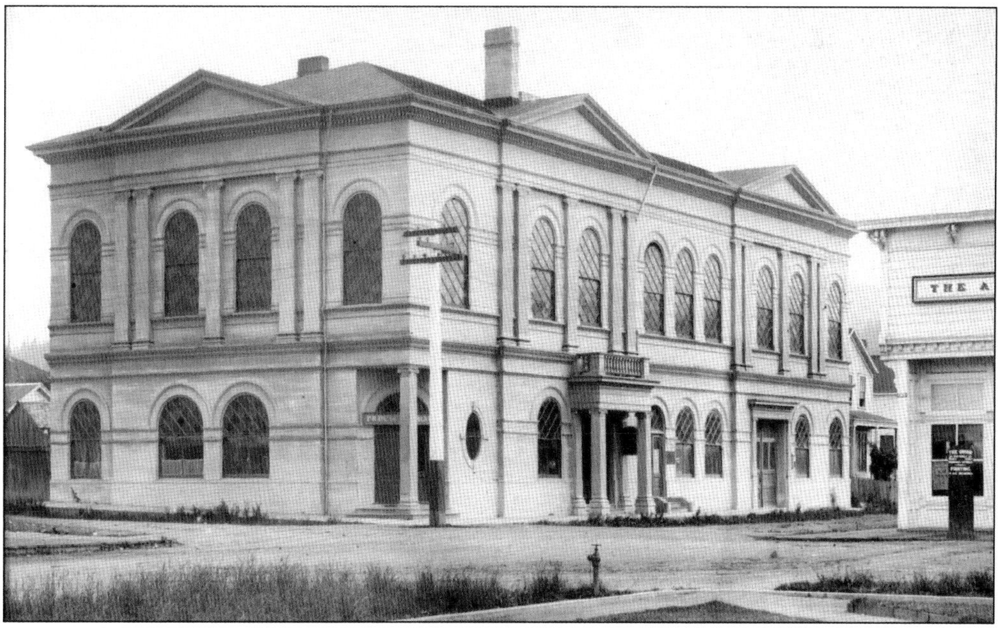

Arcata City Hall, sitting at the corner of Ninth and G Streets, provided a home for the city's business offices, a free library, fire department, and a jail on the first floor, with the upper floor shared by Arcata Lodge No. 106, Free & Associated Masons, and Anniversary Lodge No. 85, International Order of Odd Fellows. The second floor had five-foot-high curly redwood wainscoting. Built in 1896 for $8,500, the public building was demolished in 1971. (Courtesy of Humboldt County Historical Society.)

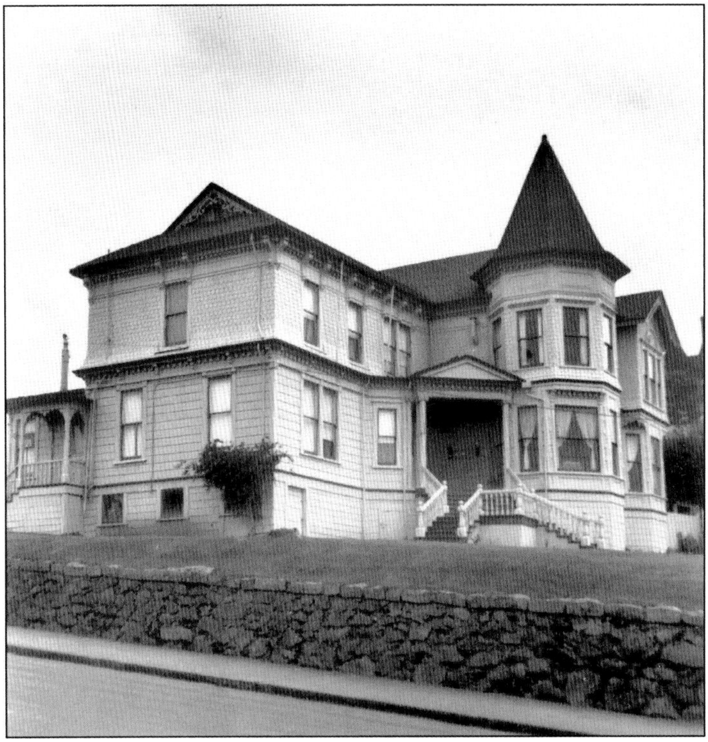

Drs. Frances Horel and John Leveringhouse established the Arcata Sanitarium, also known as the Horel Sanitarium, in 1893 at the corner of Twelfth and I Streets, offering not only standard medical care but treatment for alcohol and narcotic addictions. A few years later the treatment center moved to this building on the corner of Thirteenth and J Streets where it served as Arcata's only hospital until 1907. Still standing, the former hospital is now a private residence. (Courtesy of Humboldt County Historical Society, DeLong Collection.)

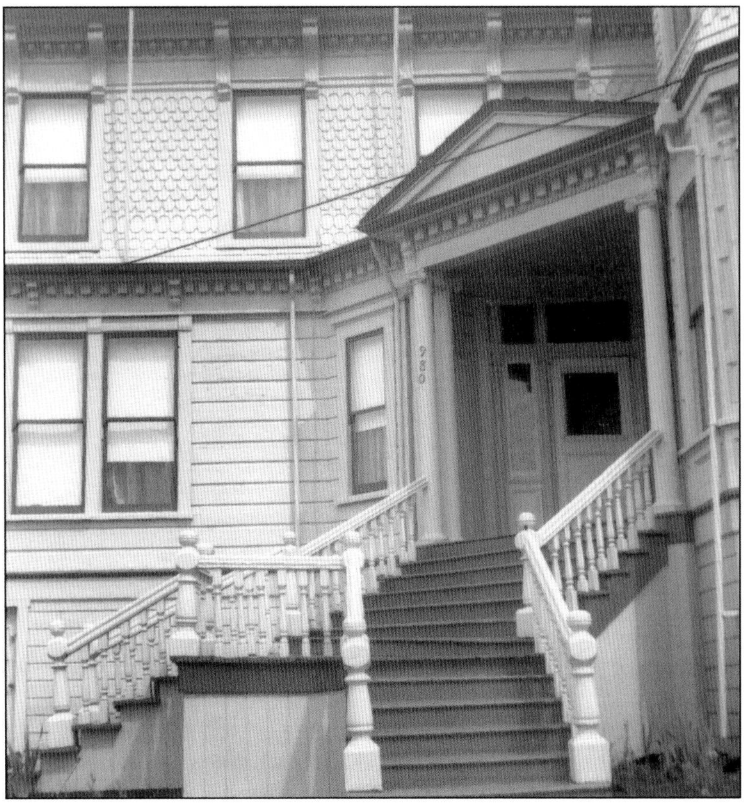

A closer look at the sanitorium reveals its architectural details. (Courtesy of Humboldt County Historical Society, DeLong Collection.)

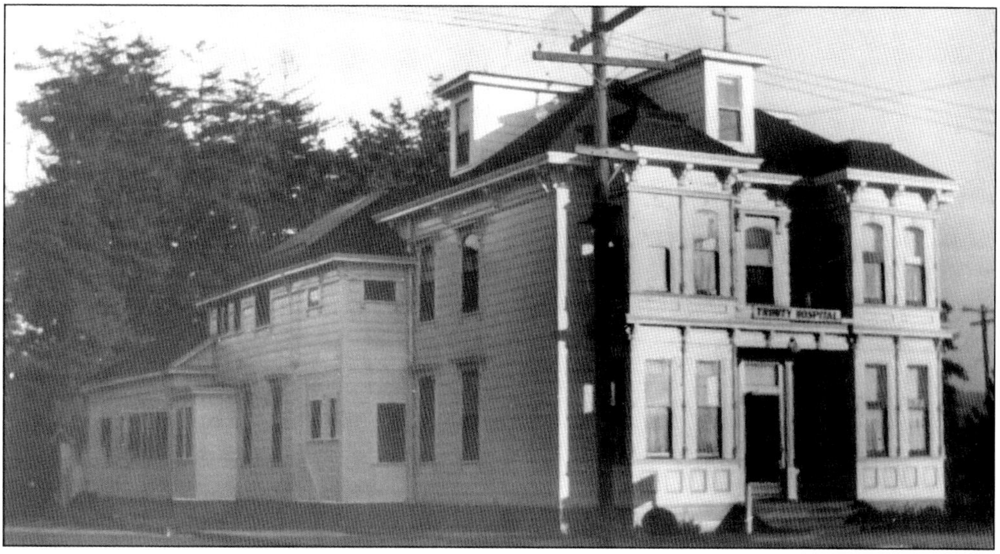

The first Trinity Hospital, shown here in 1931 on the corner of Thirteenth and G Streets, burned down in February 1943 with 23 people escaping the blaze. The hospital, established in the family home of Annie Richert McKinnon by Dr. G.W. McKinnon in 1907, was later sold to Dr. George Purlenky. In 1927 the Arcata Chamber of Commerce purchased the building for the Sisters of St. Joseph. After the fire, a new Trinity Hospital was built on C Street. It was then purchased by American Hospital Management Corporation in 1969, who leased the building to Humboldt State University after the completion of Mad River Community Hospital in 1972. (Courtesy of Humboldt County Historical Society.)

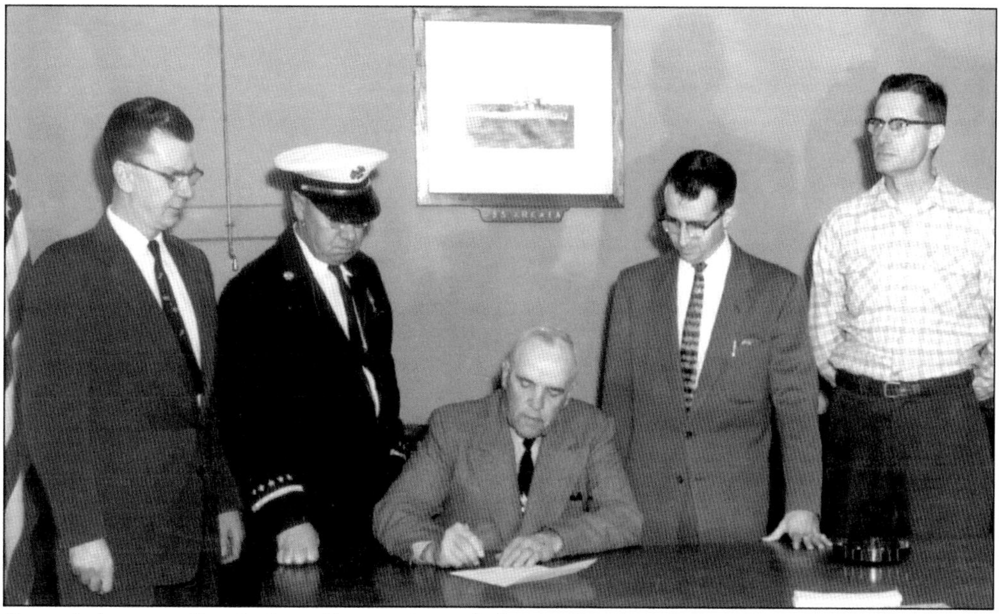

City of Arcata officials formally proclaimed the week of January 10–16, 1957, as National Electrical Week. Shown, from left to right, are Pacific Gas and Electric Company district manager S.L. Lindeblad, Arcata fire chief Roy Sorenson, Arcata mayor Ralph Lyman, R.L. Norton, and electrical inspector Marvin Krei. (Courtesy of Humboldt County Historical Society, Roscoe Collection.)

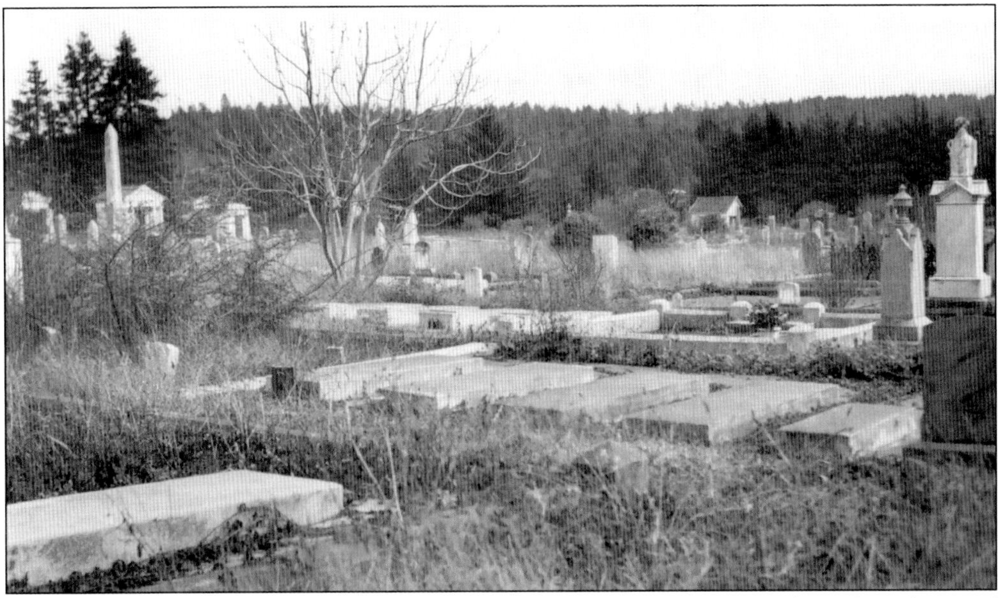

Greenwood Cemetery, stretching from the north end of J Street, was used as a burial ground in the 1850s before being officially declared a cemetery in March 1860. Concerned about the graveyard's disarray, a group of citizens organized in 1952 and developed a five-year cleanup and beautification plan. The burial ground includes the Minor mausoleum, crafted from slabs of granite taken from Isaac Minor's quarry north of Arcata and valued at $35,000 in 1909. (Courtesy of Humboldt County Historical Society, Roscoe Collection.)

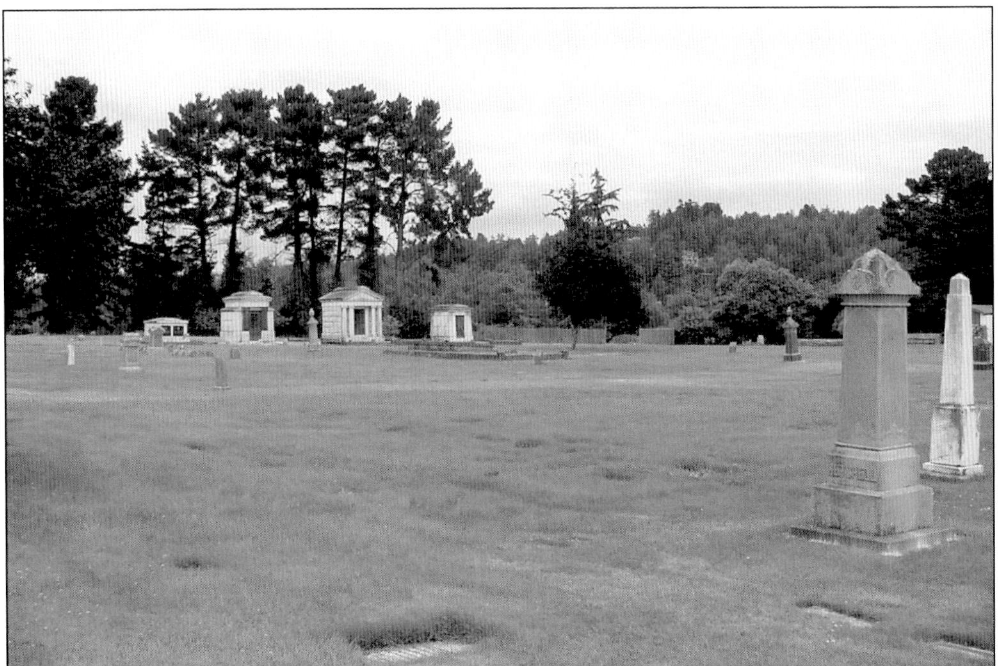

A modern-day view of Arcata's Greenwood Cemetery shows Isaac Minor's mausoleum, built with granite from his own quarry, in the middle of the three structures in the distance. (Courtesy of Col. Thomas Monroe.)

Five

Leisure and Homes

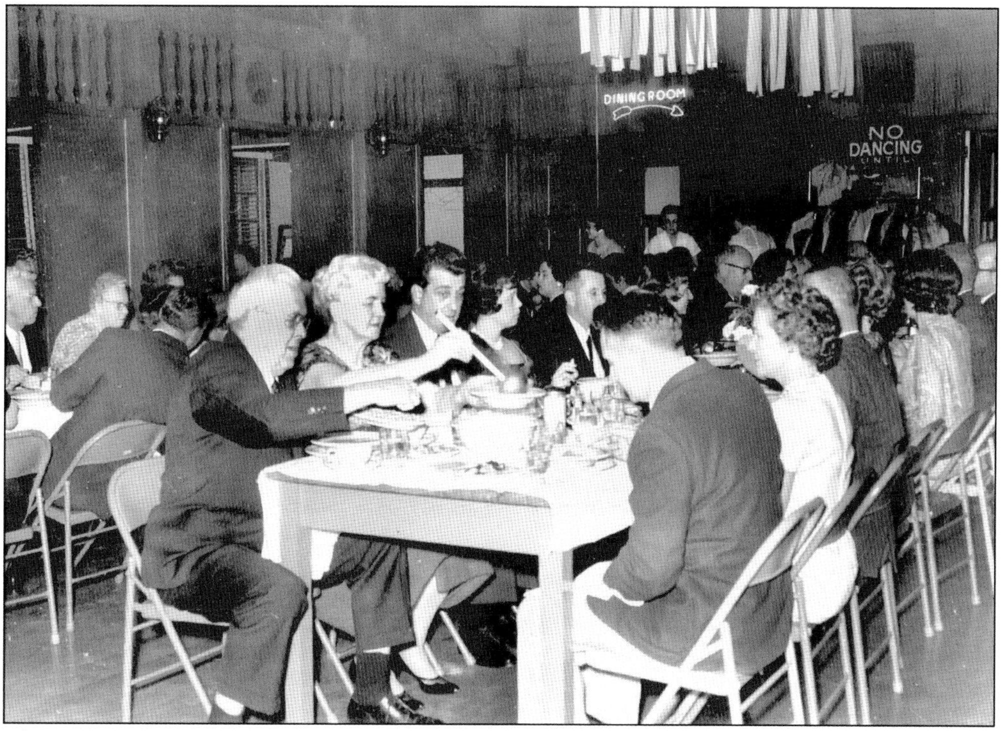

The Big 4 Inn, long a popular Italian restaurant in Humboldt County, got its start in Trinidad in 1922. The restaurant's first landlord, retired justice of the peace Tom Tighe, suggested that owners Maria and Victor Evangelista name their business the big four after railroad barons Huntington, Stanford, Crocker, and Hopkins. The Evangelistas opened their larger Arcata establishment in April 1934. Maria and Victor retired in 1945, but the business remained in the family until the expansion of Highway 101 in the early 1970s. (Courtesy of Vivian Ziegler.)

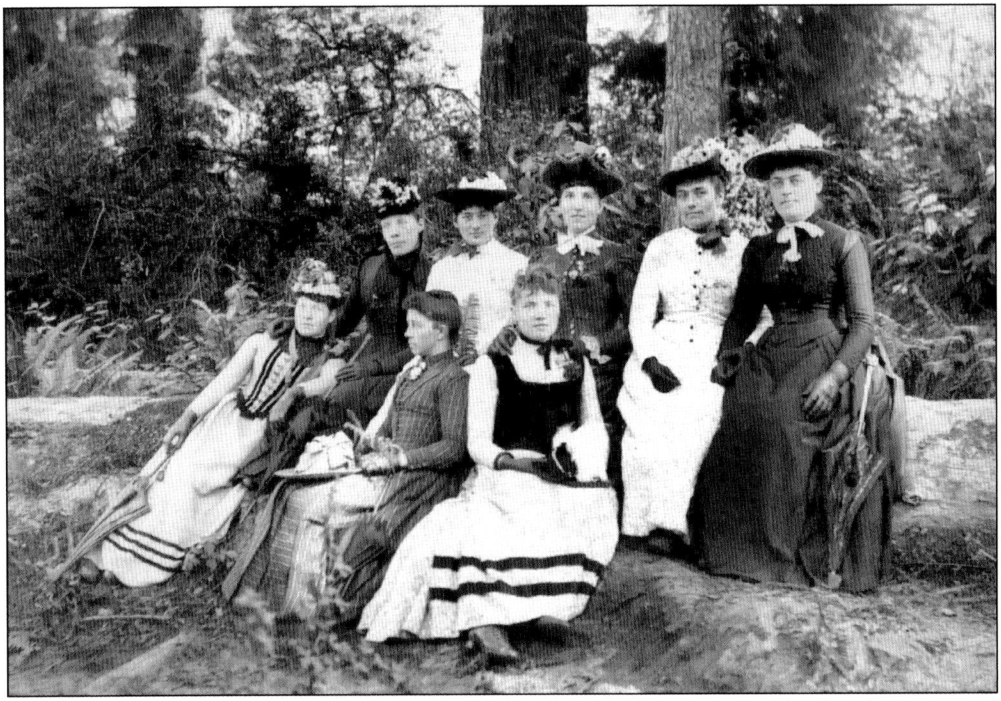

It wasn't unusual for the young women employed by Arcata's more wealthy families to spend their days off enjoying the countryside. Among those identified here are Ida Ryden (back row, second from left) and Amelia Alden (back row, far right). Lena Olson, who worked for Noah Falk's family, sits center front. (Courtesy of Vivian Ziegler.)

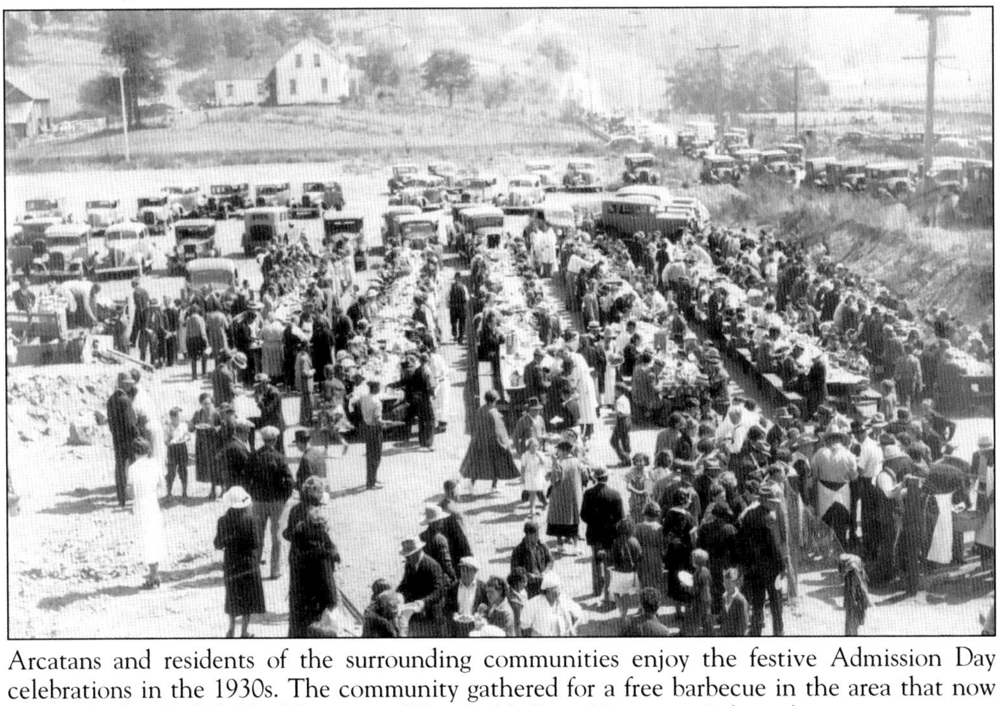

Arcatans and residents of the surrounding communities enjoy the festive Admission Day celebrations in the 1930s. The community gathered for a free barbecue in the area that now houses the baseball fields. (Courtesy of Humboldt State University Library.)

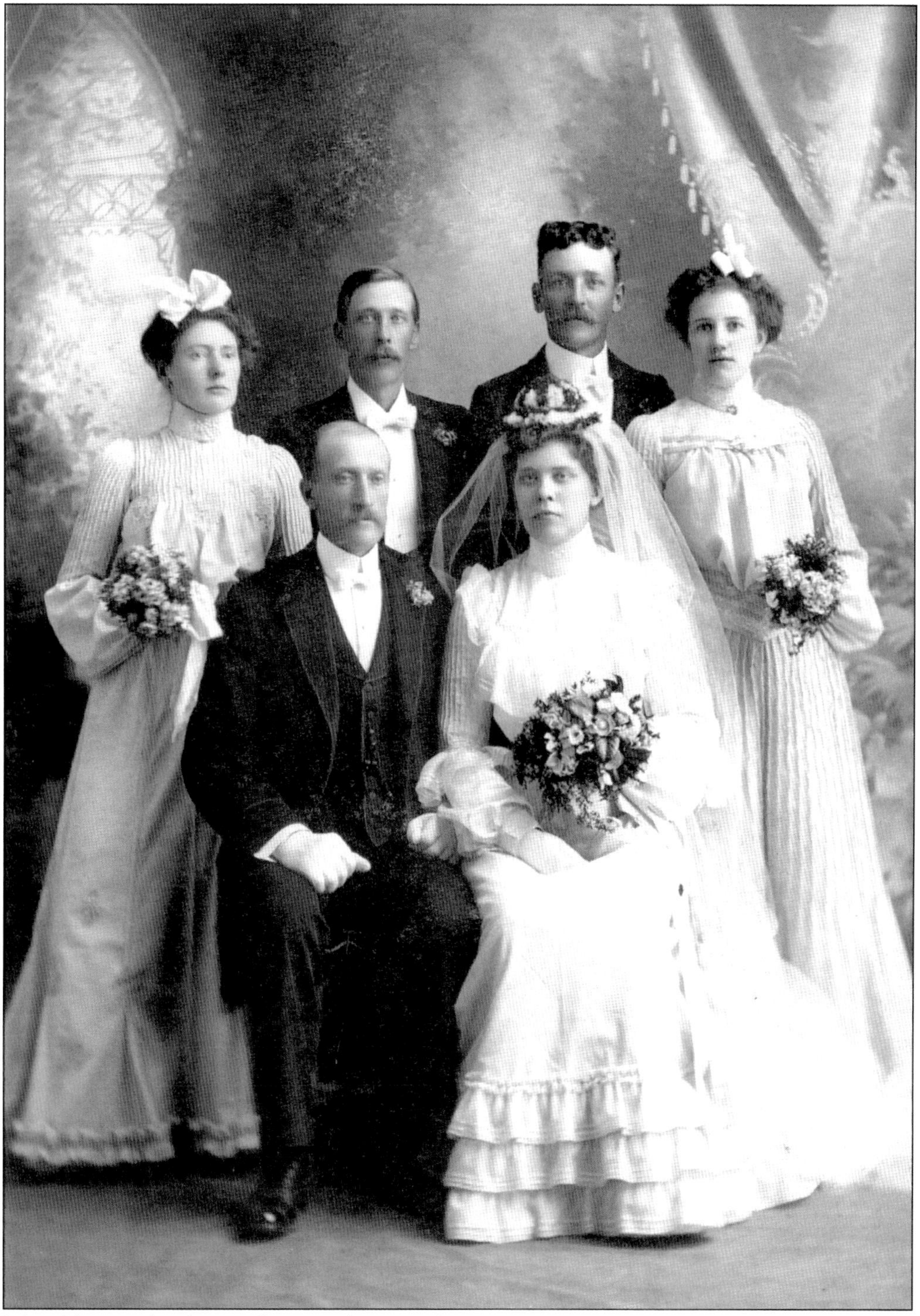

John Olson and Hilma Melgren wed on April 28, 1903, in Arcata at the B.A. Houda residence and hosted a wedding banquet at the Union Hotel in Arcata for more than 100 guests. In the back row are, from left to right, Charlotte Jacobson, Alfred Anderson, Louis Larson, and Anna Larson. (Courtesy of Vivian Ziegler.)

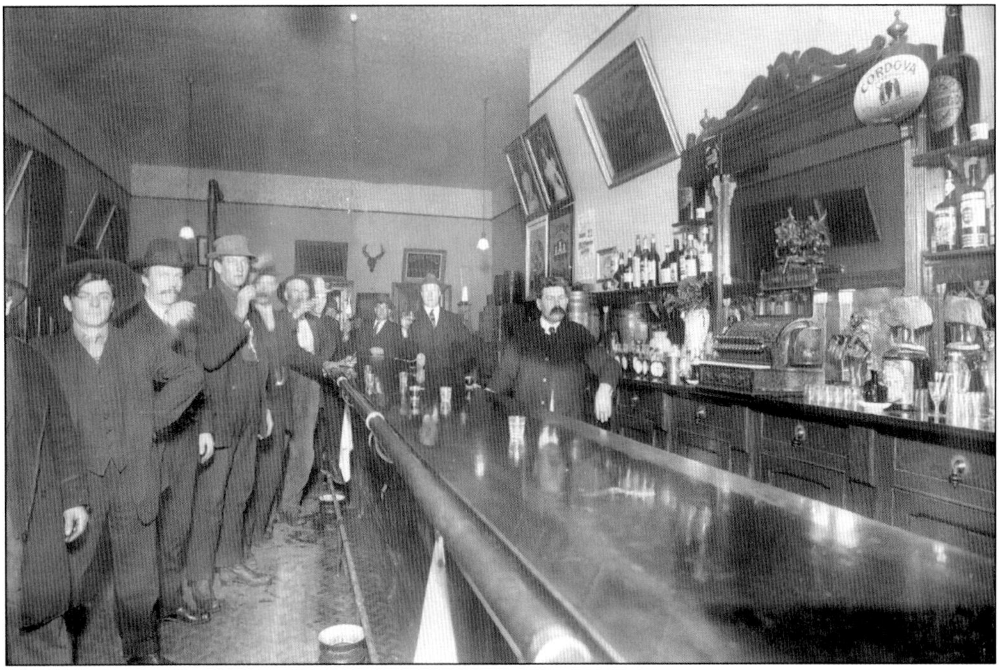

Patrons of the Arcata Opera Hall enjoy refreshments at the bar, also known as the Jacobsen Saloon. The drinking establishment, built in 1876 on the south side of the plaza, remained a saloon for 55 years. Owner Severin Jacobsen worked on the Harpst logging claim near Arcata when he lost his left leg in a logging accident. The boss and some friends then set him up in the saloon business. Jacobsen gave it up in 1920 and turned his attention to managing his other properties, including valuable Arcata real estate, until his death in 1932. (Courtesy of Humboldt County Historical Society.)

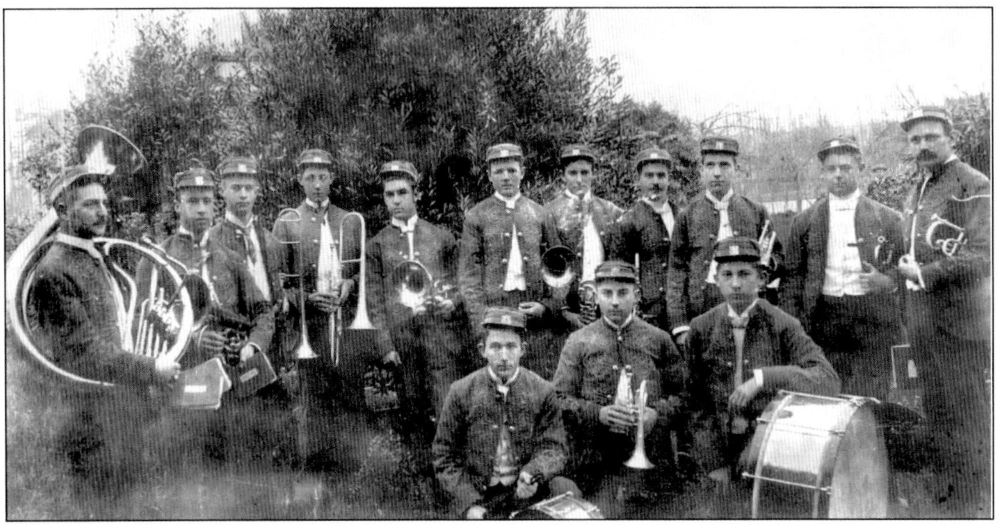

The Arcata Cornet Band, shown here in 1892, featured a variety of instruments including trombones, drums, tubas, and more. C.H. Pierce, the band's conductor, led the music made by Will Liscom, Robert Burns Jr., Paul M. Burns, Frank Mason, Harry K. Orman, George Zehndner, Walter Wiscom, Everet Spring, Thomas J. Crawford, Lee Wiley, Arthur Duprey, Leon Chevret, and Benjamin Sammons. (Courtesy of Humboldt County Historical Society.)

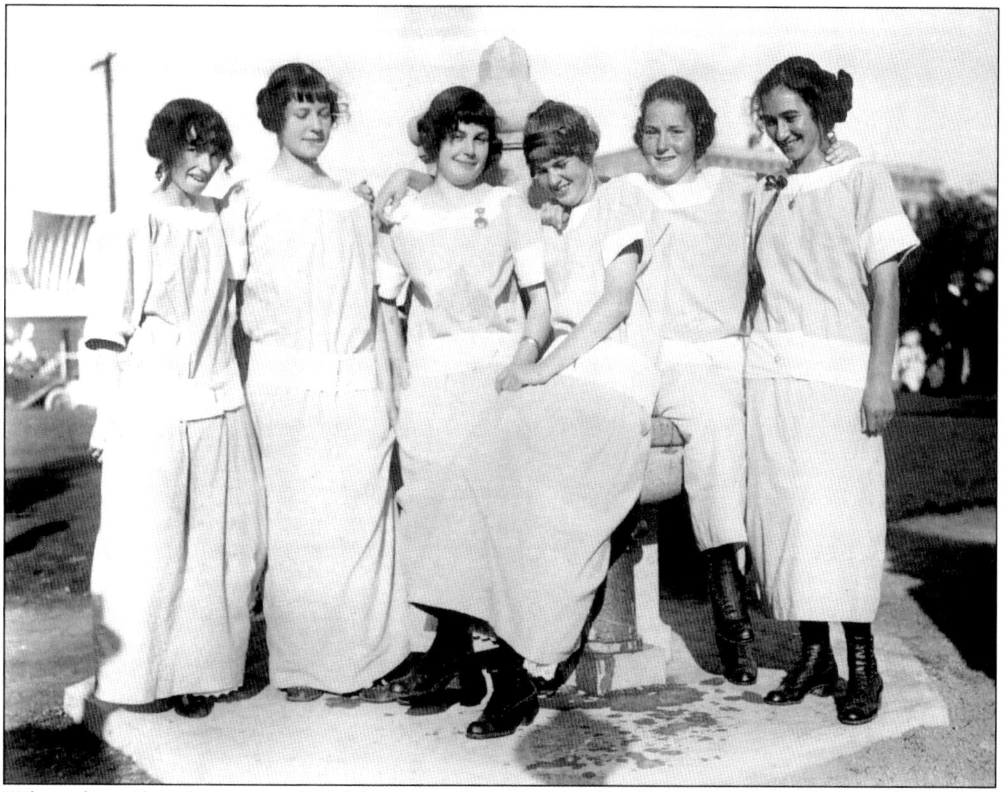

When the railroad was completed from San Francisco to Humboldt County in 1914, celebrations were held throughout the area. These young ladies, surrounding the Women's Christian Temperance Union's water fountain on the west side of the plaza, joined in. (Courtesy of Humboldt County Historical Society.)

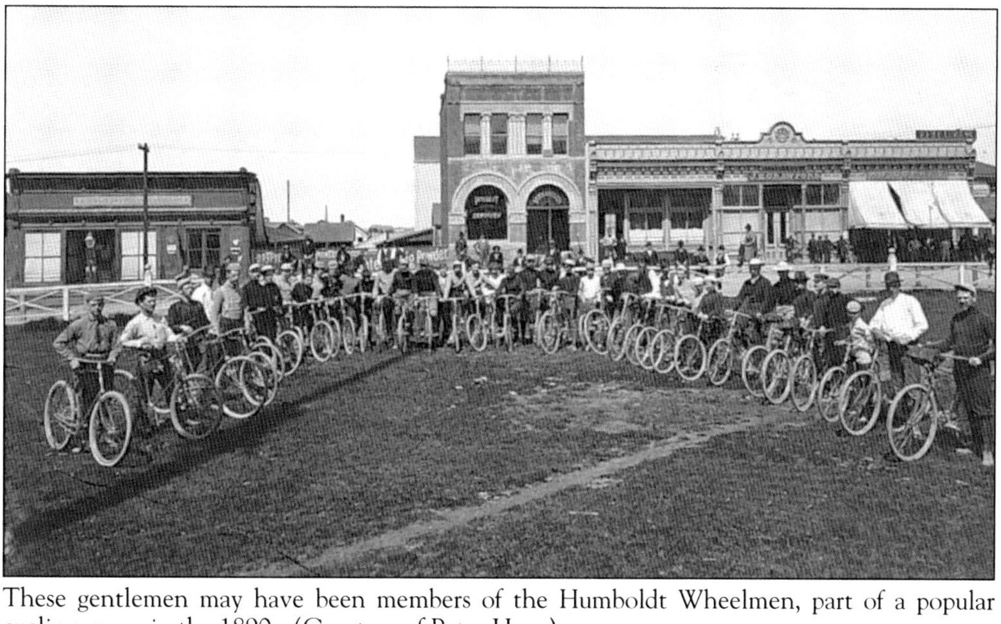

These gentlemen may have been members of the Humboldt Wheelmen, part of a popular cycling group in the 1890s. (Courtesy of Peter Hess.)

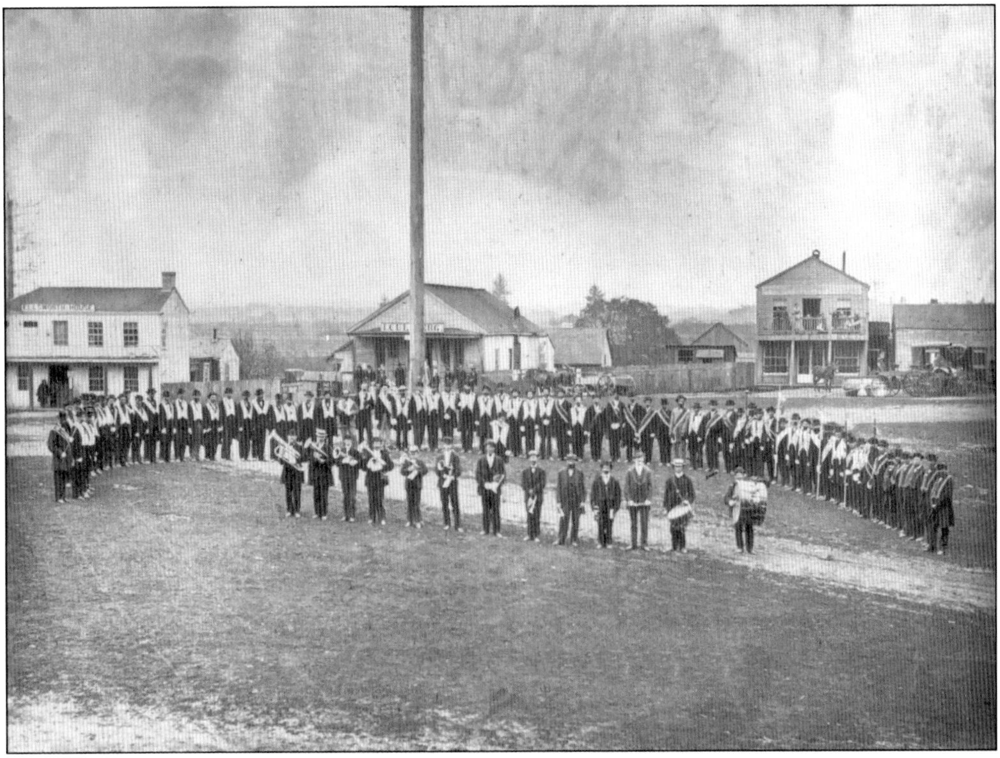

This large group of musicians gathered on the plaza some time in the late 1850s. Directly behind the pole is Isaac Cullberg's store, which opened in 1853. (Courtesy of Humboldt County Historical Society.)

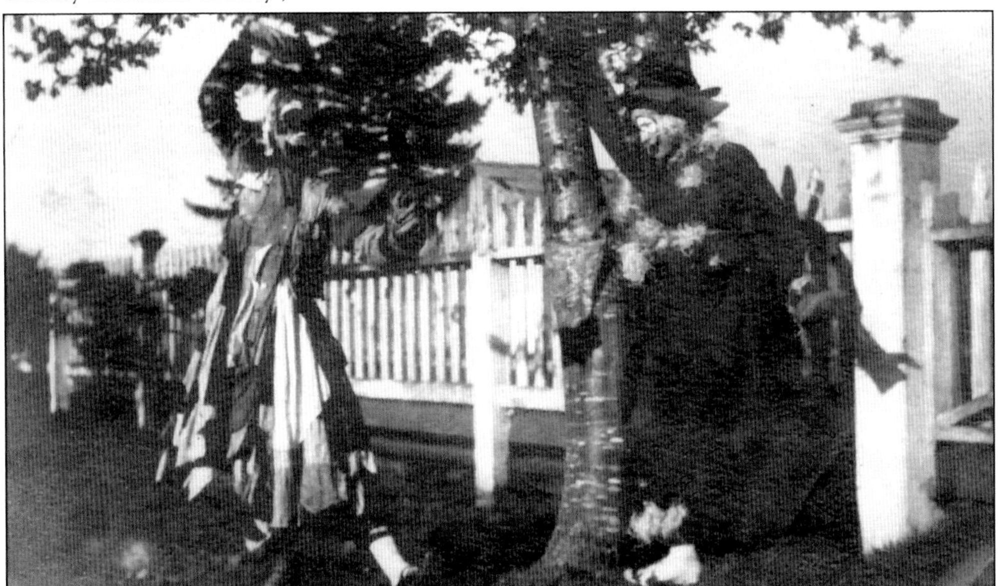

Lottie Beer as "Scraps" (left) and Helen Gaynor as a scarecrow entertain family and friends in the front yard of the Bohmansson home in the spring of 1918. (Courtesy of Humboldt County Historical Society, Roscoe Collection.)

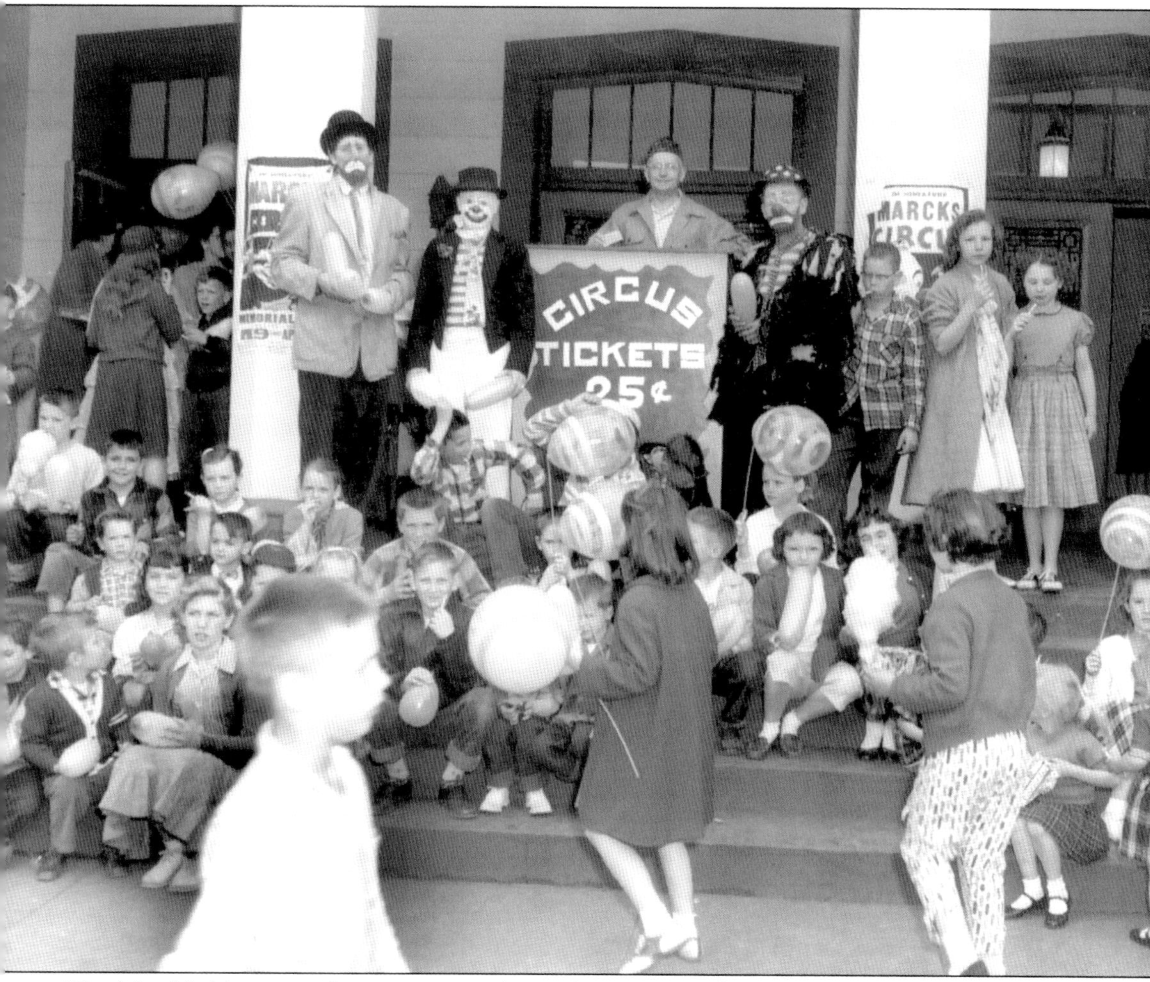

The Marck's Miniature Circus came to Arcata Veteran's Hall in April 1957. Clown Tommy "Smoky" Rouse, Bruce Fowler, and Donald Marcks entertained those attending the event, which was sponsored by the American Legion. (Courtesy of Humboldt County Historical Society, Roscoe Collection.)

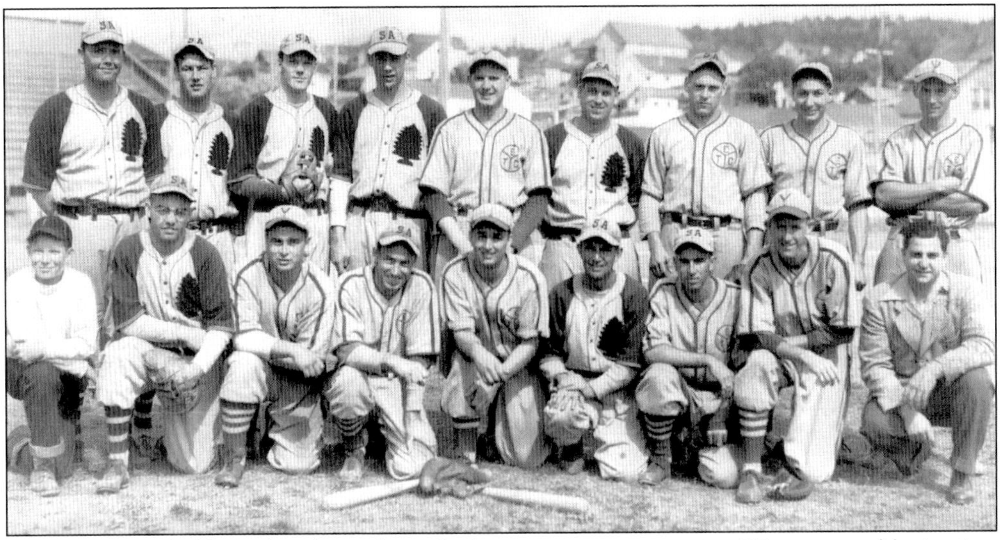

The 1946 Humboldt Crabs, shown here, had a great season, winning 37 games and losing just 12 to earn them a spot in the state semi-pro tournament finals. Organized in 1945, the Crabs continue to play today. The team, from left to right, included (front row) an unidentified bat boy, Royce Lima, Links Carranco, Rudy Tomich, Lou Bonomini, Fred Papini, Eddie Oleverio, John McDonald, and Nelo Del Porto; (back row) Charles Timmons, Charles Beauchamp, Tom Kipp, Bruce Johnson, Bunny Hadley, Clarence McLeen, Bob Mathews, Rico Pastori, and Dave Hauger. Not pictured are Wally Scott and Bill Prentice. (Courtesy of Humboldt County Historical Society, Woods Collection.)

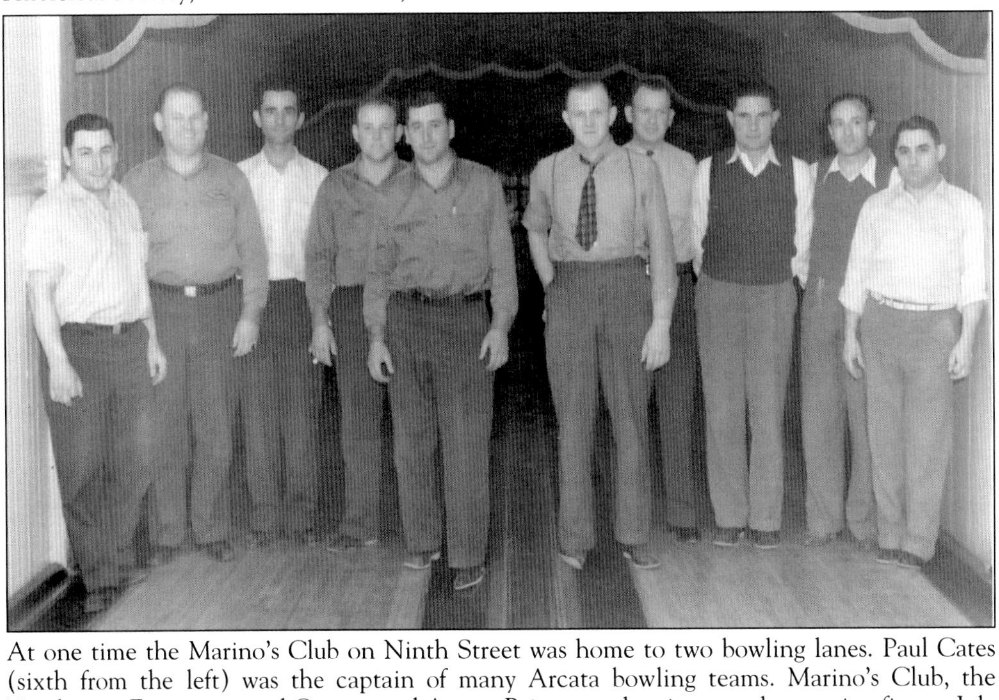

At one time the Marino's Club on Ninth Street was home to two bowling lanes. Paul Cates (sixth from the left) was the captain of many Arcata bowling teams. Marino's Club, the Northcoast Environmental Center, and Arcata Paint were lost in an early morning fire on July 26, 2001. Other Arcata bowling alleys include the New Delta Bowl, Arcata Bowl, and Redwood Lanes. (Courtesy of Humboldt County Historical Society, Cates Collection.)

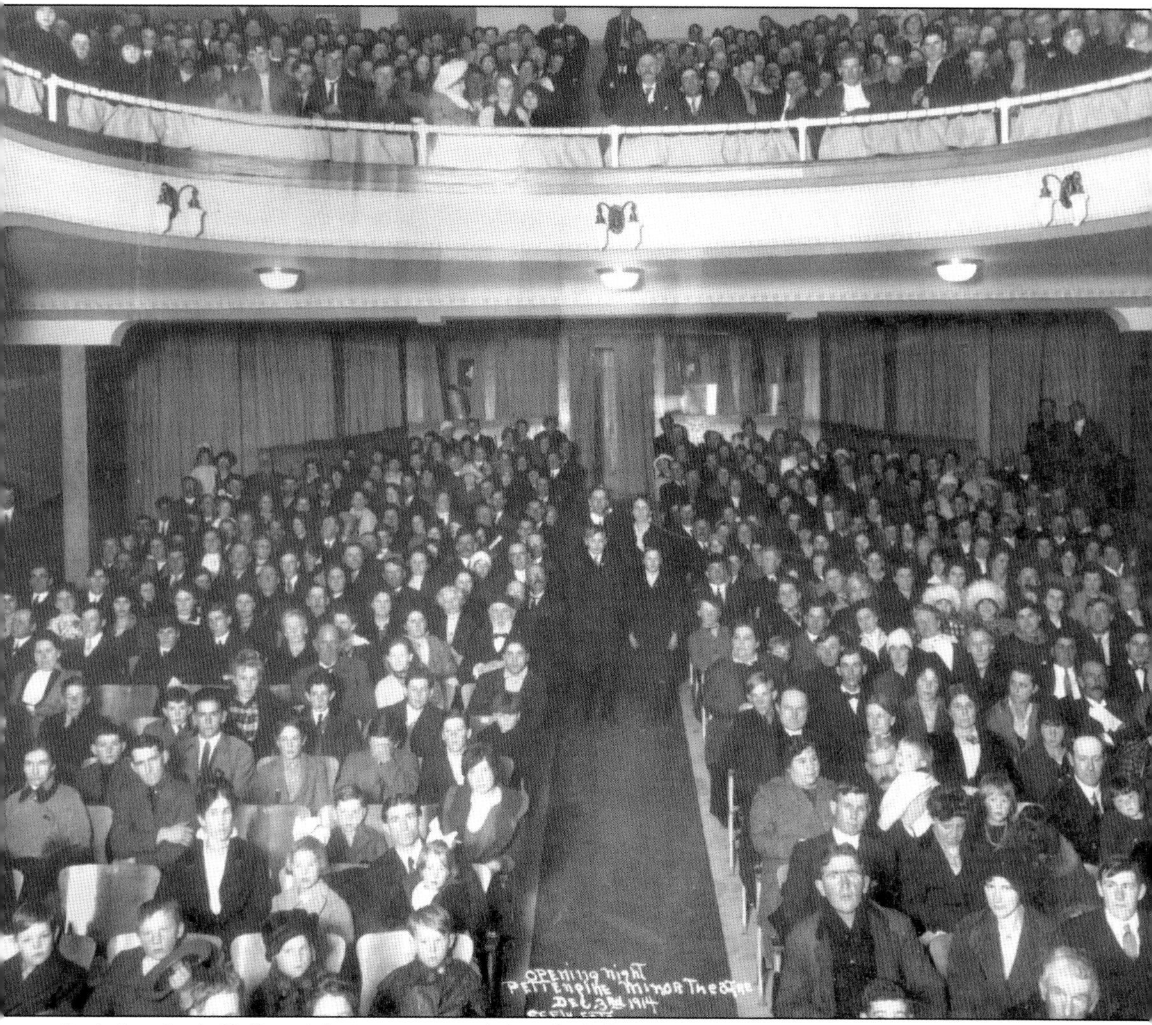

Jack London's *Valley of the Moon* topped the playbill on December 3, 1914, for the opening of Isaac Minor's new movie theater on H Street. The Pettengills were the first to lease the fine new venue, with several others following, including George Mann, who would go on to make his own way in Humboldt County's theater business. The original house balcony still serves Arcata moviegoers. (Courtesy of Humboldt County Historical Society.)

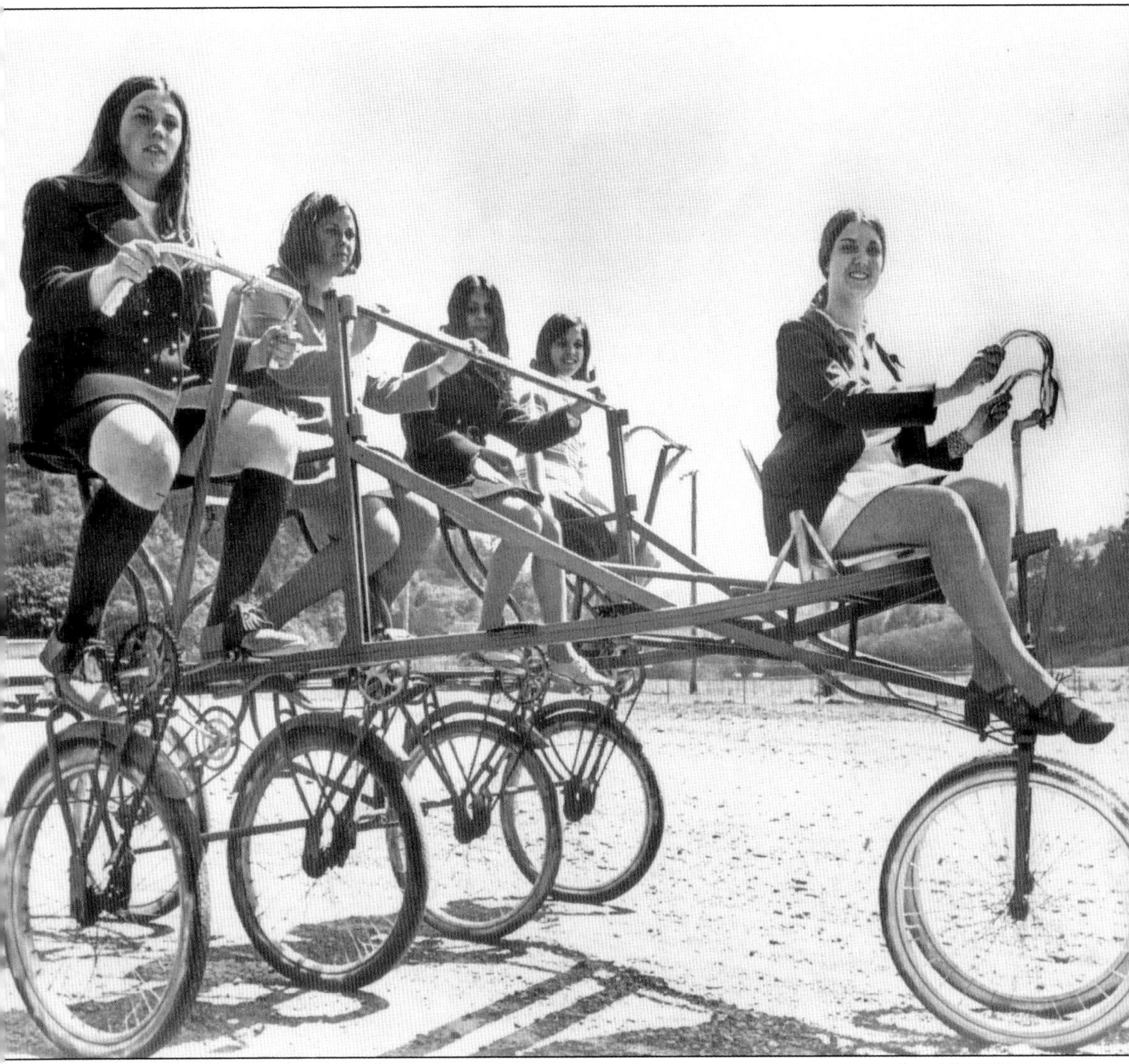

These Humboldt State College students try out an entry in preparation for the 1970 Kinetic Sculpture Race. (Courtesy of Humboldt County Historical Society.)

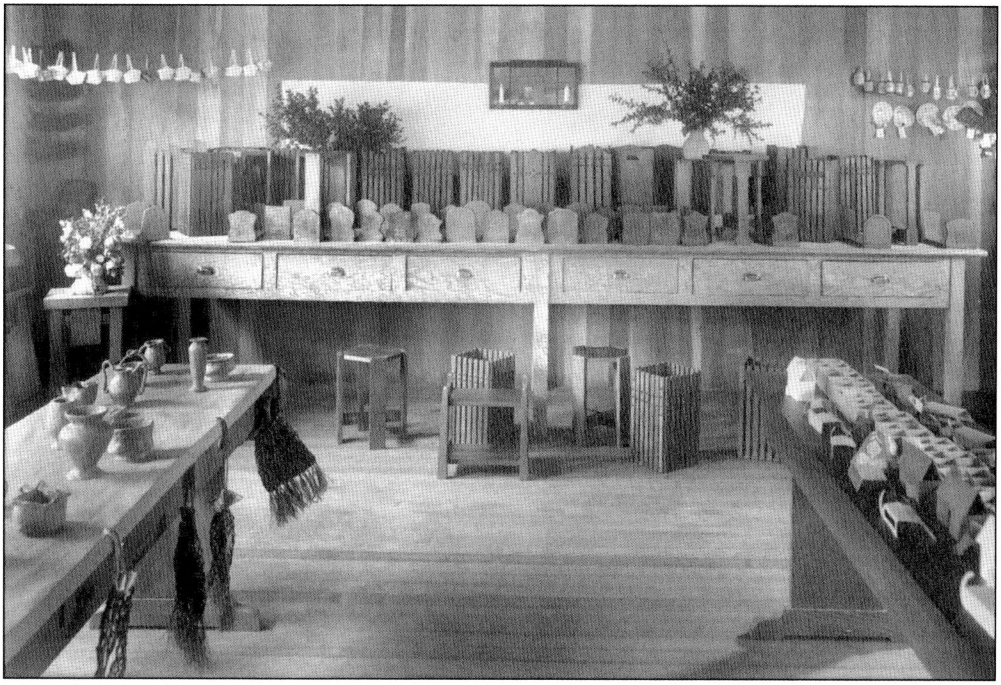

These hand-crafted wooden items were likely part of the third annual exhibition of the Northern Humboldt Fair Association held in Excelsior Hall in Arcata in 1919. (Courtesy of Humboldt State University Library.)

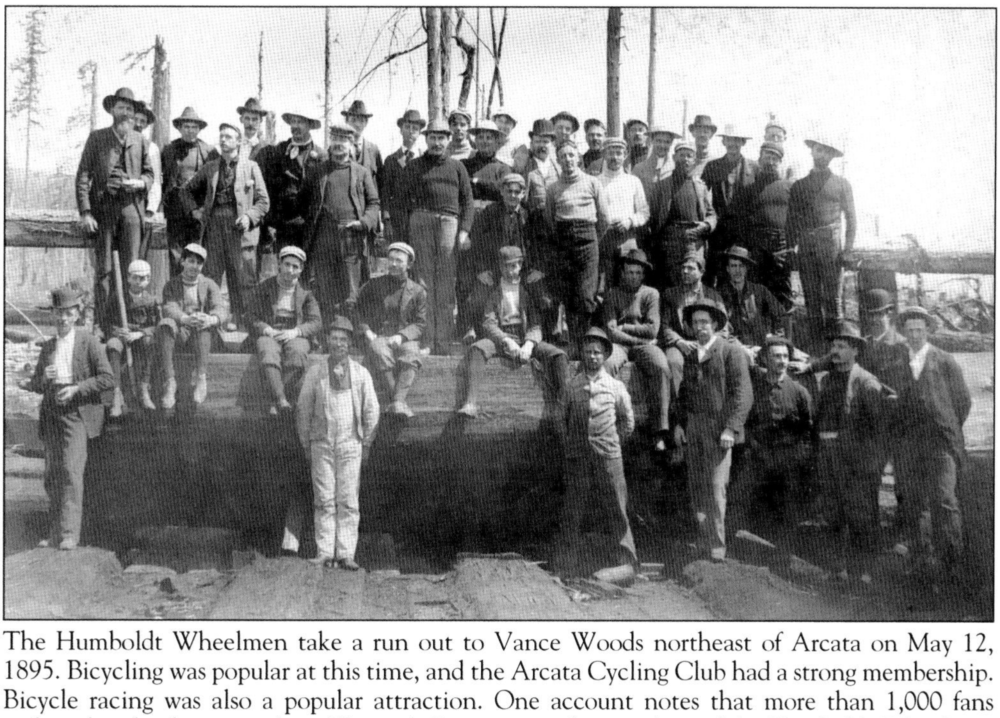

The Humboldt Wheelmen take a run out to Vance Woods northeast of Arcata on May 12, 1895. Bicycling was popular at this time, and the Arcata Cycling Club had a strong membership. Bicycle racing was also a popular attraction. One account notes that more than 1,000 fans gathered at the driving park on Eleventh Street to see the members of the Humboldt Wheelmen and Arcata Cycling Club compete. (Courtesy of Humboldt County Historical Society.)

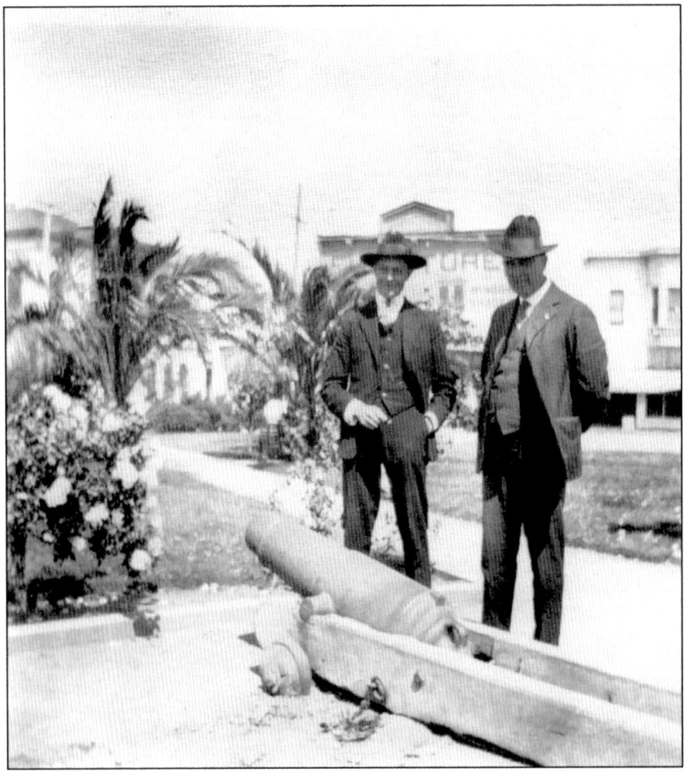

A little plaza mischief, perhaps? (Courtesy of Humboldt County Historical Society, Haffner Collection.)

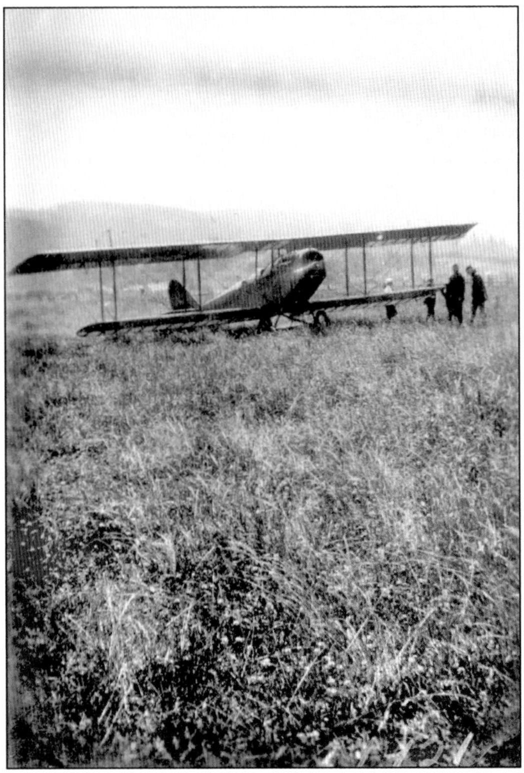

Earl "Brick" Graham was one of the first men in the area to buy an airplane and often landed on the family's Arcata Bottom ranch. Graham's father, Frank, was one of the founders of the Northern Redwood Lumber Company. In 1917 Brick signed up for the American aviation service and spent 18 months in service to the country. (Courtesy of Vivian Ziegler.)

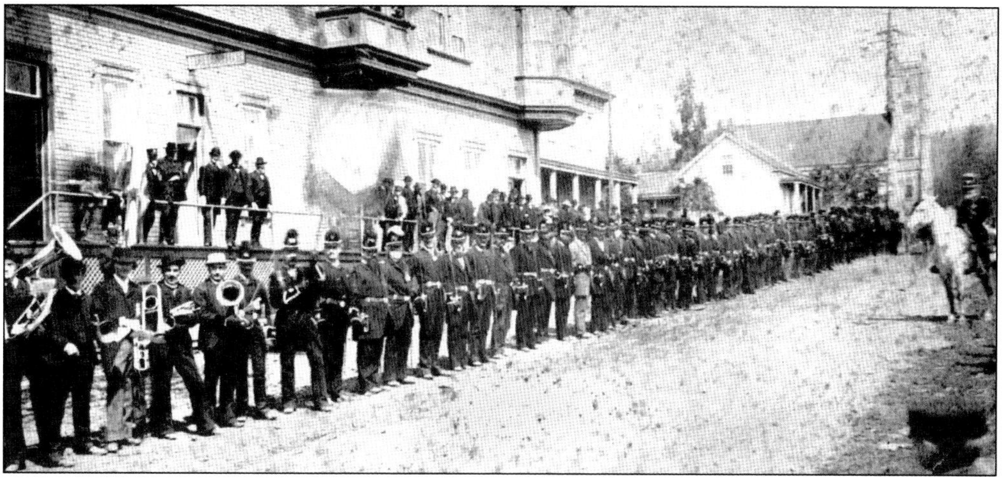

The North Star Lodge, No. 39, Knights of Pythias's band stands along Eleventh Street by its 1885 building. The lodge aimed for the "elevation, happiness, and betterment of all mankind," as well as being dedicated to youth welfare, according to the 1954 centennial issue of the *Humboldt Times*. (Courtesy Humboldt County Historical Society, Roscoe Collection.)

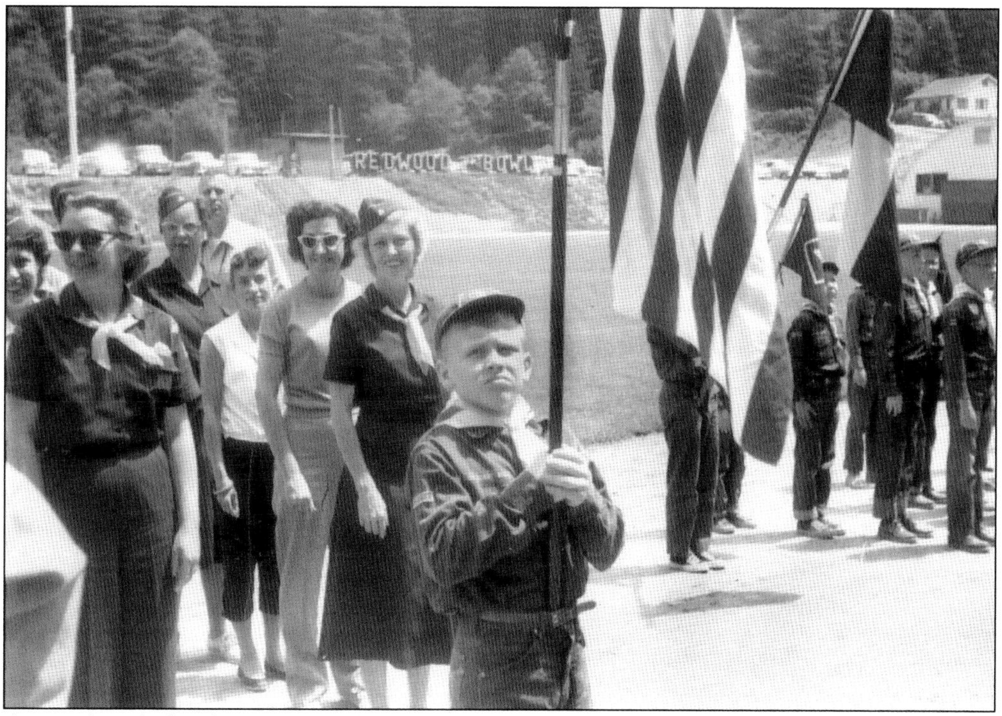

An unidentified Cub Scout proudly represents his troop during a ceremony at then Humboldt State College. (Courtesy of Humboldt County Historical Society, Goss Collection.)

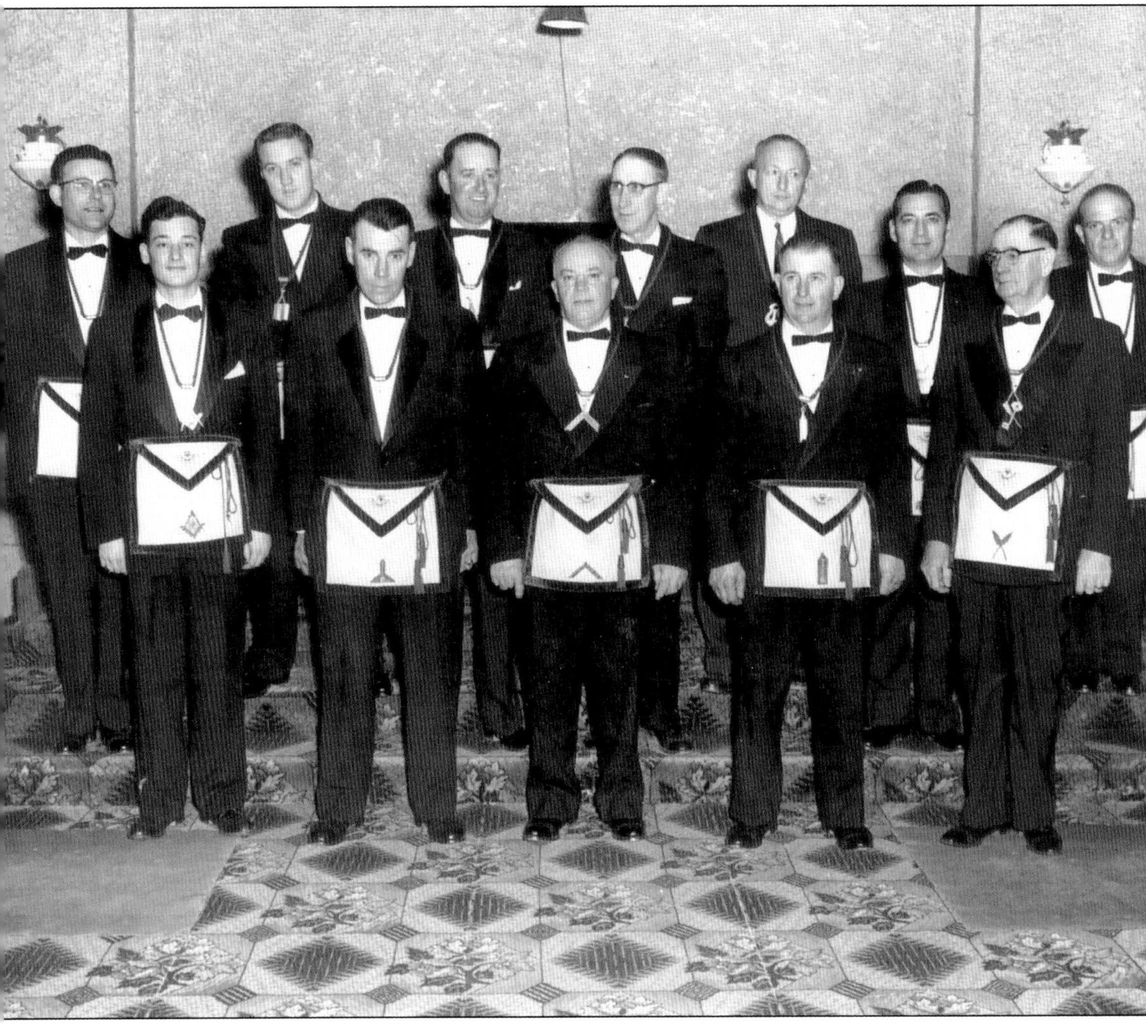

Arcata Lodge No. 106, Free and Accepted Masons, shown here in a 1957 installation ceremony, was organized in April 1856 and continues today. At one point the lodge shared the upper floor of the old city hall with the International Order of Odd Fellows. (Courtesy of Humboldt County Historical Society, Roscoe Collection.)

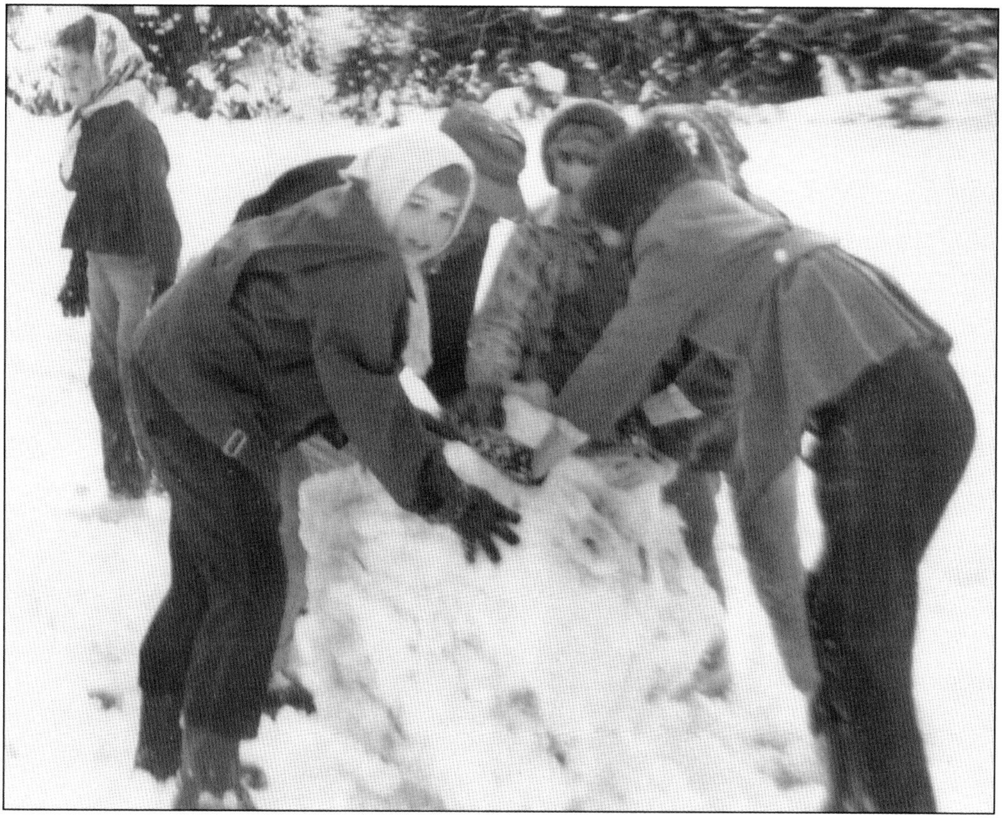

The Busy Fingers Blue Birds of Arcata made a trip to Snow Camp in February 1957, with leader Mrs. William Fulton. The Blue Birds included Katie Stokes, Diane Chetkovich, Linda Sacchi, Rose Marie Fulton, Kathy Dave, Connie Workman, Pat Heberle, and Phyllis Davis. (Courtesy of Humboldt County Historical Society, Roscoe Collection.)

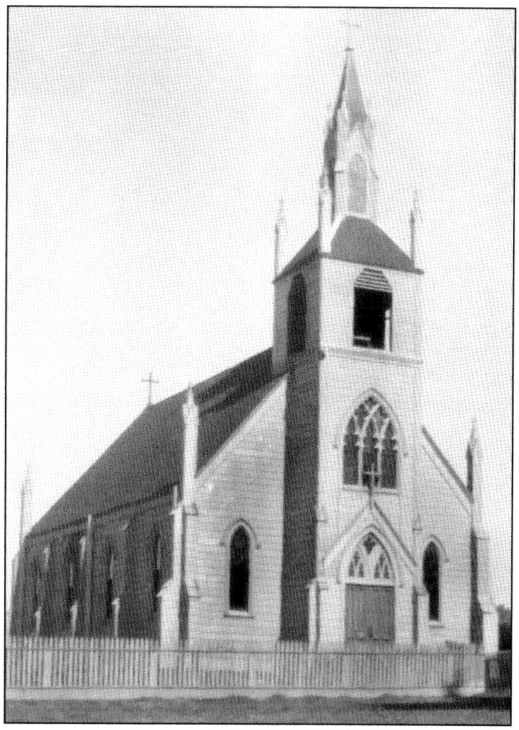

St. Mary's Catholic Church, built in 1884 on Sixteenth Street, was abandoned in 1983 after being declared structurally unsound. The Catholic portion of Greenwood Cemetery is located behind the former church site. In the interim, parish members attended services in St. Mary's School gymnasium before the new church on Janes Road was dedicated in 1996. The original church burned to the ground on February 8, 2003. (Courtesy of Peter Hess.)

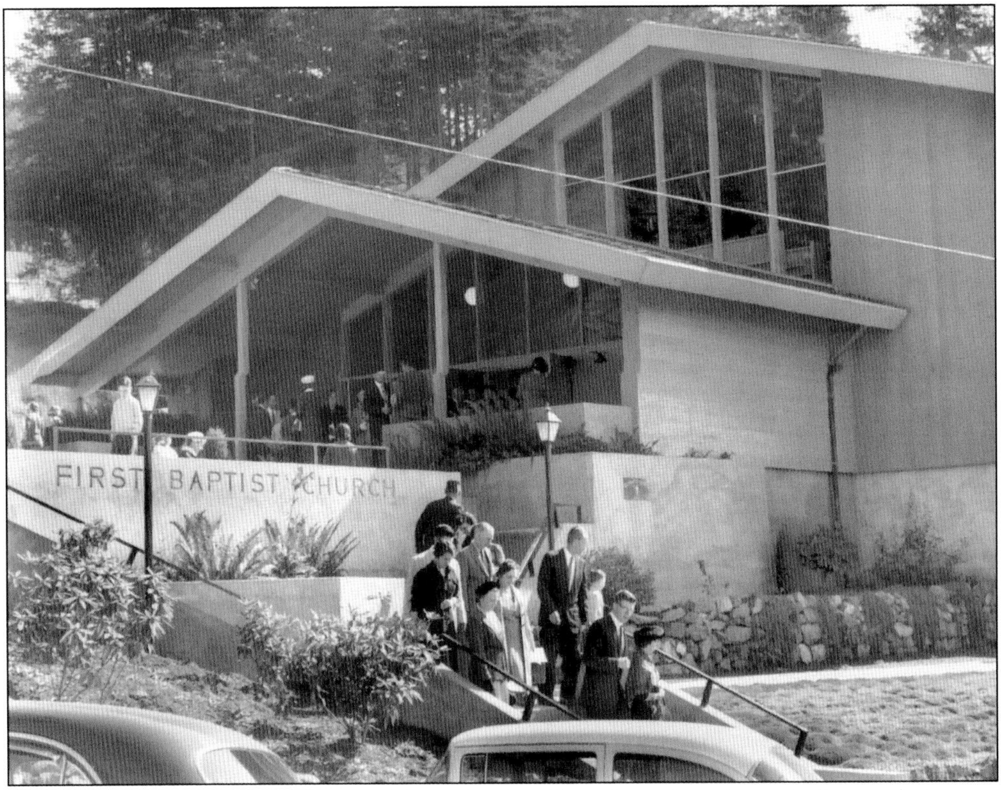

The congregation of the Arcata First Baptist Church gathered to dedicate their new Union Street building on November 29, 1957. (Courtesy of Humboldt County Historical Society, Roscoe Collection.)

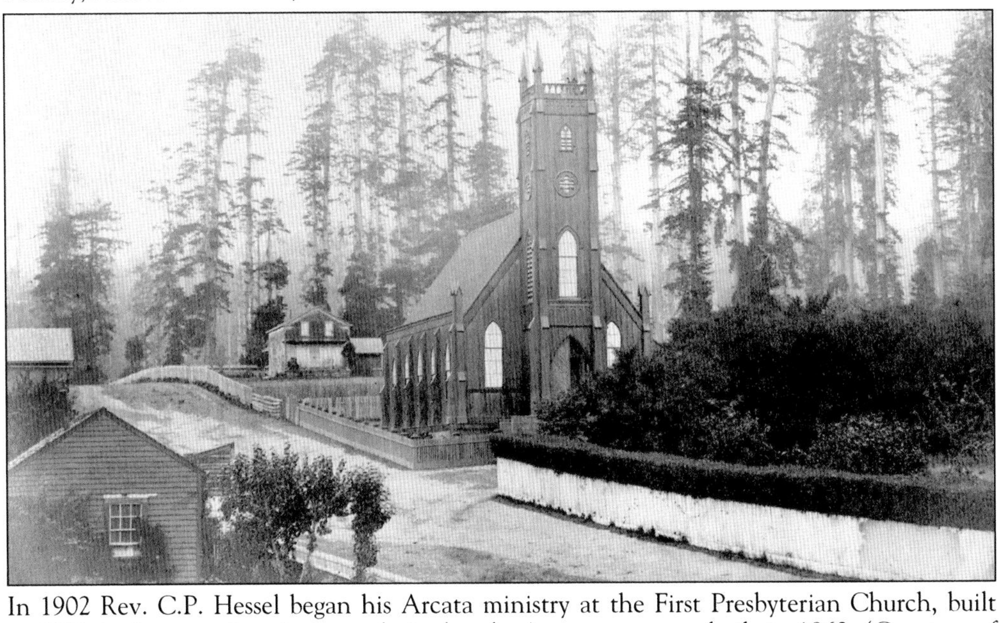

In 1902 Rev. C.P. Hessel began his Arcata ministry at the First Presbyterian Church, built in 1861 in the same location as today's church. A parsonage was built in 1862. (Courtesy of Arcata Presbyterian Church.)

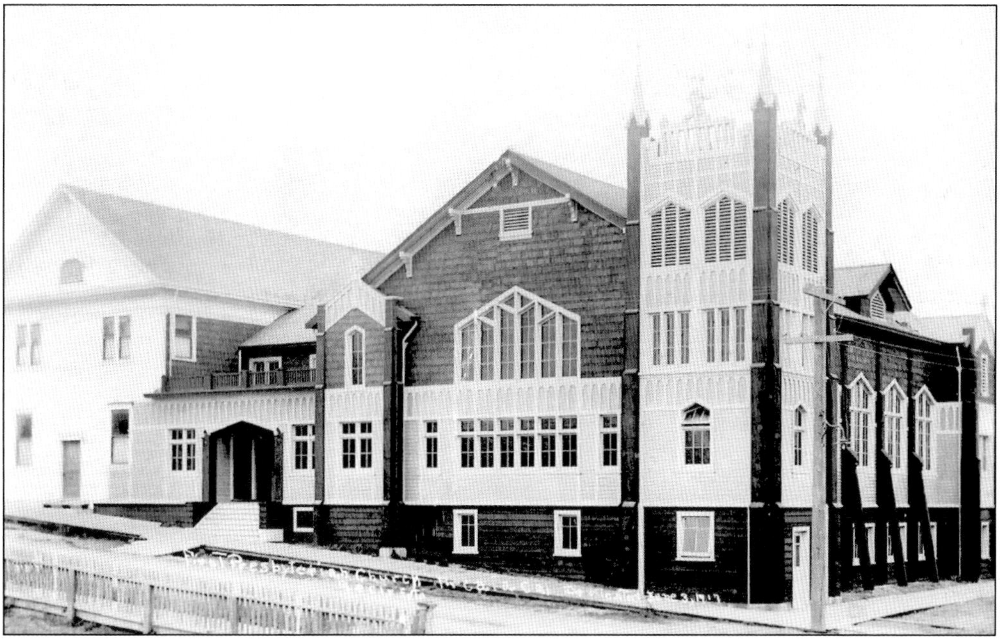

Dedicated on June 3, 1917, the current Presbyterian church has become a landmark on the corner of Eleventh and G Streets. Financed primarily through donations, the new church was completed for $7,708.75 by contract to Nelson B. Johansen and was furnished for an additional $930. The day-long dedication on that June day, according to the *Arcata Union*, included three services, many flowers, much music, and the christening of Rev. and Mrs. Hessel's one-year-old daughter, Margaret Isabel Hessel. (Courtesy of Arcata Presbyterian Church.)

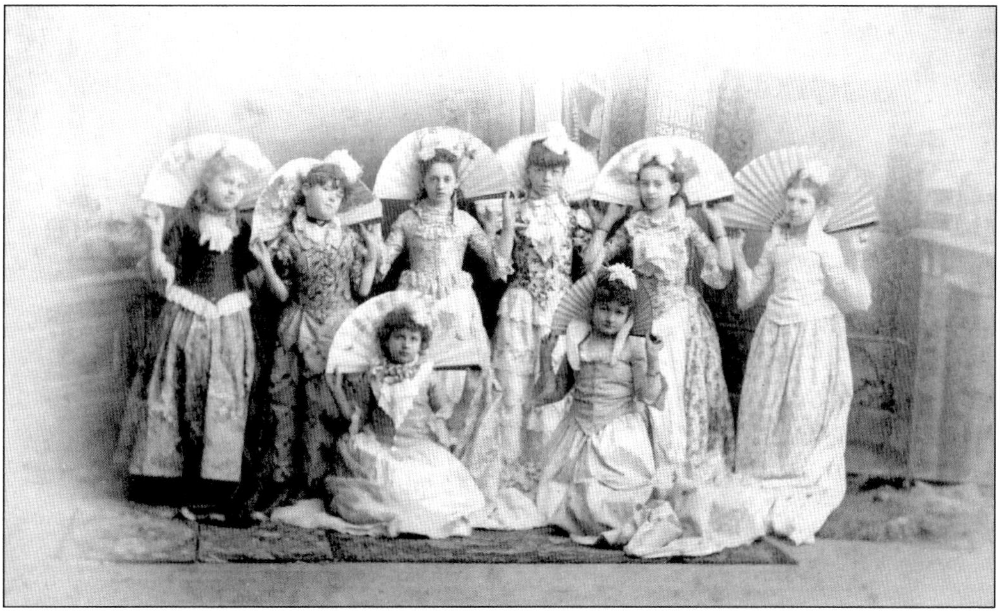

A performance of the Presbyterian church's "Fan Brigade" was identified as one of the many social events of the 1890s. Standing, from left to right, are Cecilia Stone Long, Clara H. Dorais, Jessie Minor, Olive E. Hannah, Jessie May Wiley, and Margaret Johanson. Seated are Lily Averill Lattin (left) and Grace D. Burns. (Courtesy of Arcata Presbyterian Church.)

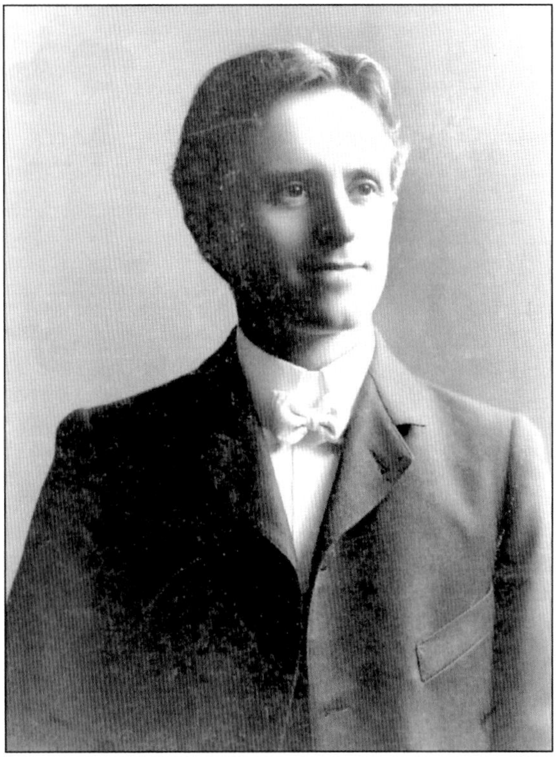

Rev. Charles P. Hessel arrived in 1902 to assume leadership of the First Presbyterian Church of Arcata and oversaw the construction of the 1917 church, which still serves the congregation. During his long tenure, Hessel was one of the organizers of the Humboldt County Ministerial Union. Prior to his arrival in Arcata, he served as a missionary in the rural Humboldt County settlements of Grizzly Bluff and Port Kenyon. (Courtesy of Vivian Ziegler.)

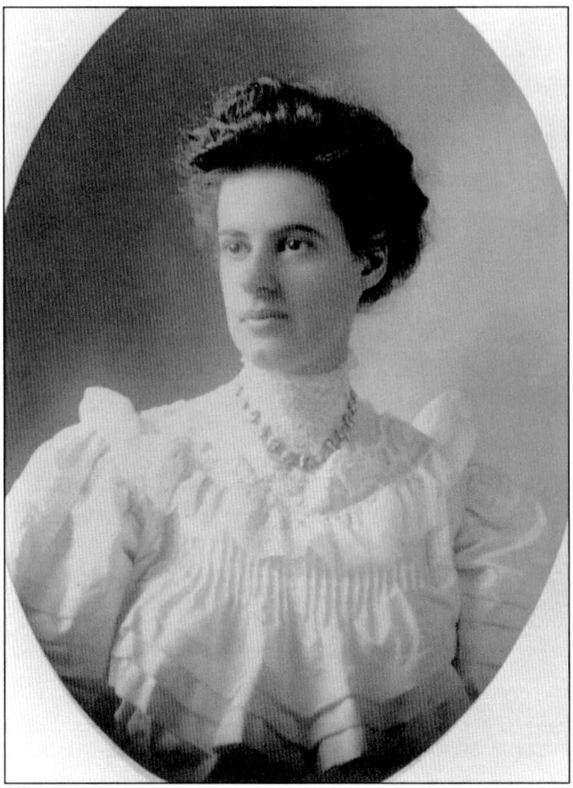

Reverend Hessel married Edna I. Protzman of Portland, Oregon, a few years after his calling to Arcata. (Courtesy of Vivian Ziegler.)

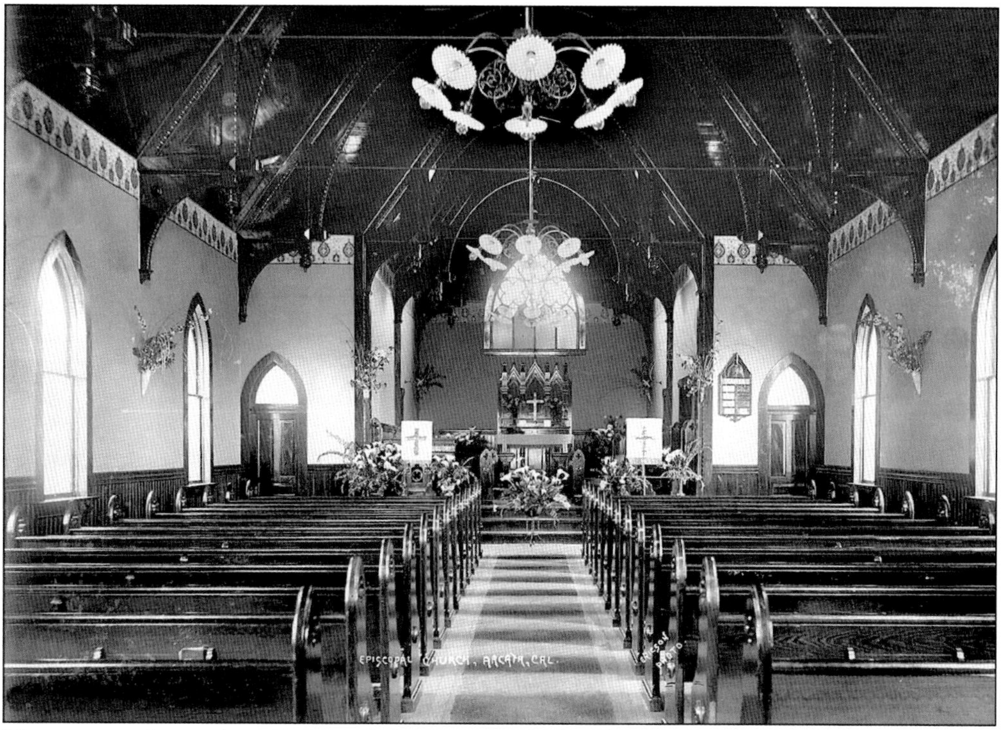

This image shows the interior of the Episcopal church. (Courtesy of Ericson Collection, Humboldt State University Library.)

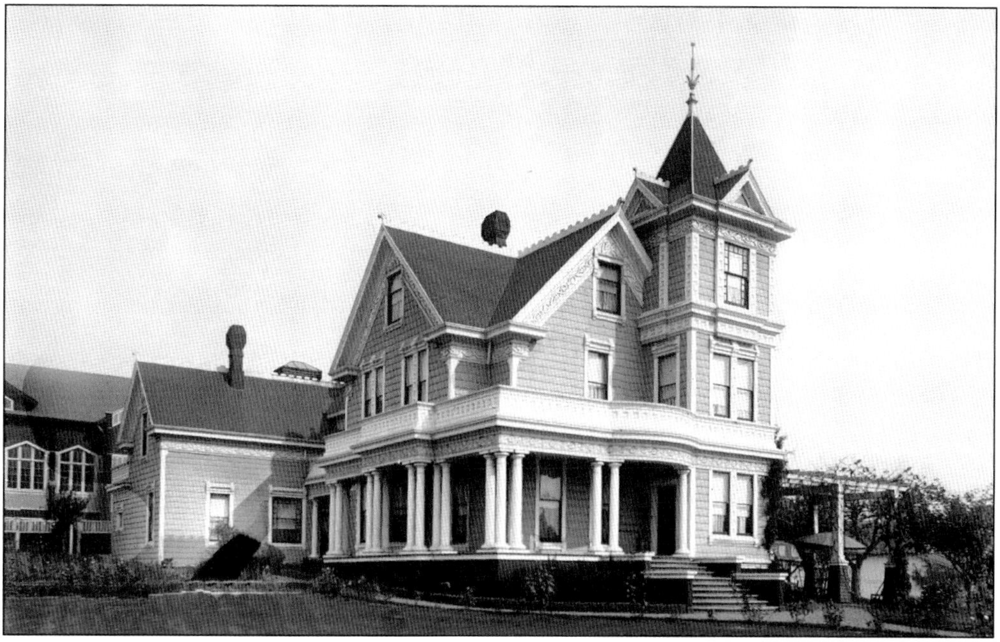

The stately Brizard home was built on G Street in 1889 and remained in the family until at least 1949. The home, rich in Victorian details, was torn down in later years to make way for businesses now occupying the east side of G Street, due north of the Arcata Theater. (Courtesy of Ericson Collection, Humboldt State University Library.)

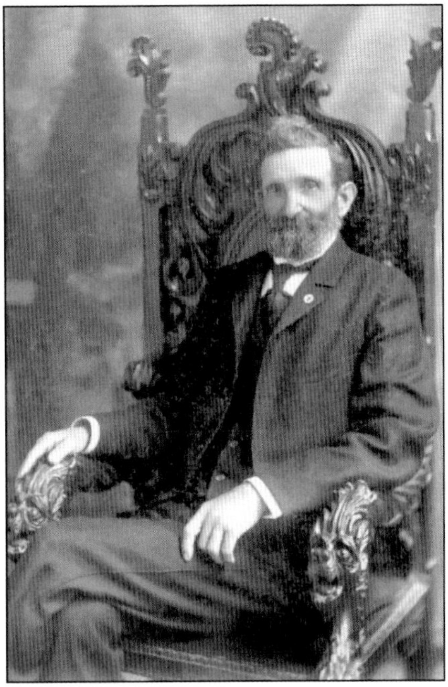

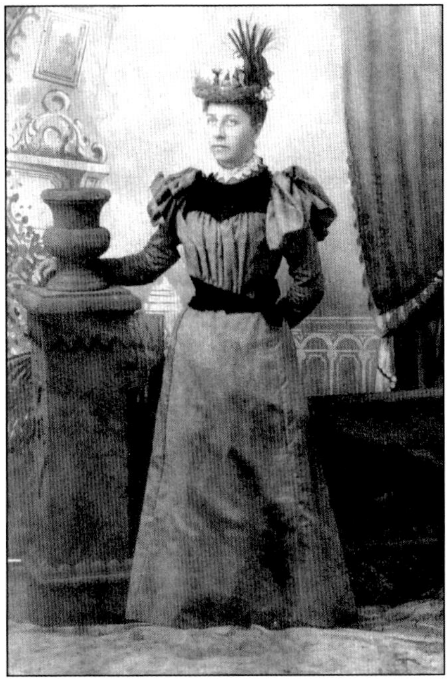

Noah Falk is pictured on the left and Lena Olson on the right. Olson worked as a domestic for the Falk family and was one of several Arcata residents who emigrated from Sweden. (Left, courtesy of Humboldt County Historical Society; right, courtesy of Vivian Ziegler.)

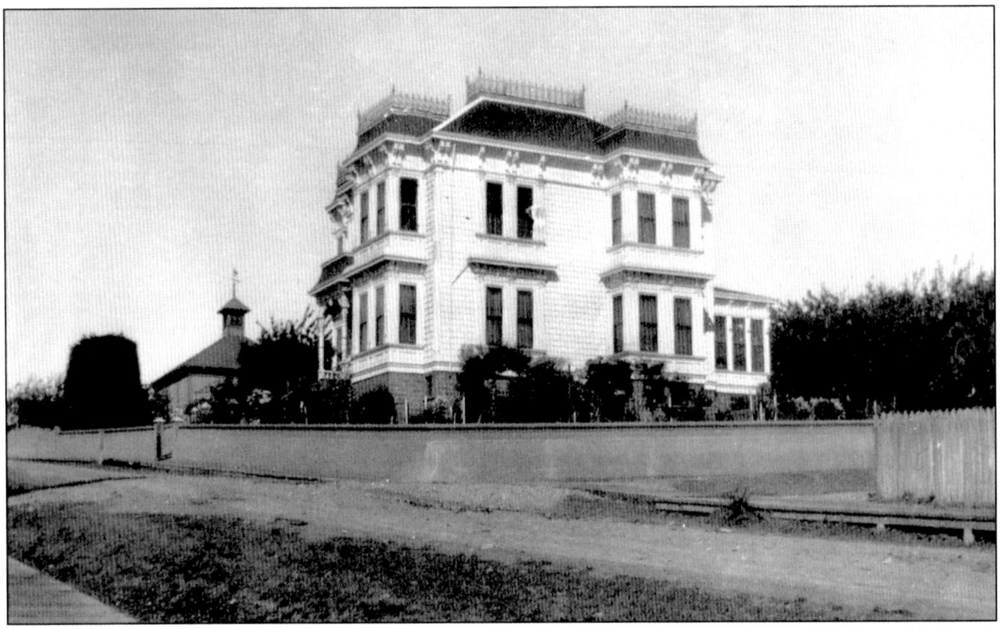

Certainly one of the grandest homes of Arcata, Noah Falk's mansion covered nearly a full block between Twelfth and Thirteenth Streets and G and H Streets. Falk, president of the Elk River Mill and Lumber Company, was also president of the Union Water Company and served on the board of directors of four area banks. He also headed the Arcata Hotel Corporation, which built Hotel Arcata. Falk designed the 1887 home that included curly and fine-grained redwood inside and formal gardens and a carriage house outside. (Courtesy of Peter Hess.)

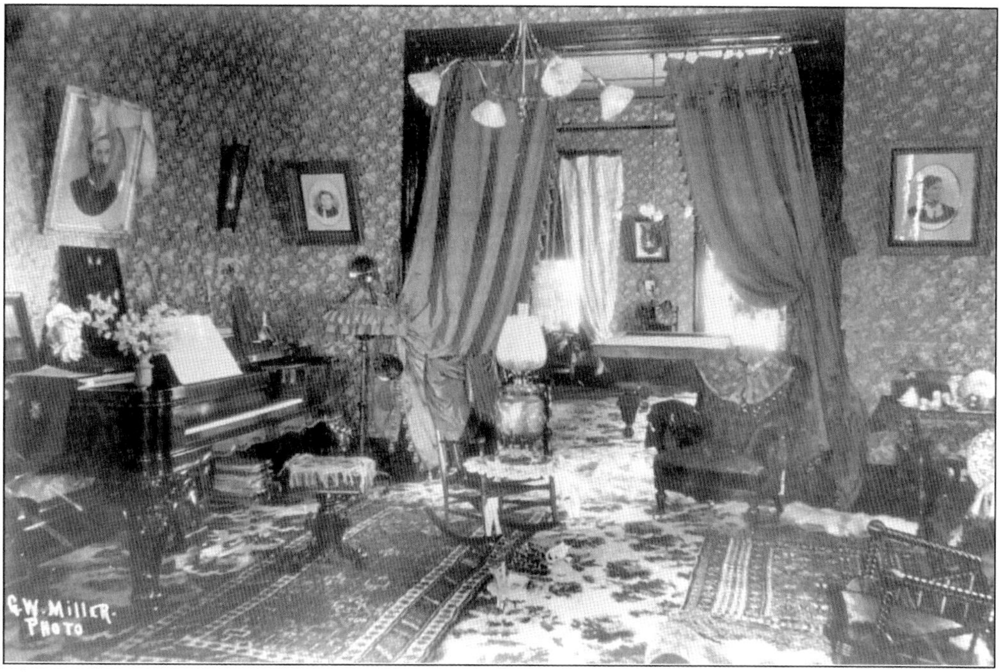

The interior of the Falk mansion was as splendid as its exterior. Those walls, however, may have contained much sadness as three of the couple's four children did not survive infancy. (Courtesy of Humboldt County Historical Society, Gates Collection.)

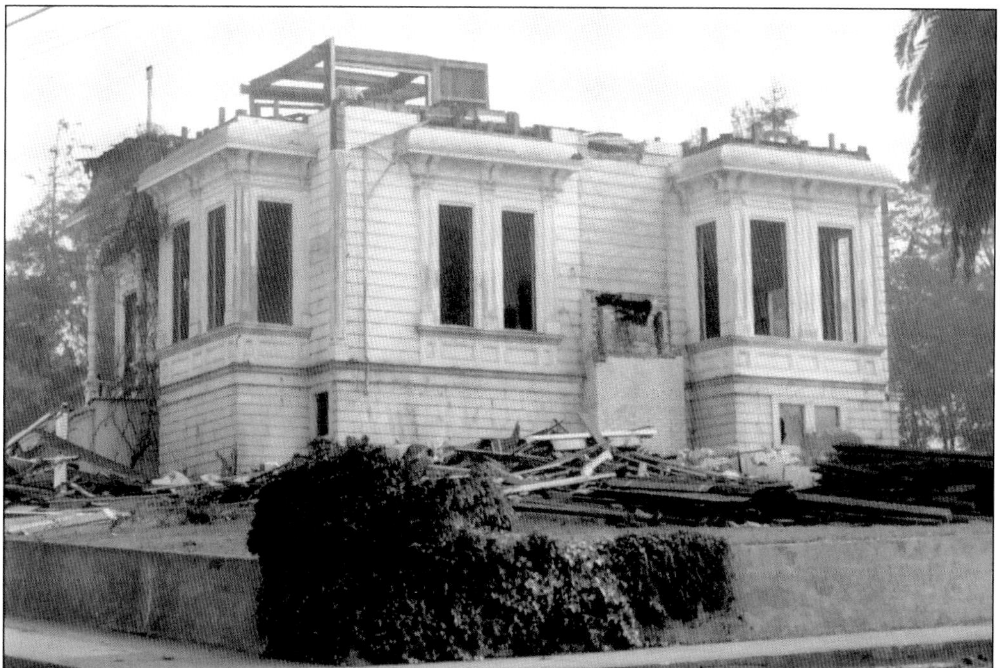

The Falk mansion was torn down in 1956 to make way for a Safeway store. Wildberries Market is now located at the hilltop site. (Courtesy of Humboldt County Historical Society, Roscoe Collection.)

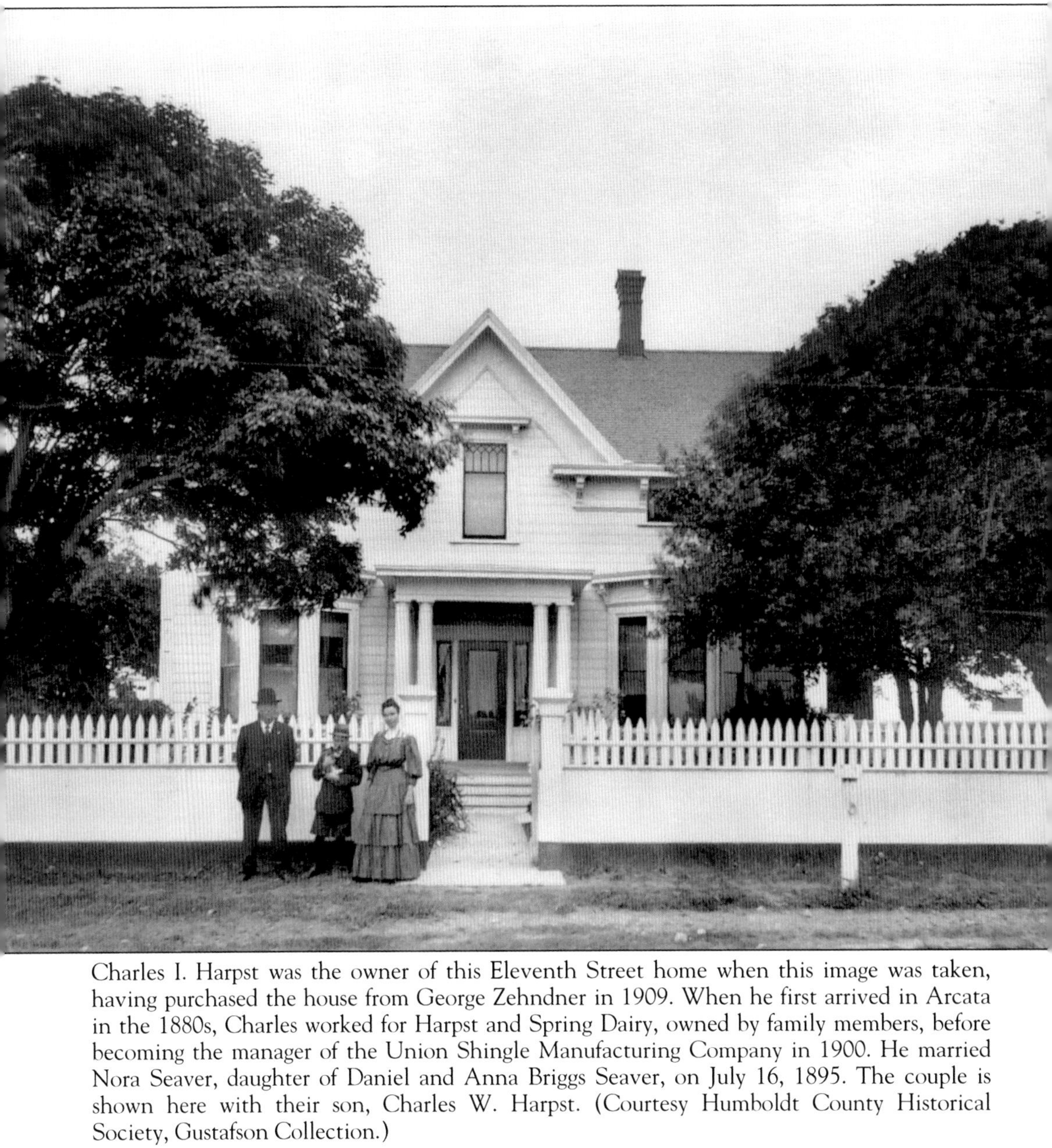

Charles I. Harpst was the owner of this Eleventh Street home when this image was taken, having purchased the house from George Zehndner in 1909. When he first arrived in Arcata in the 1880s, Charles worked for Harpst and Spring Dairy, owned by family members, before becoming the manager of the Union Shingle Manufacturing Company in 1900. He married Nora Seaver, daughter of Daniel and Anna Briggs Seaver, on July 16, 1895. The couple is shown here with their son, Charles W. Harpst. (Courtesy Humboldt County Historical Society, Gustafson Collection.)

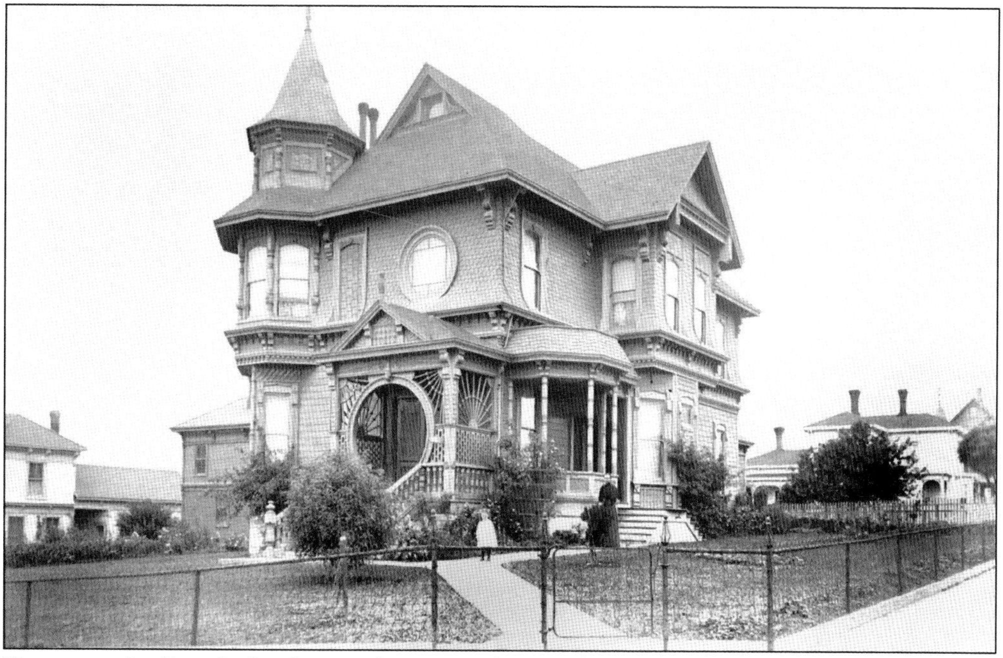

Known as the Bair-Stokes home, this 1888 Thirteenth Street house has provided shelter for a number of medical men beginning with Dr. Fred H. Bangs and his wife, Belle May. Dr. Levi Force and Dr. Frances Horel, founder of the Arcata Sanitarium, were subsequent owners prior to its purchase in 1898 by businessman Thomas Bair. The home remained in the Bair family until the mid-1940s. John and Edith Stokes purchased the distinctive residence in 1948 and lived there until they died. (Courtesy of Historic Sites Society of Arcata, Ruth Horel Collection.)

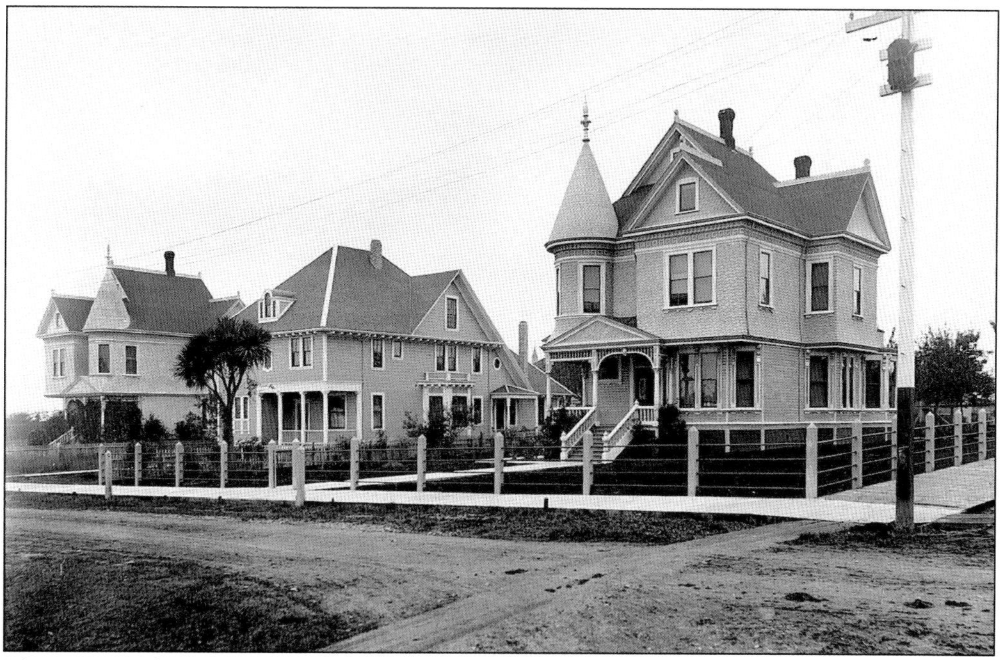

This is an early view of Fourteenth Street between Ninth and Tenth Streets. (Courtesy of Ericson Collection, Humboldt State University Library.)

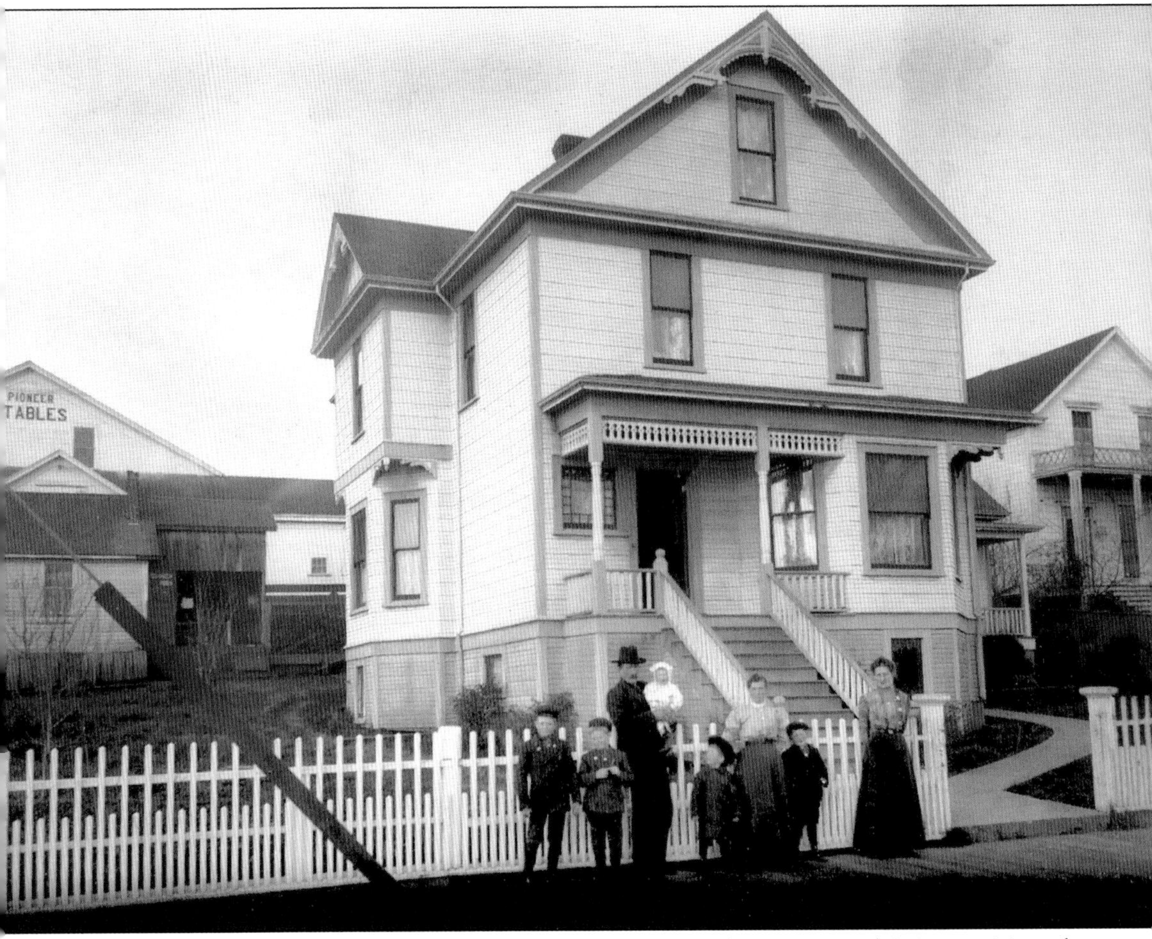

The Edward Stromberg home was located on Seventh Street between F and G Streets. Note the rear of Pioneer Stables on the left. (Courtesy of Humboldt County Historical Society.)

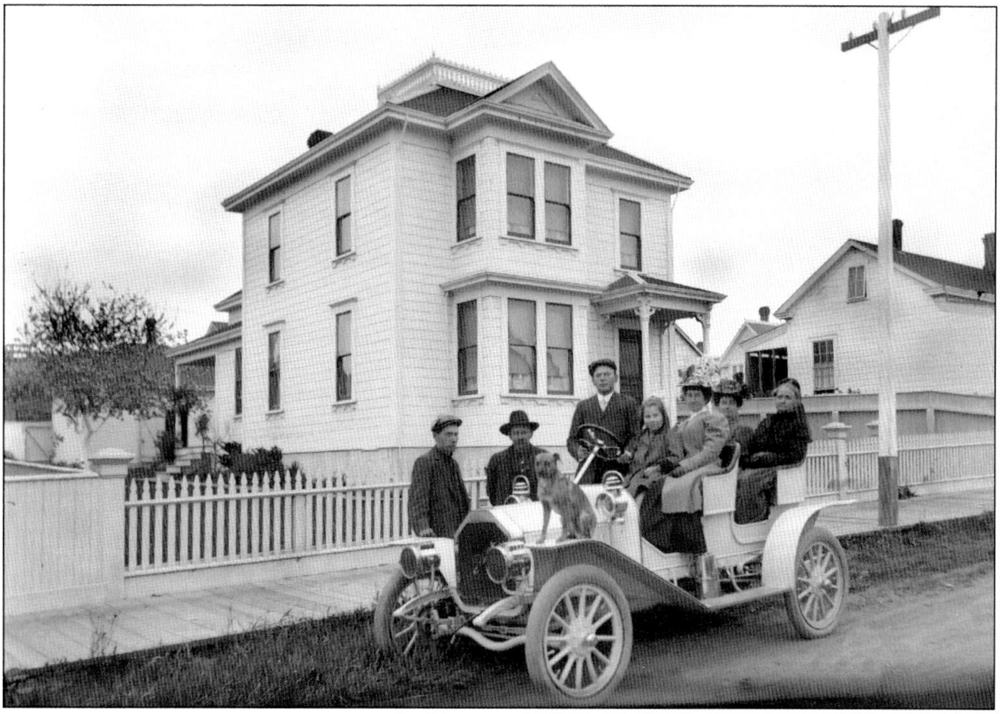

The identity of this Arcata family wasn't noted, but they appear to be headed on an outing in their open auto. (Courtesy of Ericson Collection, Humboldt State University Library.)

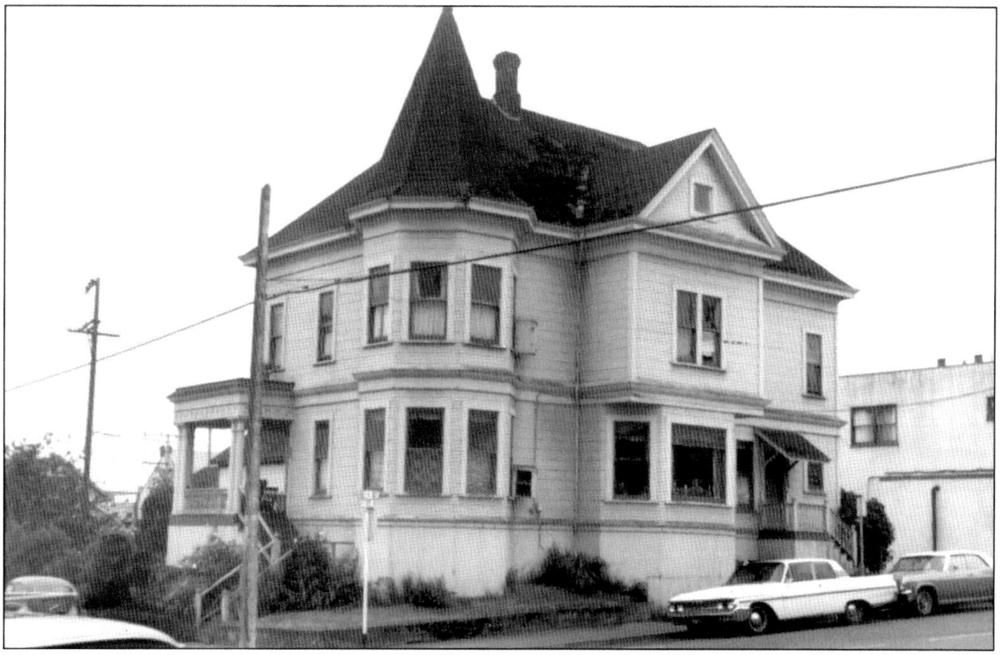

Built in 1901 for undertaker and businessman George Murray at Tenth and F Streets, this Victorian had three owners in 1904 and was best known during that time as the city's "red light" house. City leaders squelched the reputation in the fall of 1906 with their stated intention to arrest everyone found leaving the home. (Courtesy of Humboldt County Historical Society.)

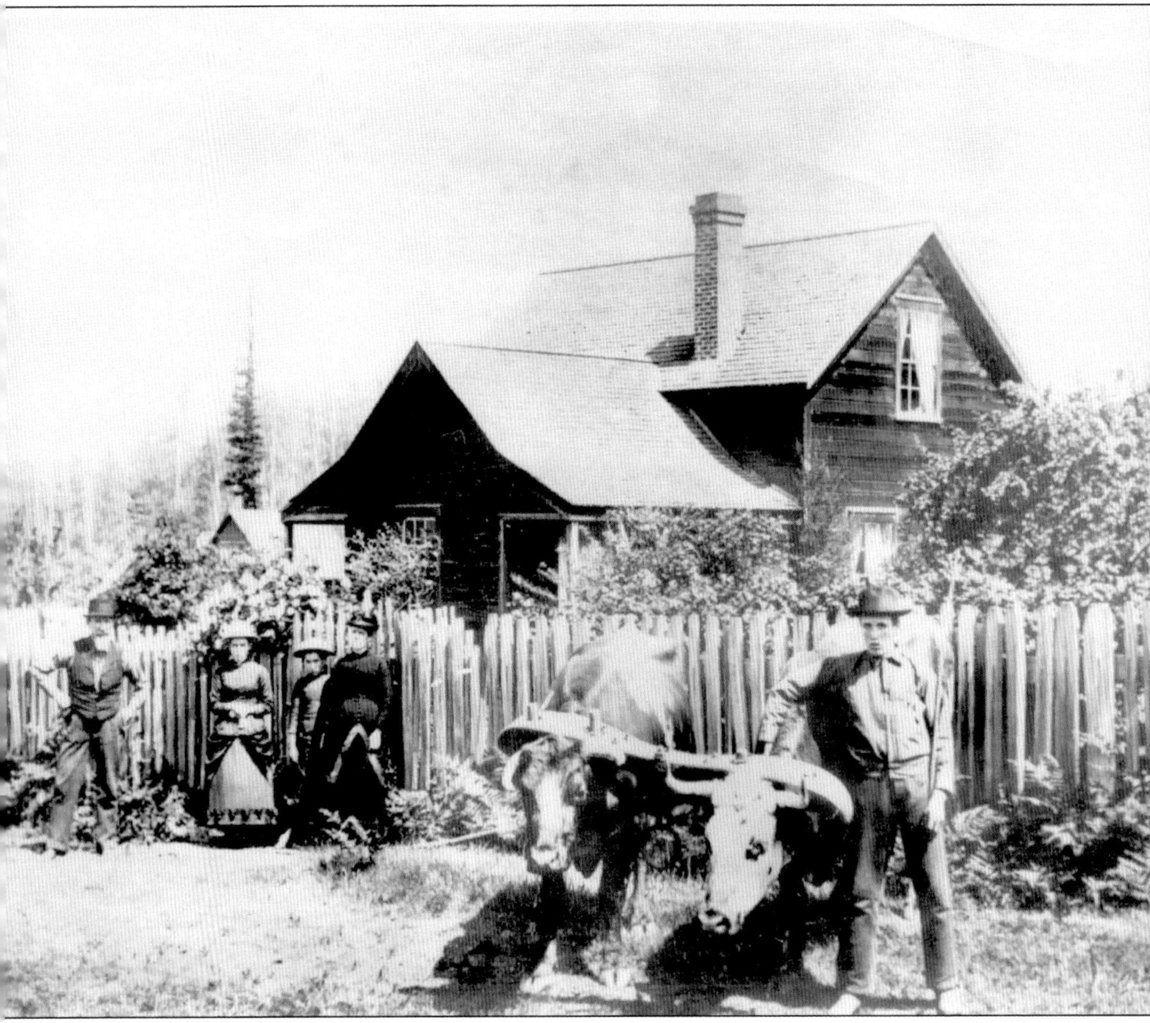

Daniel Seaver and family gather in front of their home in east Arcata around 1880. Shown, from left to right, are Daniel Seaver, Lottie Seaver, Nora Seaver, Mrs. Annie Seaver, Allen Seaver, and twin oxen Buck and Golden. (Courtesy of Humboldt County Historical Society, Roscoe Collection.)

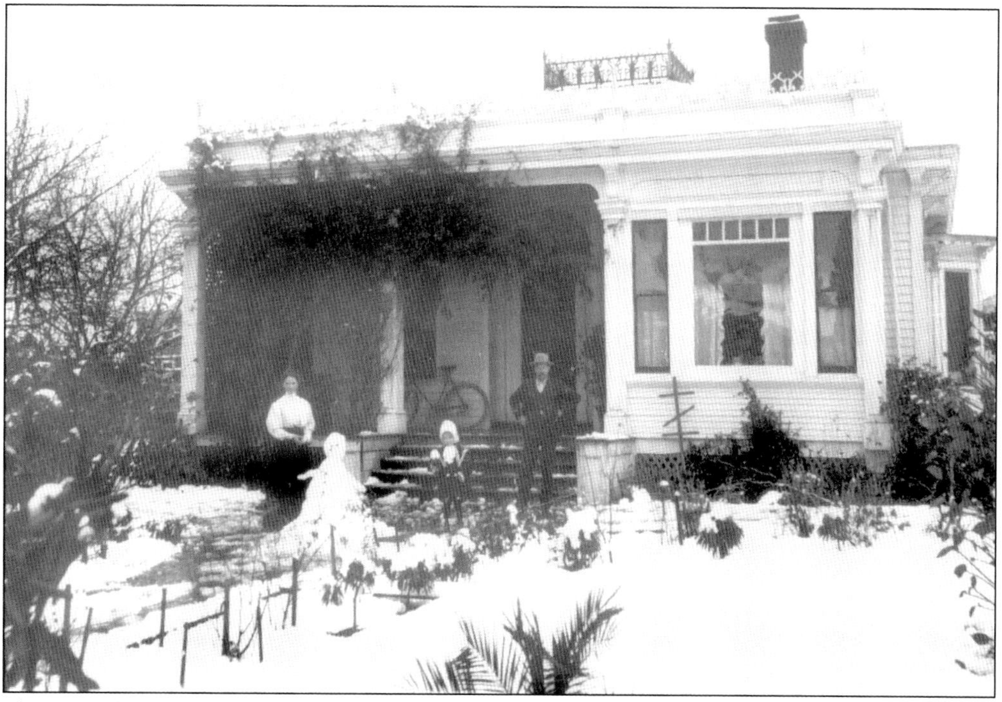

Plaza merchant Isaac Cullberg left this I Street home to his nephew, who was also named Issac Cullberg. Here the second Isaac; his wife, Hulda; and their first daughter, Ebba, enjoy a little snow, *c.* 1908. (Courtesy of Humboldt County Historical Society.)

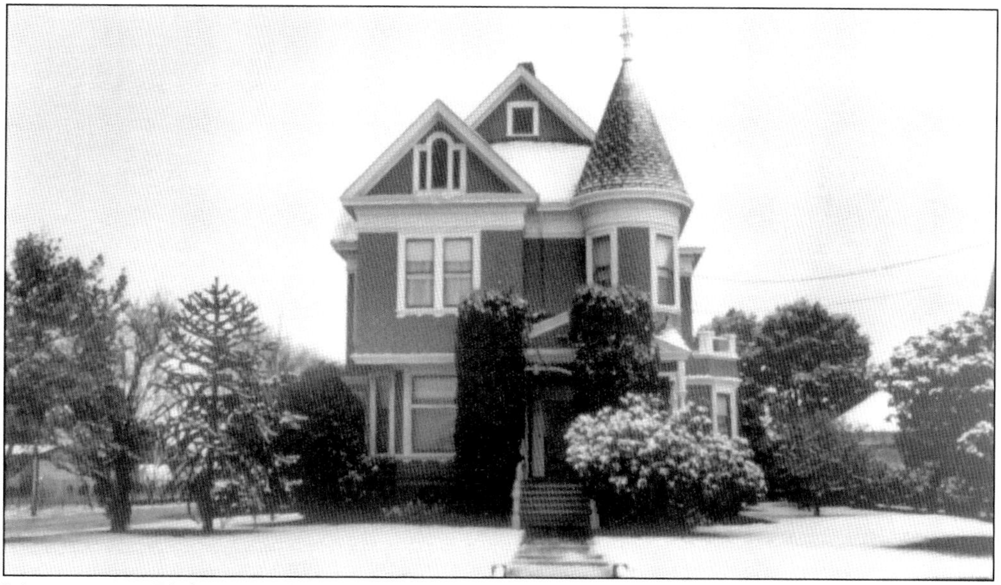

Maine native Elisha B. Jackson found financial rewards in the area's redwood timber and had this Fourteenth Street home built in 1883, 13 years after arriving in Arcata. Jackson was a founding partner of Chandler, Henderson and Company mill in Blue Lake, which moved to Riverside in 1888. The home remained in the Jackson family until 1946, when Robert Matthews purchased it. It remains in his daughter's family today. (Courtesy of Humboldt County Historical Society, DeLong Collection.)

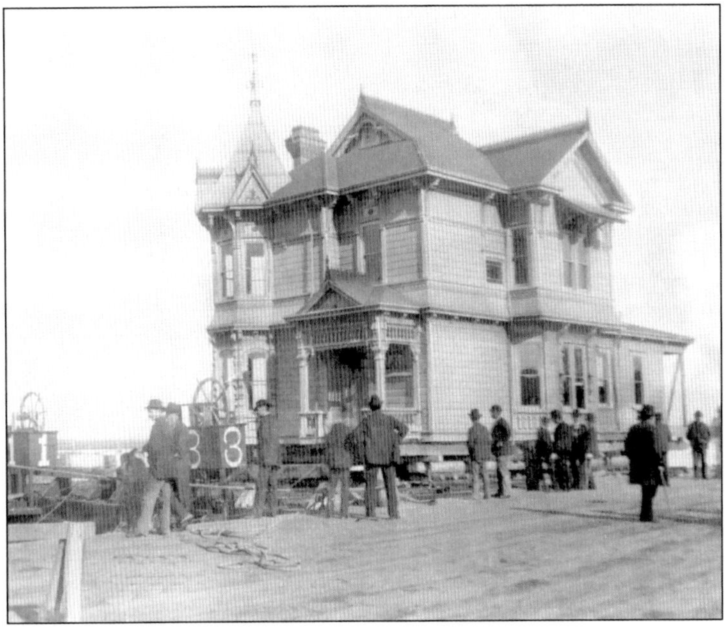

It wasn't unusual to move houses in the early days of Humboldt County, but this 1889 home, known as the Dean House, took to the Humboldt Bay in 1895 after attorney and owner Ernest Sevier left Arcata for Eureka and decided to transport his home to its new site at Sixth and N Streets. A 1935 fire reduced the structure to a single story. (Courtesy Humboldt County Historical Society, Stine Collection.)

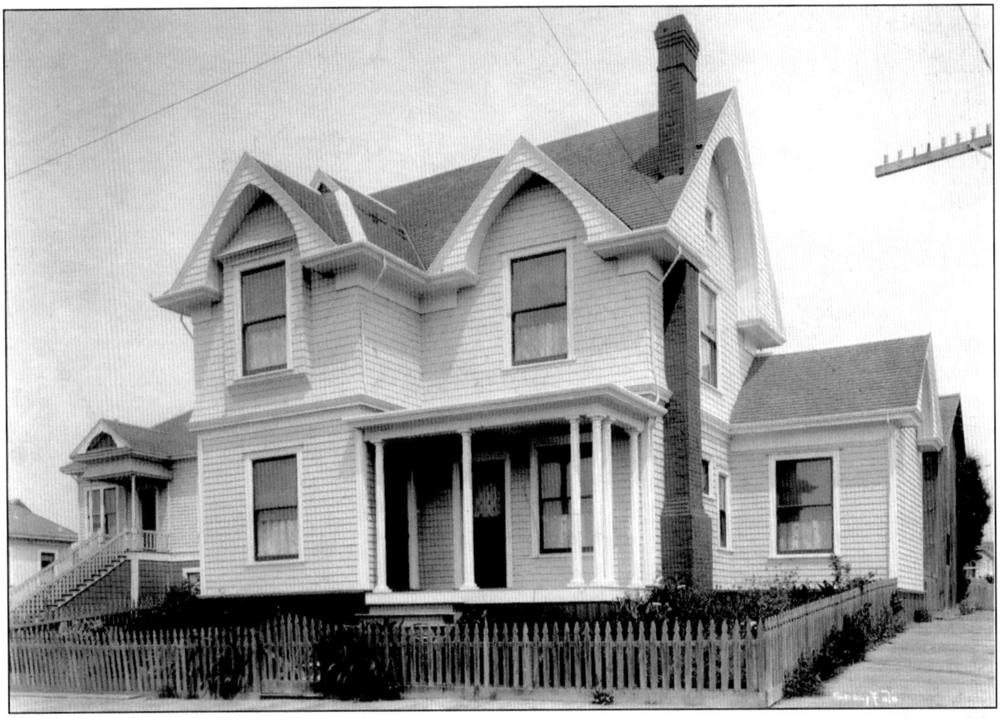

This unique style of eaves was, at one time, the dominant feature in at least two and possibly three Arcata homes and was said to be the handiwork of Nelson B. Johansen. This house once stood at the corner of Fifth and H Streets and was home to the Johan Ryden family. Ryden began as a farmer in the Arcata Bottom before launching his tailoring business in 1902. According to Vivian Ziegler, who lived with her family in the house to the left, Herr Ryden was known for nearly always wearing a top hat and long formal coat. The house burned in the 1960s. (Courtesy of Vivian Ziegler.)

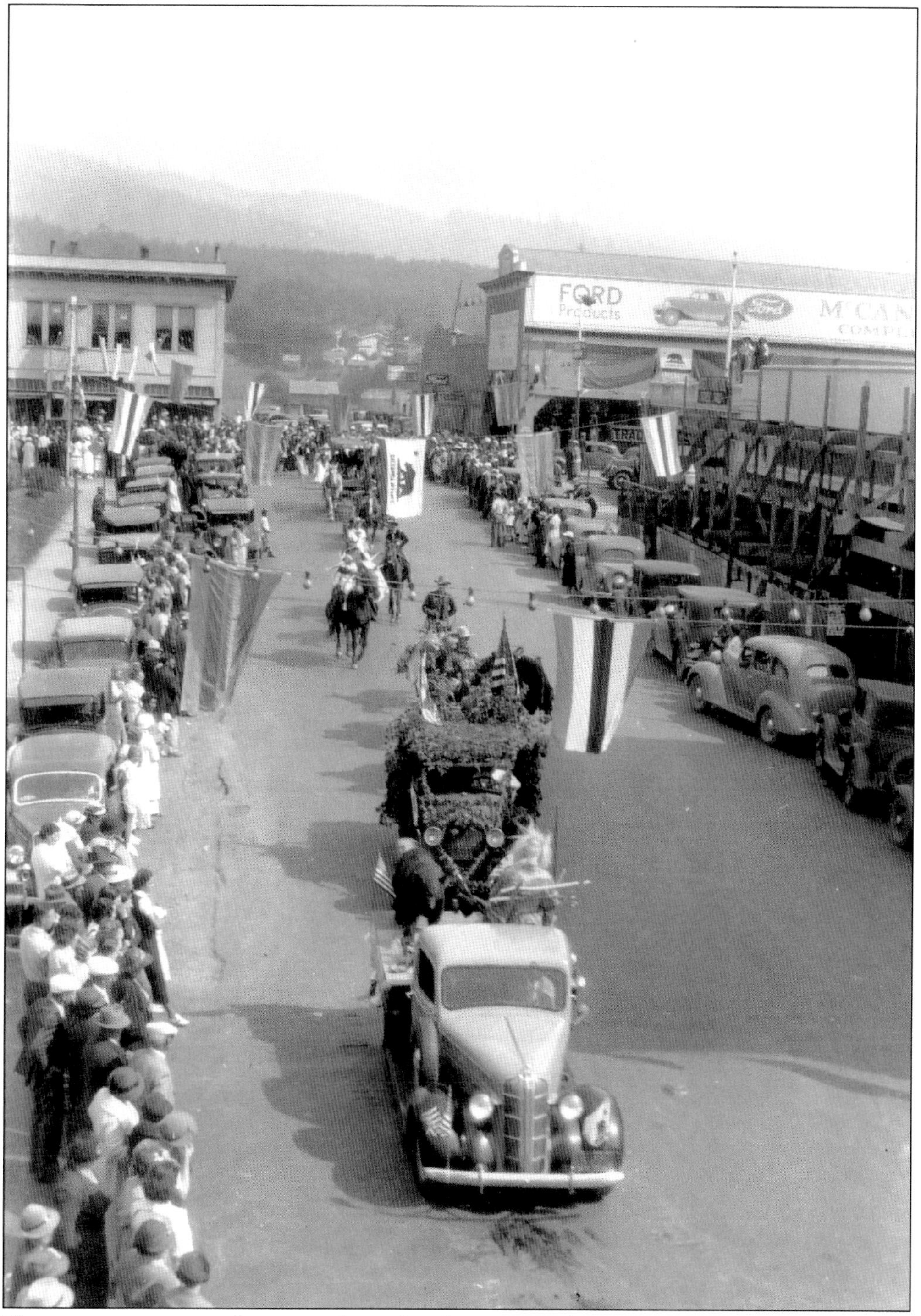

The community turned out in force for the 1938 Admission Day parade, shown here making its way along Eighth Street. (Courtesy of Humboldt County Historical Society, Trinidad Museum Collection.)

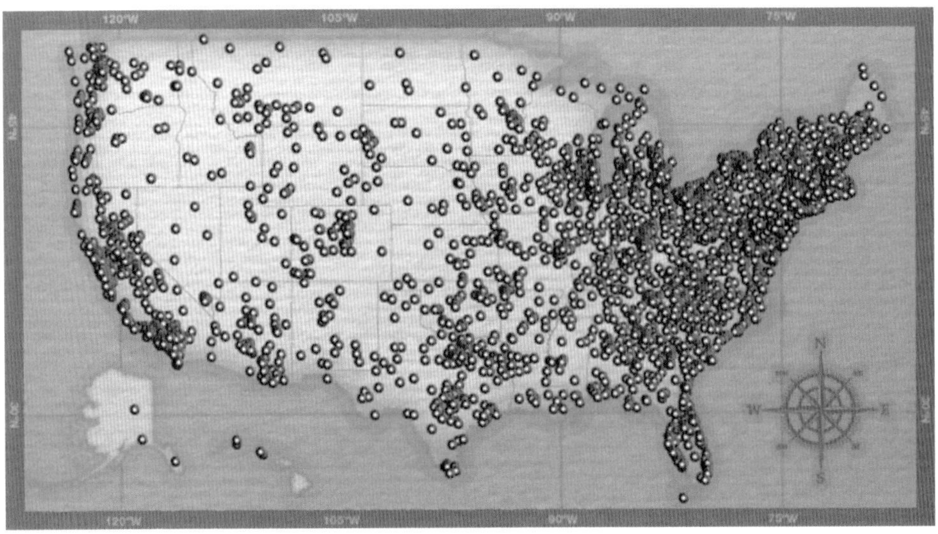

Consistent with our mission to preserve history on a local level, this book was printed in South Carolina on American-made paper and manufactured entirely in the United States. Products carrying the accredited Forest Stewardship Council (FSC) label are printed on 100 percent FSC-certified paper.

MADE IN THE USA